Elements of Literature®
Fourth Course

Holt Assessment: Literature, Reading, and Vocabulary

- Entry-Level Test and End-of-Year Test
- Collection Diagnostic Tests
- Selection Tests
- Collection Summative Tests
- Answer Key

HOLT, RINEHART AND WINSTON
A Harcourt Education Company
Orlando • Austin • New York • San Diego • London

Copyright © by Holt, Rinehart and Winston

All rights reserved. No part of this publication may be reproduced or transmitted in any form or by any means, electronic or mechanical, including photocopy, recording, or any information storage and retrieval system, without permission in writing from the publisher.

Teachers using **ELEMENTS OF LITERATURE** may photocopy blackline masters in complete pages in sufficient quantities for classroom use only and not for resale.

ELEMENTS OF LITERATURE, HOLT, and the **"Owl Design"** are trademarks licensed to Holt, Rinehart and Winston, registered in the United States of America and/or other jurisdictions.

Printed in the United States of America

If you have received these materials as examination copies free of charge, Holt, Rinehart and Winston retains title to the materials and they may not be resold. Resale of examination copies is strictly prohibited.

Possession of this publication in print format does not entitle users to convert this publication, or any portion of it, into electronic format.

ISBN 0-03-078997-4

4 5 6 7 179 08 07

Contents

Overview of ELEMENTS OF LITERATURE Assessment Program viii
About This Book xi

Entry-Level Test 1

Collection 1   Plot and Setting • Synthesizing Sources

Collection 1 Diagnostic Test 13
Selection Tests

    Contents of the Dead Man's Pocket • *Jack Finney* 15

    Double Daddy • *Penny Parker*
    Diary of a Mad Blender • *Sue Shellenbarger*
    The Child's View of Working Parents • *Cora Daniels* 18

    The Leap • *Louise Erdrich* 20

    The Pedestrian • *Ray Bradbury* 24

Collection 1 Summative Test 27

Collection 2   Character • Using Primary and Secondary Sources

Collection 2 Diagnostic Test 32
Selection Tests

    Everyday Use • *Alice Walker* 34

    Interview with Alice Walker • *Roland L. Freeman*
    Interview with Nikki Giovanni • *Roland L. Freeman*
    "Thinkin' on Marryin'" • *Patricia Cooper* and *Norma Bradley Allen*
    A Baby's Quilt to Sew Up the Generations • *Felicia R. Lee* 37

    Two Kinds • *Amy Tan* 39

    By Any Other Name • *Santha Rama Rau* 42

Collection 2 Summative Test 45

Collection 3   Narrator and Voice • Generating Research Questions

Collection 3 Diagnostic Test 51
Selection Tests

    By the Waters of Babylon • *Stephen Vincent Benét* 53

    The Storyteller • *Saki* 56

    The Cold Equations • *Tom Godwin* 59

Taste—The Final Frontier • *Esther Addley*	62
Typhoid Fever *from* Angela's Ashes • *Frank McCourt*	64
An Ancient Enemy Gets Tougher • *Karen Watson*	67
Collection 3 Summative Test	69

Collection 4 Comparing Themes • Evaluating Arguments: Pro and Con

Collection 4 Diagnostic Test	74
Selection Tests	
Catch the Moon • *Judith Ortiz Cofer*	76
The Bass, the River, and Sheila Mant • *W. D. Wetherell*	79
And of Clay Are We Created • *Isabel Allende*, translated by *Margaret Sayers Peden* Ill-Equipped Rescuers Dig Out Volcano Victims • *Bradley Graham*	82
The Man in the Water • *Roger Rosenblatt* The Parable of the Good Samaritan • *King James Bible* A State Championship Versus Runner's Conscience • *John Christian Hoyle*	86
If Decency Doesn't, Law Should Make Us Samaritans • *Gloria Allred* and *Lisa Bloom* Good Samaritans U.S.A. Are Afraid to Act • *Ann Sjoerdsma*	89
Collection 4 Summative Test	91

Collection 5 Irony and Ambiguity • Generating Research Questions and Evaluating Sources

Collection 5 Diagnostic Test	95
Selection Tests	
Lamb to the Slaughter • *Roald Dahl*	97
R.M.S. Titanic • *Hanson W. Baldwin* A Fireman's Story • *Harry Senior* From a Lifeboat • *Mrs. D. H. Bishop*	100
from Into Thin Air • *Jon Krakauer*	103
Explorers Say There's Still Lots to Look For • *Helen O'Neill*	106
Notes from a Bottle • *James Stevenson*	108
Collection 5 Summative Test	111

Collection 6 Symbolism and Allegory • Synthesizing Sources

Collection 6 Diagnostic Test **115**

Selection Tests

Through the Tunnel • *Doris Lessing* **117**

Coming of Age, Latino Style: Special Rite Ushers Girls into Adulthood • *Cindy Rodriguez*
Vision Quest *from* Encyclopaedia Britannica
Crossing a Threshold to Adulthood • *Jessica Barnes* **120**

The Masque of the Red Death • *Edgar Allan Poe*
The Black Death *from* When Plague Strikes • *James Cross Giblin* **122**

Stopping by Woods on a Snowy Evening • *Robert Frost*
After Apple-Picking • *Robert Frost* **126**

Collection 6 Summative Test **129**

Collection 7 Poetry

Collection 7 Diagnostic Test **133**

Selection Tests

A Storm in the Mountains • *Aleksandr Solzhenitsyn, translated by Michael Glenny* **135**

Same Song • *Pat Mora* **138**

Eating Together • *Li-Young Lee*
Grape Sherbet • *Rita Dove* **141**

The Legend • *Garrett Hongo* **144**

Simile • *N. Scott Momaday* **147**

I Am Offering This Poem • *Jimmy Santiago Baca*
since feeling is first • *E. E. Cummings* **149**

Heart! We will forget him! • *Emily Dickinson*
Three Japanese Tankas • *Ono Komachi, translated by Jane Hirshfield with Mariko Aratani* **152**

Shall I Compare Thee to a Summer's Day? • *William Shakespeare* **155**

Ode to My Socks • *Pablo Neruda, translated by Robert Bly* **158**

Sea Fever • *John Masefield* **161**

Bonny Barbara Allan • *Anonymous* **164**

The Flying Cat • *Naomi Shihab Nye* **167**

Ex–Basketball Player • *John Updike*
miss rosie • *Lucille Clifton* **170**

Remember • *Joy Harjo* **173**

Contents   v

    We Real Cool • *Gwendolyn Brooks* 176

    Jazz Fantasia • *Carl Sandburg* 178

Collection 7 Summative Test 180

Collection 8   Evaluating Style • Evaluating an Argument

Collection 8 Diagnostic Test 184

Selection Tests

    Geraldo No Last Name • *Sandra Cisneros* 186

    Night Calls • *Lisa Fugard*
    Waiting for *E. gularis* • *Linda Pastan* 189

    Call of the Wild—Save Us! • *Norman Myers* 193

    A Very Old Man with Enormous Wings • *Gabriel García Márquez*, translated by *Gregory Rabassa*
    Sonnet for Heaven Below • *Jack Agüeros* 195

Collection 8 Summative Test 199

Collection 9   Biographical and Historical Approach • Using Primary and Secondary Sources

Collection 9 Diagnostic Test 204

Selection Tests

    Where Have You Gone, Charming Billy? • *Tim O'Brien*
    The Friendship Only Lasted a Few Seconds • *Lily Lee Adams* 206

    The War Escalates *from* The American Nation • *Paul Boyer*
    Dear Folks • *Kenneth W. Bagby*
    from Declaration of Independence from the War in Vietnam • *Martin Luther King, Jr.* 210

    The Sword in the Stone *from* Le Morte d'Arthur • *Sir Thomas Malory*, retold by *Keith Baines*
    "The Magic Happened" • *John Steinbeck* 212

    The Tale of Sir Launcelot du Lake *from* Le Morte d'Arthur • *Sir Thomas Malory*, retold by *Keith Baines*
    The Romance: Where Good Always Triumphs • *David Adams Leeming* 215

    Theseus • retold by *Edith Hamilton*
    "All We Need Is That Piece of String" • *Bill Moyers* with *Joseph Campbell* 219

    Sigurd, the Dragon Slayer • retold by *Olivia E. Coolidge* 222

Collection 9 Summative Test 225

Collection 10   Drama • Evaluating an Argument

Collection 10 Diagnostic Test 231

Selection Tests

    The Brute: A Joke in One Act • *Anton Chekhov*, translated by *Eric Bentley* 233

    The Tragedy of Julius Caesar, Act I • *William Shakespeare* 237

    The Tragedy of Julius Caesar, Act II • *William Shakespeare* 240

    The Tragedy of Julius Caesar, Act III • *William Shakespeare* 243

    The Tragedy of Julius Caesar, Act IV • *William Shakespeare* 246

    The Tragedy of Julius Caesar, Act V • *William Shakespeare*
    The Fear and the Flames • *Jimmy Breslin* 249

    Julius Caesar in an Absorbing Production • *John Mason Brown* 252

Collection 10 Summative Test 254

Collection 11   Consumer and Workplace Documents: Music on the E-frontier

Collection 11 Diagnostic Test 259

Selection Tests

    Evaluating the Logic of Functional Documents 261

    Following Technical Directions 263

    Analyzing Functional Workplace Documents 265

    Citing Internet Sources 267

    Reading Consumer Documents 269

Collection 11 Summative Test 271

End-of-Year Test 276

Answer Sheets 294

Answer Key 297

Skills Profile 335

FOR THE TEACHER

Overview of ELEMENTS OF LITERATURE Assessment Program

Two assessment booklets have been developed for ELEMENTS OF LITERATURE.

(1) Assessment of student mastery of selections and specific literary, reading, and vocabulary skills in the **Student Edition:**

- *Holt Assessment: Literature, Reading, and Vocabulary*

(2) Assessment of student mastery of workshops and specific writing, listening, and speaking skills in the **Student Edition:**

- *Holt Assessment: Writing, Listening, and Speaking*

Diagnostic Assessment

Holt Assessment: Literature, Reading, and Vocabulary contains two types of diagnostic tests:

- The Entry-Level Test is a diagnostic tool that helps you determine (1) how well students have mastered essential prerequisite skills needed for the year and (2) to what degree students understand the concepts that will be taught during the current year. This test uses multiple tasks to assess mastery of literary, reading, and vocabulary skills.

- The Collection Diagnostic Tests help you determine the extent of students' prior knowledge of literary, reading, and vocabulary skills taught in each collection. These tests provide vital information that will assist you in helping students master collection skills.

Holt Online Essay Scoring can be used as a diagnostic tool to evaluate students' writing proficiency:

- For each essay, the online scoring system delivers a holistic score and analytic feedback related to five writing traits. These two scoring methods will enable you to pinpoint the strengths of your students' writing as well as skills that need improvement.

> **NOTE:** You may wish to address the needs of students who are reading below grade level. If so, you can administer the Diagnostic Assessment for Reading Intervention, found in the front of *Holt Reading Solutions*. This assessment is designed to identify a student's reading level and to diagnose the specific reading comprehension skills that need instructional attention.

Ongoing, Informal Assessment

The **Student Edition** offers systematic opportunities for ongoing, informal assessment and immediate instructional follow-up. Students' responses to their reading; their writing, listening, and speaking projects; and their work with vocabulary skills all serve as both instructional and ongoing assessment tasks.

FOR THE TEACHER

Overview of ELEMENTS OF LITERATURE Assessment Program *(continued)*

- Throughout the **Student Edition,** practice and assessment are immediate and occur at the point where skills are taught.

- In order for assessment to inform instruction on an ongoing basis, related material repeats instruction and then offers new opportunities for informal assessment.

- Skills Reviews at the end of each collection offer a quick evaluation of how well students have mastered the collection skills.

Progress Assessment

Students' mastery of the content of the **Student Edition** is systematically assessed in two test booklets:

- *Holt Assessment: Literature, Reading, and Vocabulary* offers a test for every selection. Multiple-choice questions focus on comprehension, the selected skills, and vocabulary development. In addition, students write answers to constructed-response prompts that test their understanding of the skills.

- *Holt Assessment: Writing, Listening, and Speaking* provides both multiple-choice questions for writing and analytical scales and rubrics for writing, listening, and speaking. These instruments assess proficiency in all the writing applications appropriate for each grade level.

Summative Assessment

Holt Assessment: Literature, Reading, and Vocabulary contains two types of summative tests:

- The Collection Summative Tests, which appear at the end of every collection, ask students to apply their recently acquired skills to a new literary selection. These tests contain both multiple-choice questions and constructed-response prompts.

- The End-of-Year Test helps you determine how well students have mastered the skills and concepts taught during the year. This test mirrors the Entry-Level Test and uses multiple tasks to assess mastery of literary, reading, and vocabulary skills.

Holt Online Essay Scoring can be used as an end-of-year assessment tool:

- You can use *Holt Online Essay Scoring* to evaluate how well students have mastered the writing skills taught during the year. You will be able to assess student

FOR THE TEACHER

Overview of Elements of Literature Assessment Program (continued)

	mastery using a holistic score as well as analytic feedback based on five writing traits.
Monitoring Student Progress	Both *Holt Assessment: Literature, Reading, and Vocabulary* and *Holt Assessment: Writing, Listening, and Speaking* include skills profiles that record progress toward the mastery of skills. Students and teachers can use the profiles to monitor student progress.
One-Stop Planner® CD-ROM with ExamView® Test Generator	All of the questions in this booklet are available on the *One-Stop Planner® CD-ROM with ExamView® Test Generator*. You can use the ExamView Test Generator to customize any of the tests in this booklet. You can then print a test or post it to the *Holt Online Assessment* area at my.hrw.com.
Holt Online Assessment	You can use *Holt Online Assessment* to administer and score the diagnostic and summative tests online. You can then generate and print reports to document student growth and class results. For your students, this online resource provides individual assessment of strengths and weaknesses and immediate feedback.

FOR THE TEACHER
About This Book

Holt Assessment: Literature, Reading, and Vocabulary accompanies ELEMENTS OF LITERATURE. The booklet includes copying masters for diagnostic tests, selection tests, and summative tests to assess students' knowledge of prerequisite skills, their comprehension of the readings in the **Student Edition,** and their mastery of the skills covered in each collection.

Entry-Level Test

The **Entry-Level Test** is a diagnostic tool that enables you to evaluate your students' mastery of essential skills at the start of the year. This objective, multiple-choice test contains several reading selections followed by questions assessing students' comprehension of their reading and their knowledge of select literary skills. Other sections of the test evaluate students' command of vocabulary skills.

Collection Tests

The copying masters in *Holt Assessment: Literature, Reading, and Vocabulary* are organized by collection. There are three types of tests for each collection:

- A **Collection Diagnostic Test** is included for every collection. These multiple-choice tests cover literary terms and devices as well as reading and vocabulary skills. These tests will enable you to assess students' prior knowledge of the skills taught in each collection.

- A **Selection Test** accompanies every major selection in the **Student Edition.** Each Selection Test includes objective questions that assess students' comprehension of the selection, mastery of literary skills as they apply to the selection, and acquisition of vocabulary words. In addition, students write a brief essay in response to a constructed-response prompt that asks them to formulate answers independently using their newly acquired skills.

- A **Collection Summative Test** follows the selection tests for each collection. This test asks students to apply their new skills to a selection that does not appear in the **Student Edition.** Students are asked to read a brief selection and then respond to multiple-choice questions and constructed-response prompts that assess their comprehension of the selection and vocabulary, reading, and literary skills.

End-of-Year Test

The **End-of-Year Test** is a summative tool that assesses students' mastery of the skills and concepts taught during the year. Like the Entry-Level Test, this test uses a multiple-choice format to assess students' comprehension of several reading selections and their mastery of literary and vocabulary skills.

FOR THE TEACHER
About This Book *(continued)*

Answer Sheets and Answer Key **Answer Sheets** are provided for the Entry-Level Test and the End-of-Year Test. If you prefer, students may mark their answers on the tests themselves. For all collection tests, students should write their answers on the tests. The **Answer Key** provides answers to objective questions. It also provides model responses to constructed-response prompts.

Skills Profile The **Skills Profile** lists the skills assessed by the tests in this booklet. You can use the Skills Profile to create a developmental record of your students' progress as they master each skill.

Administering the Tests The format of the Entry-Level Test and the End-of-Year Test, with their accompanying answer sheets, replicates that of most standardized tests. You can use these tests to help familiarize your students with the types of standardized tests they will take in the future.

To administer these tests, prepare a copy of the appropriate test and answer sheet for each student. Some sections of the tests have sample items. Before students begin these sections, you may want to select the correct answer for the sample items with the class. Then, answer any questions students have about the samples. When students demonstrate that they understand how to do the items, have them begin these sections. Students may record their answers on the answer sheets or on the tests.

To administer the collection tests, prepare a copy of each test for your students. Students should mark their answers on the tests themselves. When administering Selection Tests that cover poetry, you may want to allow students to use the textbook, since these tests often require a response to the precise wording, rhythm, or meter of a particular poem. You also have the option of making any Selection Test an open-book test.

One-Stop Planner® CD-ROM with ExamView® Test Generator The tests in this booklet are included on the *One-Stop Planner*® **CD-ROM with ExamView® Test Generator.** Use the ExamView Test Generator to customize and print a test tailored to the needs of your students.

Holt Online Assessment With *Holt Online Assessment* you can administer and score the diagnostic and summative tests online. Use this online tool to generate and print reports to record student mastery and class performance.

Entry-Level Test

Reading and Literary Analysis

DIRECTIONS Read the passage below, and answer the following questions.

SAMPLE A

Antarctica is the most isolated place on earth. It is also the world's largest, driest, and windiest desert. Such extreme conditions have led to interesting adaptations in some Antarctic organisms. Small groups of scientists have learned to endure the continent's harsh conditions in order to study the mutations in these fascinating creatures.

One of these creatures is a type of fish that survives in some of the world's coldest waters by manufacturing a chemical that keeps its blood and tissues from freezing. Phytoplankton are another. These tiny organisms have developed their own built-in sunscreen for protection from radiation. Scientists are excited about these discoveries and the possibility that they will someday be used to help humanity.

A Scientists live in the extreme conditions of Antarctica because they want to —

- A adapt to extreme conditions
- B study some of its organisms
- C evaluate the effects of isolation
- D measure radiation levels

B The *easiest* way to learn more about scientists currently working in Antarctica would be to —

- F fly to Antarctica to meet them
- G search for articles about them in newspapers
- H read about them on the Internet
- J look for books about them at the library

Entry-Level Test

Reading and Literary Analysis

DIRECTIONS Read the selection, and answer the following questions.

Home
by Gwendolyn Brooks

What had been wanted was this always, this always to last, the talking softly on this porch, with the snake plant in the jardiniere[1] in the southwest corner, and the obstinate slip from Aunt Eppie's magnificent Michigan fern at the left side of the friendly door. Mama, Maud Martha, and Helen rocked slowly in their rocking chairs, and looked at the late afternoon light on the lawn and at the emphatic iron of the fence and at the poplar tree. These things might soon be theirs no longer. Those shafts and pools of light, the tree, the graceful iron, might soon be viewed possessively by different eyes.

Papa was to have gone that noon, during his lunch hour, to the office of the Home Owners' Loan. If he had not succeeded in getting another *extension*, they would be leaving this house in which they had lived for more than fourteen years. There was little hope. The Home Owners' Loan was hard. They sat, making their plans.

"We'll be moving into a nice flat[2] somewhere," said Mama. "Somewhere on South Park, or Michigan, or in Washington Park Court." Those flats, as the girls and Mama knew well, were burdens on wages twice the size of Papa's. This was not mentioned now.

"They're much prettier than this old house," said Helen. "I have friends I'd just as soon not bring here. And I have other friends that wouldn't come down this far for anything, unless they were in a taxi."

Yesterday, Maud Martha would have attacked her. Tomorrow she might. Today she said nothing. She merely gazed at a little hopping robin in the tree, her tree, and tried to keep the fronts of her eyes dry.

"Well, I do know," said Mama, turning her hands over and over, "that I've been getting tireder and tireder of doing that firing.[3] From October to April, there's firing to be done."

---

1. **jardiniere** (jär′də·nir′): ornamental pot or stand for plants.
2. **flat:** apartment.
3. **firing:** starting a coal fire.

"Home" from *Maud Martha* by Gwendolyn Brooks. Copyright © 1993 by Gwendolyn Brooks. Published by Third World Press, Chicago. Reproduced by permission of **Brooks Permissions**.

"But lately we've been helping, Harry and I," said Maud Martha. "And sometimes in March and April and in October, and even in November, we could build a little fire in the fireplace. Sometimes the weather was just right for that."

She knew, from the way they looked at her, that this had been a mistake. They did not want to cry.

But she felt that the little line of white, sometimes ridged with smoked purple, and all that cream-shot saffron[4] would never drift across any western sky except that in back of this house. The rain would drum with as sweet a dullness nowhere but here. The birds on South Park were mechanical birds, no better than the poor caught canaries in those "rich" women's sun parlors.

"It's just going to *kill* Papa!" burst out Maud Martha. "He loves this house! He *lives* for this house!"

"He lives for us," said Helen. "It's us he loves. He wouldn't want the house, except for us."

"And he'll have us," added Mama, "wherever."

"You know," Helen sighed, "if you want to know the truth, this is a relief. If this hadn't come up, we would have gone on, just dragged on, hanging out here forever."

"It might," allowed Mama, "be an act of God. God may just have reached down and picked up the reins."

"Yes," Maud Martha cracked in, "that's what you always say—that God knows best."

Her mother looked at her quickly, decided the statement was not suspect, looked away.

Helen saw Papa coming. "There's Papa," said Helen.

They could not tell a thing from the way Papa was walking. It was the same dear little staccato walk,[5] one shoulder down, then the other, then repeat, and repeat. They watched his progress. He passed the Kennedys', he passed the vacant lot, he passed Mrs. Blakemore's. They wanted to hurl

---

4. **saffron:** yellow-orange color.
5. **staccato** (stə·kät′ō) **walk:** walk of short, abrupt steps.

themselves over the fence, into the street, and shake the truth out of his collar. He opened his gate—the gate—and still his stride and face told them nothing.

"Hello," he said.

Mama got up and followed him through the front door. The girls knew better than to go in too.

Presently Mama's head emerged. Her eyes were lamps turned on.

"It's all right," she exclaimed. "He got it. It's all over. Everything is all right."

The door slammed shut. Mama's footsteps hurried away.

"I think," said Helen, rocking rapidly, "I think I'll give a party. I haven't given a party since I was eleven. I'd like some of my friends to just casually see that we're homeowners."

---

1 This story takes place during —

  A the late afternoon
  B two full days
  C a week and a half
  D fourteen years

2 How does the emotional dialogue among the sisters and the mother affect the plot?

  F Causes external conflicts
  G Builds suspense
  H Hints at the way the story ends
  J Motivates the family to move

3 The climax of the story occurs when —

  A Helen sees Papa coming up the street
  B Papa opens the gate and tells them nothing
  C Mama exclaims, "It's all right. . . . He got it."
  D the door slams and Mama hurries away

4 Which of the following phrases conveys the author's distinctive voice in this story?

  F "'Hello,' he said," "some of my friends," "the vacant lot," "Home Owners' Loan"
  G "graceful iron," "poor caught canaries," "the talking softly," "magnificent Michigan fern"
  H "in October," "There's Papa," "his lunch hour," "into the street"
  J "their rocking chairs," "He got it," "the poplar tree," "this old house"

Entry-Level Test continued

READING AND LITERARY ANALYSIS

5 The dialogue in this story reveals that —

A the family is hoping to move
B the sisters do not get along
C Mama and Papa are elderly
D this is a loving family

6 Why do Mama and Helen argue that moving might be a good thing?

F They want to move into an apartment.
G They dislike their run-down house.
H They are putting up a brave front.
J They are trying to sell the house.

7 The dialogue in this story creates a tone that is —

A tender
B morose
C cheerful
D critical

8 What does the word *extension* mean in this sentence from the story?

> "If he had not succeeded in getting another extension, they would be leaving this house in which they had lived for more than fourteen years."

F An outward movement of the arms
G A structural addition to the house
H A larger amount of space
J Extra time to repay a loan

9 When the narrator says that Maud Martha "tried to keep the fronts of her eyes dry," it means that she —

A struggled to keep from crying
B reacted to the effects of the sun
C tried to keep from arguing
D attempted to watch the robin

10 Which sentence *best* expresses the universal theme of this story?

F Hard work always pays off.
G New experiences are educational.
H There's no place like home.
J Don't judge a book by its cover.

11 Read this sentence from the story.

> "'It's just going to kill Papa!' burst out Maud Martha."

Which of the following words would have the *least* emotional connotation of the word *kill*?

A Destroy
B Devastate
C Upset
D Shatter

The following question is not about the selection. Read and answer the question.

12 In a flashback a writer —

F comments directly on the events in the plot
G tells about a character's life in the future
H gives a short summary of the plot
J interrupts the story to show a past event

Entry-Level Test

5

Reading and Literary Analysis (continued)

DIRECTIONS Read the selection, and answer the following questions.

The Tropics in New York
Claude McKay

Bananas ripe and green, and ginger-root,
    Cocoa in pods and alligator pears,°
And tangerines and mangoes and grape fruit,
    Fit for the highest prize at parish fairs,

5   Set in the window, bringing memories
    Of fruit-trees laden by low-singing rills,°
And dewy dawns, and mystical blue skies
    In benediction° over nun-like hills.

My eyes grew dim, and I could no more gaze;
10   A wave of longing through my body swept,
And, hungry for the old, familiar ways,
    I turned aside and bowed my head and wept.

---

2. **alligator pears:** avocados, tropical fruits. All the foods mentioned in this stanza grow in Jamaica, the Caribbean island where the poet was born.
6. **rills:** streams; brooks.
8. **benediction:** blessing.

Entry-Level Test — continued

READING AND LITERARY ANALYSIS

13 The first-person narration of this poem adds to its tone of —

- A fear
- B yearning
- C bitterness
- D anger

14 The speaker of this poem is remembering —

- F a place where he used to live
- G how hungry he is
- H where to buy some fruit
- J going to church to pray

15 The title of the poem, "The Tropics in New York," is ironic because —

- A it is a very unusual title for a poem
- B sometimes it gets extremely hot in New York
- C we don't expect to find the tropics in New York
- D the weather is a lot nicer in the tropics

16 From the narration in this poem, you can tell that the speaker is —

- F happy-go-lucky
- G homesick
- H competitive
- J hungry

17 What topic do the short story "Home" and the poem "The Tropics in New York" share?

- A Fruits and vegetables
- B Keeping your house
- C Wanting to go home
- D Feelings about home

18 What universal theme could apply to *both* "Home" and "The Tropics in New York"?

- F Home is where the heart is.
- G Home is where they have to take you in.
- H Memories stir powerful feelings.
- J We often long for the past.

19 The poet used the word *gaze* in line 9 instead of its synonym *look* probably because *gaze* has connotations of —

- A seeing what isn't there
- B looking longingly
- C glancing quickly
- D looking very closely

20 Both the story and the poem express their theme through —

- F dialogue
- G multiple characters
- H soliloquies
- J figurative language

GO ON

Entry-Level Test

Reading and Literary Analysis (continued)

DIRECTIONS Read the selection, and answer the following questions.

Henna Body Painting

In many cultures in Africa, India, and the Middle East, the plant dye henna has been used for adorning the body for more than five thousand years. People in the United States and Europe have only recently become interested in its possibilities beyond its old-fashioned use as a hair coloring.

Henna dye comes in shades of brown, russet, and crimson. It is made from the dried leaves, flowers, and twigs of the henna shrub, which are ground into a fine powder. One mixes the powder with water and an oil to form a paste, which is the basis for the paint that outlines the intricate designs.

Henna painting varies from country to country and spans different cultures and religious traditions. African henna designs have angular geometric patterns that are large and striking. Arabic henna painting features broad, floral patterns on hands and feet. Indian henna painting uses fine, lacelike floral and paisley designs that cover the entire hands, forearms, and feet.

Often the painting is done to celebrate special occasions. In North Africa, red palms signal a young person's passage into a new stage in life. In Morocco, a soldier's right hand might be painted with henna designs to protect him in battle. In the northern and western parts of India, henna painting is an important part of the wedding ritual. There is a romantic notion that the deeper the color obtained on the skin, the longer the love in the marriage will last.

If the custom of henna body painting has existed in other cultures for so long, why is it only now receiving attention in the United States and Europe? Its growing popularity may be related to the increased interest in tattooing. However, henna enjoys a prime advantage over tattooing—it doesn't hurt! Composed of harmless ingredients, the henna dye washes away after a period of time, and the application of a simple design takes less than thirty minutes. Henna painting also avoids the health risks connected with tattooing.

If you decide to give henna body painting a try, not only will you get a hip look without pain or health hazards but you'll be following an honorable and ancient tradition.

Entry-Level Test continued

READING AND LITERARY ANALYSIS

21 The writer's *main* purpose in writing this article is to —

A warn people against using henna hair dye

B criticize those who use henna coloring

C persuade readers to try henna painting

D inform readers about henna painting

22 Which of the following is *not* evidence given for the benefits of henna painting over tattooing?

F Tattooing is painful.

G Henna painting is more beautiful than tattooing.

H Henna painting is not bad for your health.

J Henna painting can be done in a short amount of time.

23 Which evidence supports the argument that henna is a "natural skin decoration"?

A Henna decorations vary from culture to culture.

B Henna has been used for five thousand years.

C Henna paint is made from the henna shrub.

D Henna decorations are used on special occasions.

24 Which research question would *best* lead to more information about the topic of this article?

F When do the flowers on the henna shrub bloom?

G What types of traditional henna painting are used today?

H What is the typical age at which people marry in India?

J How many people in the United States use henna hair dye?

25 For research about painting hands and feet with henna, the *best* source of information would be —

A an atlas with maps of the Middle East

B do-it-yourself directions for tattooing

C reading a romance novel set in India

D typing "henna" into a search engine

26 Which reference belongs in a bibliography of sources about henna body painting?

F Walter, Cindy, and Jennifer Priestly. *The Basic Guide to Dyeing and Painting Fabric*. Iola, Wisconsin: Krause Publications, 2002.

G Patrick, Diane. *Family Celebrations*. New York: Silver Moon Press, 1993.

H Weinberg, Norma Pasekoff. *Henna from Head to Toe!* North Adams, Massachusetts: Storey Books, 1999.

J Frazer, Sir James. *The Golden Bough*. Ware, Hertfordshire: Cumberland House.

GO ON

Entry-Level Test

Entry-Level Test continued

READING AND LITERARY ANALYSIS

27 All of the following could be connections to the ideas in this article *except* —

  A Some henna body designs may be similar to some fabric designs.
  B With mass communications, many ideas spread across cultures.
  C Originally all paints were made from natural sources.
  D Ancient pottery gives archaeologists clues to its creators and their society.

28 To know that *henna* comes from the Arabic word *hinnā'* is to understand its —

  F connotation
  G denotation
  H derivation
  J pronunciation

29 When the writer says that henna painting uses "floral patterns," this means that the designs look like —

  A shrubs
  B flowers
  C paisley
  D angles

The following question is not about the selection. Read and answer the question.

30 We borrow words as well as customs from other cultures. From the names of the Norse gods Odin, Thor, and Freya we get which words?

  F Wednesday, Thursday, Friday
  G origin, thirsty, frightened
  H alpha, beta, kappa
  J January, February, March

Vocabulary

Entry-Level Test

DIRECTIONS Choose the word or group of words that has the same, or about the same, meaning as the underlined word. Then, mark the space for the answer you have chosen.

SAMPLE A

A <u>prodigy</u> is someone who is —

- A cautious
- B patient
- C talented
- D mischievous

31 A <u>refuge</u> is a —

- A shelter
- B dessert
- C bit of garbage
- D refusal

32 Something that is <u>inevitable</u> is —

- F inedible
- G capable
- H unavoidable
- J interesting

33 Someone who is <u>serene</u> is —

- A kind
- B critical
- C cheerful
- D calm

34 An <u>omen</u> is a —

- F scary monster
- G sign of the future
- H happy event
- J body of work

35 <u>Remorse</u> is another word for —

- A power
- B argument
- C guilt
- D resolve

36 Something that is <u>luminous</u> is —

- F glowing
- G puzzling
- H questioning
- J unfeeling

GO ON

Entry-Level Test

Entry-Level Test

Vocabulary

DIRECTIONS Read each sentence in the box. Then, choose the answer in which the underlined word is used in the same way. Mark the space for the answer you have chosen.

SAMPLE B

The winter decorations have been taken down, and there is a spring display in the store window.

- A That lively man always seems to have a spring in his step.
- B By summer we will have blooms from our spring planting.
- C If that spring dries up, there will be no water for the horses.
- D The animal was crouched and ready to spring.

37 Who is the authority in charge here?

- A You must ask an authority to sign this document.
- B The court has final authority for that decision.
- C We have it on good authority that the claim is false.
- D Using reliable sources will lend authority to your report.

38 If we hurry we can see the 7:00 P.M. feature at the theater.

- F I have been told that my nose is my best feature.
- G The fashion collection will feature silks and wools.
- H He wrote the feature story in the newspaper.
- J When does the next feature begin?

39 There were scores of people at the ballgame.

- A He plans to settle some old scores.
- B Did you get good scores on your exams?
- C Scores of visitors lined up to enter the museum.
- D She will bring the musical scores for the production.

40 When the strain of the work ended, his health improved.

- F Do not strain my patience by teasing me.
- G The constant strain of the deadlines was exhausting.
- H Be sure to save the juice when you strain the pineapple slices.
- J He has to strain to hit the low notes when he sings.

STOP

12 Holt Assessment: Literature, Reading, and Vocabulary

COLLECTION 1 DIAGNOSTIC TEST

LITERATURE
INFORMATIONAL TEXT
VOCABULARY

Plot and Setting

On the line provided, write the letter of the *best* answer to each of the following items. *(100 points; 10 points each)*

_____ 1. The struggle that gets the plot under way is called the —
   A narration
   B conflict
   C climax
   D dialogue

_____ 2. Writers use plot **complications** in order to —
   F introduce the main character
   G resolve the central problem
   H intensify the main character's problems
   J create a chronological sequence of events

_____ 3. **Suspense** is —
   A a feeling that the main character is about to be killed
   B the reader's desire for a happy ending
   C the reader's first impression of the main character
   D the reader's uncertainty about what will happen in the story

_____ 4. In a **flashback** a writer —
   F comments directly on the events in the plot
   G tells about a character's life in the future
   H gives a short summary of the plot
   J interrupts the story to show a past event

_____ 5. The **setting** pulls the reader into a story by —
   A showing how the characters interact with each other
   B giving the reader the feeling of being in a situation with the characters
   C describing the main character's actions
   D revealing an insight about human experience

Collection 1 Diagnostic Test

13

_____ 6. What kind of **mood** would a writer create by describing children laughing in a park on a sunny afternoon?
   F   Somber
   G   Cheerful
   H   Tense
   J   Chaotic

_____ 7. Which of the following steps is an example of **synthesizing**?
   A   Combine the ideas from two sources to create a new work.
   B   Create an outline for a report.
   C   Restate a paragraph in your own words.
   D   Underline or highlight important information in an article.

_____ 8. A writer would probably use **statistics** in an essay to —
   F   indicate the topic
   G   reveal his or her attitude toward the topic
   H   support the main idea
   J   help readers relate the topic to their own experiences

_____ 9. Which of the following words does *not* contain a **prefix**?
   A   rejected
   B   unnecessary
   C   manageable
   D   submarine

_____ 10. A word's **etymology** gives information about its —
   F   connotation
   G   plural form
   H   spelling
   J   origin

| NAME | CLASS | DATE | SCORE |

SELECTION TEST LITERARY RESPONSE AND ANALYSIS

Contents of the Dead Man's Pocket Jack Finney

COMPREHENSION *(40 points; 4 points each)*
On the line provided, write the letter of the *best* answer to each of the following items.

_____ 1. The two settings of this story are a(n) —
   A living room and a ledge
   B bedroom and a living room
   C apartment and an elevator
   D window and a bathroom

_____ 2. Tom Benecke stays behind when his wife goes to see a movie because he —
   F has work he wants to do
   G and his wife had an argument
   H doesn't want to see the movie his wife wants to see
   J and his wife need to spend less money on entertainment

_____ 3. Tom's major conflict in this story is to —
   A get his work done on time
   B retrieve a crucial paper without being killed
   C save his troubled marriage
   D persuade his wife that his new idea is a good one

_____ 4. Which event early in the story creates Tom's conflict?
   F His wife wants to go to see a movie.
   G He smashes the window with his fist.
   H The yellow sheet flies out the window.
   J He and his wife move to an apartment on Lexington Avenue.

_____ 5. Which word *best* describes the relationship between Tom and his wife?
   A jealous
   B suspicious
   C uncaring
   D caring

_____ 6. The *main* danger Tom faces in the story is the danger of falling —
   F in love with another woman
   G for a practical joke
   H to his death on the street below
   J into the hands of criminals

Contents of the Dead Man's Pocket   15

NAME _____ CLASS _____ DATE _____ SCORE _____

_____ 7. One part of Tom's apartment that does *not* play a role in the story is the —
  A windowpane
  B windowsill
  C kitchen
  D front door

_____ 8. What role does a cigarette play in the story?
  F Tom uses it to start a signal fire.
  G It is part of the contents of Tom's pockets.
  H Its presence tempts Tom and so he loses his balance.
  J Its burning shows Tom how much time has passed.

_____ 9. Which tactic does Tom *not* use to get out of trouble?
  A Shouting to passersby
  B Lighting matches
  C Smashing glass
  D Waiting for his wife to return

_____ 10. At the end of the story, Tom does something that contradicts everything that went before. He —
  F leaves his work behind and goes to see a movie
  G rolls on the floor with laughter, glad to be alive
  H falls to the cement sidewalk, eleven stories below
  J saves himself by getting over his fear and taking action

LITERARY FOCUS *(20 points; 5 points each)*
On the line provided, write the letter of the *best* answer to each of the following items.

_____ 11. In a plot the term **sequence** refers to the —
  A fact that every event has a cause and effect
  B order in which events happen
  C reasons characters make choices
  D outcome, or final situation, of the story

_____ 12. What is the difference between **foreshadowing** and **flashback**?
  F Foreshadowing looks to the future; flashback looks to the past.
  G Flashback refers to plot; foreshadowing refers to character.
  H One involves a change of setting, but the other doesn't.
  J One involves the main character's conflict, but the other doesn't.

NAME _____ CLASS _____ DATE _____ SCORE _____

_____ 13. What is unusual about the use of time in this story?

  A The story is told in chronological order, from first event to last event.

  B Events are narrated in a jumbled sequence, so it is sometimes hard to know whether time is moving forward or backward.

  C The entire story contains only one instant of time during which the main character remembers the events.

  D The amount of time it takes to read the story is about the same amount of time the events take to happen.

_____ 14. Approximately how much time passes throughout the story?

  F One minute

  G Ten minutes

  H One hour

  J One night

VOCABULARY DEVELOPMENT (20 points; 4 points each)

Match the definition on the right with the Vocabulary word on the left.
On the line provided, write the letter of the word or phrase that *best* defines each Vocabulary word.

_____ 15. interminable   a. not relating to the situation
_____ 16. discarding   b. getting rid of
_____ 17. confirmation   c. endless
_____ 18. irrelevantly   d. not understandable
_____ 19. incomprehensible   e. proof

CONSTRUCTED RESPONSE (20 points)

20. As Tom tries to solve his problem in this story, his mind sometimes flashes forward, imagining possible outcomes. Find an example of this kind of flash-forward in the story. On a separate sheet of paper, describe the flash-forward, and analyze how it affects Tom's choices and the reader's sense of suspense.

Contents of the Dead Man's Pocket   **17**

NAME	CLASS	DATE	SCORE

SELECTION TEST **INFORMATIONAL READING**

Double Daddy Penny Parker
Diary of a Mad Blender Sue Shellenbarger
The Child's View of Working Parents Cora Daniels

COMPREHENSION *(50 points; 10 points each)*
On the line provided, write the letter of the *best* answer to each of the following items.

_____ 1. The authors of all three articles would probably agree that —
   A work is more important than family life
   B workers need to balance their jobs and their family duties
   C a solution to work problems means family conflict
   D it is easier to be a working father than a working mother

_____ 2. In order to balance work and family life, Sue Shellenbarger —
   F decided to work only three fourths as many hours as before
   G vowed not to do work when she went on vacation
   H tried to use the tips she found in many books on time management
   J looked for a perfect blend of work time and playtime

_____ 3. According to Penny Parker, "daddy stress" is the —
   A stress that comes from making too little money
   B fear of ever missing a child's ballgame or play
   C difficulty of being a father in an age of working mothers
   D strain of trying to spend more time with family while also working hard

_____ 4. What did Shellenbarger learn about the effects of being a "blender"?
   F Her kids didn't need her as much as she had thought they did.
   G The more she "blended" work and family, the calmer she became.
   H When she took time for her family, her work didn't suffer after all.
   J Her experiment left her with little time for creative thought.

_____ 5. What did Ellen Galinsky, the researcher in "The Child's View of Working Parents," learn about kids' feelings?
   A Two thirds of kids worry about their working parents.
   B Kids have learned that work puts their parents in a bad mood.
   C The present generation of kids has decided to become "slackers."
   D Kids don't care whether their parents work in an office or at home.

18 Holt Assessment: Literature, Reading, and Vocabulary

| NAME | CLASS | DATE | SCORE |

VOCABULARY DEVELOPMENT *(50 points; 10 points each)*
On the lines provided, write the Vocabulary word that fits *best* in each sentence.

phenomenon   **poignant**   **colleague**   **autonomy**   **integrate**

6. A kid who cries out, "Let me live my own life!" is asking for more _____.

7. It is truly _____ to see how much the members of a family care about one another.

8. Stress because of conflicts between work and family is a well-known _____ of life today.

9. How can we successfully _____ the demands of job and home?

10. Is it right to care as much about a(n) _____, a fellow worker, as about the members of one's own family?

Double Daddy ... The Child's View of Working Parents

| NAME | CLASS | DATE | SCORE |

SELECTION TEST LITERARY RESPONSE AND ANALYSIS

The Leap Louise Erdrich

COMPREHENSION *(40 points; 4 points each)*
On the line provided, write the letter of the *best* answer to each of the following items.

_____ 1. What was the mother's job before the narrator was born?
  A Nurse
  B Trapeze artist
  C Rodeo clown
  D Writer

_____ 2. When the narrator says that her mother "has never . . . bumped into a closet door left carelessly open," the narrator is referring to the fact that —
  F her mother is unable to walk
  G the narrator always keeps her closet doors shut
  H the narrator's mother is blind
  J the narrator's father liked to play practical jokes

_____ 3. Why has the narrator returned to her mother's house?
  A Her mother needs someone to read to her.
  B The narrator's marriage has recently broken up.
  C The narrator has not been able to earn her own living.
  D Her mother needs help going up and down stairs.

_____ 4. "I owe her my existence three times," the narrator says. Which of the following is *not* one of those three times?
  F The time her mother survived a circus accident
  G The time her mother rescued her from a fire
  H The time her mother and father first met
  J The fact that the narrator's sister died

_____ 5. The narrator's mother deals with the past in an unusual way. She —
  A keeps old photographs, posters, and clippings all over her house
  B often tells highly exaggerated stories about her youth
  C hardly talks about it and has kept very few souvenirs
  D still seems to think she is living in the time when she was young

_____ 6. What does the narrator's mother tell her about the act of falling?
  F Once you start, you keep going faster and faster till you hit bottom.
  G You can get up and try again, no matter how often you fall.
  H It's amazing how many things you can do while you're falling.
  J Whether you fall isn't important; what's important is how you fall.

20 Holt Assessment: Literature, Reading, and Vocabulary

NAME _____ CLASS _____ DATE _____ SCORE _____

_____ 7. At the time the narrator tells the story, she is living in —
    A her mother's house in the New Hampshire woods
    B North Dakota, where she grew up
    C a tent at the Avalon Circus
    D a hospital where she is recovering from a fall

_____ 8. How did the narrator's mother and father meet?
    F They performed together in a circus.
    G The father was a doctor in the hospital where the mother was a patient.
    H They were traveling in the same tour group to Rome, France, and Spain.
    J They met when the house caught on fire.

_____ 9. The narrator's mother performs a heroic act when she —
    A directs the firefighters in putting out the fire
    B puts out the fire with her own hands, burning them severely
    C gives up her own life to save her daughter
    D does a circus leap up to the window to rescue the narrator

_____ 10. The narrator's father taught the narrator's mother to —
    F read
    G listen
    H fly
    J speak

LITERARY FOCUS *(20 points; 5 points each)*
On the line provided, write the letter of the *best* answer to each of the following items.

_____ 11. Another word for *foreshadowing* is —
    A guess
    B inference
    C hint
    D device

_____ 12. Which line in the story most clearly foreshadows the fire?
    F "My mother is the surviving half of a blindfold trapeze act. . . ."
    G "She has never upset an object or as much as brushed a magazine onto the floor."
    H "Suddenly the room goes dark, the stitches burn beneath my fingers. . . ."
    J "No hot sun beat upon the striped tent. . . ."

The Leap

NAME	CLASS	DATE	SCORE

_____ 13. Which event in the story is *not* told in a flashback?

    A The narrator remembers events that happened in her youth.

    B The Flying Avalons' act is destroyed by an accident.

    C The narrator's sister is buried.

    D The narrator's mother goes blind.

_____ 14. Which of the following four events happens earliest in time?

    F The narrator's mother and father meet.

    G Harold Avalon is killed by lightning.

    H The narrator goes to live with her mother.

    J The narrator's mother saves the narrator's life.

VOCABULARY DEVELOPMENT *(20 points; 4 points each)*
On the line provided, write the letter of the *best* answer for each item.

_____ 15. The prefix *il–* and the Latin root word *litteratus* tell you that the word *illiterate* means —

    A sick; diseased; subject to illness

    B not legal; not permitted

    C expert in the Latin language

    D unable to read and write

_____ 16. The prefix *ex–* helps you understand that *extricating* means —

    F getting something out from where it was stuck

    G pushing something into a place where it fits

    H giving something to someone as a gift

    J looking back from a great distance

_____ 17. Which word is *not* closely related to *commemorates*?

    A memory

    B month

    C memorial

    D remember

_____ 18. The derivation of the word *radiance* shows that the word has to do with —

    F the dark of night

    G rays of light

    H rates of growth

    J dances of joy

_____ **19.** *Generate* comes from a Latin word meaning —
   A give
   B write
   C enjoy
   D create

CONSTRUCTED RESPONSE *(20 points)*

20. Choose an event in "The Leap" that happened *before* the narrator was born. On a separate sheet of paper, identify the event, and then relate the event to the following elements: (a) the device the author uses to put the event into the narrative; (b) where the event belongs in the story's chronological sequence (that is, what happens before and after it); (c) how the event affects the narrator's life.

The Leap

NAME	CLASS	DATE	SCORE

SELECTION TEST   LITERARY RESPONSE AND ANALYSIS

The Pedestrian Ray Bradbury

COMPREHENSION *(40 points; 4 points each)*
On the line provided, write the letter of the *best* answer to each of the following items.

_____ 1. Problems begin for Leonard Mead one evening when he —
   A has an argument with his wife
   B goes out for a walk
   C picks up a stray cat
   D runs from the police

_____ 2. Why is there only one police car left in the city?
   F Criminals have taken over the city and abolished the police.
   G The one police car is so heavily armed that it can handle many crimes at once.
   H There is almost no crime anymore in the city where Mead lives.
   J No one wants to be a police officer anymore in Mead's city.

_____ 3. Something that everyone else in Mead's city enjoys that he does *not* is —
   A watching television
   B taking walks
   C reading books
   D laughter

_____ 4. Which of the following statements about Mead is *false*?
   F He has walked the streets alone every night for years.
   G He is happily married and has two children.
   H He wears sneakers so that the dogs won't hear him.
   J His house is the only brightly lit house in the neighborhood.

_____ 5. Why does Mead agree that writing is *not* a profession?
   A Writers do not need a professional license.
   B Writers are not needed for television shows.
   C Mead no longer earns a living from writing.
   D Mead doesn't consider writing to be important.

_____ 6. Why is there no one in the police car?
   F Mead only imagines the car.
   G The lights are too bright to see anyone inside it.
   H The police are hidden nearby.
   J The car is completely computerized.

24   Holt Assessment: Literature, Reading, and Vocabulary

NAME _____ CLASS _____ DATE _____ SCORE _____

_____ 7. The police probably consider all the following behaviors to be regressive *except* —
   A walking at night
   B being single
   C seeking fresh air outside
   D owning a viewing screen

_____ 8. Which of the following statements *best* expresses the main idea of "The Pedestrian"?
   F People should be aware of police brutality.
   G Writers will be unemployed in the future.
   H Technology deadens feelings and life in people.
   J The future will be better for all humans.

_____ 9. Why does Mead claim he should *not* be arrested?
   A His wife can give him an alibi.
   B He has not committed a crime.
   C The police have confused him with someone else.
   D He has important business at home.

_____ 10. The police car takes Mead to a place where he will be —
   F kept in jail without a trial
   G tortured without mercy
   H given a choice of prison or exile
   J given psychiatric treatment

LITERARY FOCUS *(20 points; 5 points each)*
On the line provided, write the letter of the *best* answer to each of the following items.

_____ 11. The setting of "The Pedestrian" is a city —
   A resembling Los Angeles in 2053
   B resembling New York in 2003
   C in the Midwest in 2103
   D on Mars in 2103

_____ 12. In the opening paragraph, Mead peers "down long moonlit avenues of sidewalk." As the story proceeds, the emotion of the description shifts from —
   F dreary to encouraging
   G innocently friendly to suddenly scary
   H oddly familiar to definitely chilling
   J bleak to bland

The Pedestrian

_____ 13. What kind of mood or atmosphere does the setting suggest?
  A Cheerful and optimistic
  B Extremely terrifying
  C Eerie and surreal
  D Private and serene

_____ 14. If the story were set in France instead of the United States, which of the following factors would result?
  F American readers would not so easily identify the story with their own country.
  G The story would not be written in English.
  H The whole plot would have to be scrapped and rewritten.
  J The police would not be nasty to Mead.

VOCABULARY DEVELOPMENT (20 points; 4 points each)
On the lines provided, write the Vocabulary word that has the *opposite* meaning of the italicized word or phrase in each of the following sentences.

| ebbing | regressive | manifest | intermittent | antiseptic |

_____ 15. The sounds of gunfire came in *regular* bursts from the televisions.

_____ 16. Mead's dislike of television is *kept hidden* in the story.

_____ 17. Mead's good humor was *growing greater* as he continued to be questioned.

_____ 18. In the futuristic culture portrayed in the story, having no television is considered to be *forward thinking*.

_____ 19. The *dirty* police car ordered Mead to get inside.

CONSTRUCTED RESPONSE (20 points)

20. Stories can mean different things to different readers. On a separate sheet of paper, state a meaning you find in "The Pedestrian," and then discuss how the story's setting is relevant to that meaning.

COLLECTION 1 SUMMATIVE TEST

Plot and Setting

This test asks you to use the skills and strategies you have learned in this collection. Read this excerpt from "Distillation," a story about a father in a poor family in the 1930s who pulls his four sons in a wagon to the Chicago dump every Saturday, searching for usable items. Answer the questions that follow the story.

FROM "Distillation"
by Hugo Martinez-Serros

By noon the sky was overcast. We pulled the wagon away from the dumping area and sat on the ground to eat what we had brought from home. By then the stench no longer bothered us. My father handed us bean and potato tacos that were still warm. Hunger made them exquisite, and I sat there chewing slowly, deliberately, making them last, too happy to say anything. We shared the jug of water, bits of damp earth clinging to our hands after we set it down.

Before us was the coming and going of trucks, the movement of men, rats scurrying everywhere, some dogs, and just beyond us, under a tentlike tarp, a big gas-powered pump that was used to drain water from that whole area, which flooded easily in a heavy rain. Behind us was a tiny shack, crudely assembled with cardboard, wood, and sheet metal, home of the dump's only dweller, Uñas. He was nowhere in sight, but my mind saw him—a monstrous dung beetle rolling balls endlessly, determination on his pockmarked face, jaws in constant motion and his hands thrashing nervously, searching the grounds with a frenzy unleashed by the appearance of intruders.

By 12:30 the sky's blue was completely eclipsed. Above us an ugly gray was pressing down the sky, flattening it by degrees. My father stood up and looked hard at the sky as he spun on his heel. The temperature dropped abruptly and a strong wind rose, blowing paper, cans, boxes, and other objects across the grounds in all directions. He issued orders rapidly: "¡Pronto! Block the wheels and cover the wagon with the lona! Tie it down!" Then he took a sack and hurried off to a heap he had been eyeing while we ate.

We leapt forward, the two youngest scurrying in search of something to anchor the wheels with, while the two eldest raised the wagon's sides and unfolded the tarp my father had designed for such an emergency. The wheels blocked, we turned to help our brothers. We had seen our father tie down the tarp many times. We pulled it taut over the wagon and carefully drew the ends down and under, tying securely the lengths of rope that hung from its edges.

Huddled around the wagon, we watched the day grow darker. Big black clouds, their outlines clearly visible, scudded across the sky. It was cold and we shivered in our shirtsleeves. Now the wind blew with such force that it lifted things and flung them into spasmodic flight. We moved in together and bent down to shield and anchor ourselves. Frightened, we held our silence and pressed in closer until one of us, pointing, gasped, "Look! No one's out there! No one! Jus' look! We're all alone!"

A bolt of lightning ripped the sky and a horrendous explosion followed. Terror gripped us and we began to wail. The clouds dumped their load of huge, cold drops. And suddenly my father appeared in the distance. He looked tiny as he ran, flailing his arms, unable to shout over the sound of wind and water. He was waving us into the shack and we obeyed at once. Inside, cowed by the roar outside and pressing together, we trembled as we waited for him. He had almost reached us when the wind sheared off the roof. Part of one side was blown away as the first small pebbles of ice began to fall. He was shouting as he ran, "Salgan, come out, come out!"

Collection 1 Summative Test

We tumbled out, arms extended as we groped toward him, clutched his legs when he reached us and pulled us away seconds before the wind leveled what remained of the shack. A knot of arms and legs, we stumbled to the wagon. There was no shelter for hundreds of yards around and we could not see more than several yards in front of us. The rain slashed down, diminished, and hail fell with increasing density as the size of the spheres grew. Now we cried out with pain as white marbles struck us. My father's head pitched furiously and he bellowed with authority, "¡Cállense! Be still! Don't move from here! I'll be right back, ahorita vuelvo!"

In seconds he was back, dragging behind him the huge tarp he had torn from the pump, moving unflinchingly under the cold jawbreakers that were pummeling us. With a powerful jerk he pulled it up his back and over his head, held out his arms like wings, and we instinctively darted under. The growing force of the hailstorm crashed down on him. Thrashing desperately under the tarp, we found his legs and clung to them. I crawled between them. We could not stop bawling.

Once more he roared over the din. "There's nothing to fear! ¡Nada! You're safe with me, you know that, ya lo saben!" And then little by little he lowered his voice until he seemed to be whispering, "I would never let anything harm you, nunca, nunca. Ya, cállense, cállense ya. Cálmense, be still, you're safe, seguros, you're with me, with Papá. It's going to end now, very soon, very soon, it'll end, you'll see, ya verán, ya verán. Be still, be still, you're with me, with me. Ya, ya, cállense. . . ."

Bent forward, he held fast, undaunted, fixed to the ground, and we tried to cast off our terror. Huddled under the wings of that spreading giant, we saw the storm release its savagery, hurl spheres of ice like missiles shot from slings. They came straight down, so dense that we could see only a few feet beyond us. Gradually the storm abated, and we watched the spheres bounce with great elasticity from hard surfaces, carom when they collided, spring from the wagon's tarp like golf balls dropped on blacktopped streets. When it stopped hailing, the ground lay hidden under a vast white beaded quilt. At a distance from us and down, the highway was a string of stationary vehicles with their lights on. Repeatedly, bright bolts of lightning tore the sky from zenith to horizon and set off detonations that seemed to come from deep in the earth. At last the rain let up. My father straightened himself, rose to his full height, and we emerged from the tarp as it slid from his shoulders. He ordered us with a movement of his head and eyes, and as he calmly flexed his arms, the four of us struggled to cover the damaged pump with his great canvas mantle.

His unexpected "¡Vámonos!" filled us with joy and we prepared to leave. Hail and water were cleared from the wagon's cover. My brothers and I dug through the ice to free the wheels, and when my father took up the handle and pulled, we pushed from behind with all our might, slipping, falling, rising, moving the wagon forward by inches, slowly gaining a little speed, and finally holding at a steady walk to keep from losing control. Where the road met the highway, we waded through more than a foot of water and threw our shoulders into the wagon to shove it over the last bump. Long columns of stalled cars lined the highway as drivers examined dents and shattered or broken windows and windshields. We went home in a dense silence, my father steering and pulling in front, we propelling from behind.

Entering the yard from the alley, we unloaded the wagon without delay. While my father worked his wagon into the coal shed and locked the door, my brothers and I carried the sacks up to our second-floor flat. It was almost four when we finished emptying the sacks on newspapers spread on the kitchen floor. There we began to pare while my mother, scrubbing carefully, washed in the sink. We chattered furiously, my brothers and I, safe now from the danger outside.

NAME	CLASS	DATE	SCORE

Lázaro brought the knife down on the orange, the orange slipped from his hand, and the blade cut the tip of his thumb. He held his thumb in his fist and I got up to bring him gauze and tape from the bathroom. I knew my father would let me in even if he had already started to bathe.

Some object fallen between the bathroom door and its frame had kept it ajar, but he did not hear me approach. I froze. He was standing naked beside a heap of clothes, running his hands over his arms and shoulders, his fingertips pausing to examine more closely. His back and arms were a mass of ugly welts, livid flesh that had been flailed again and again until the veins beneath the skin had broken. His arms dropped to his sides and I thought I saw him shudder. Suddenly he seemed to grow, to swell, to fill the bathroom with his great mass. Then he threw his head back, shaking his black mane, smiled, stepped into the bathtub, and immersed himself in the water. Without knowing why, I waited a moment before timidly entering—even as I have paused all these years, and pause still, in full knowledge now, before entering that distant Saturday.

VOCABULARY SKILLS (25 points; 5 points each)
Each of the underlined words below has also been underlined in the selection. Re-read those passages in which the underlined words appear, and then use your knowledge of literal and figurative language to select an answer. On the line provided, write the letter of the word or words that *best* complete each sentence.

_____ 1. A sky that is eclipsed is —

　　A sunny

　　B as dark as a bad mood

　　C rainy

　　D as cold as ice

_____ 2. If you make a rope taut, you are —

　　F pulling it tight as a drum

　　G bringing it toward you

　　H making it skillfully

　　J tying a knot in it

_____ 3. Snow falling with great density is —

　　A falling fast as a cheetah

　　B blown by a strong wind

　　C likely to melt soon

　　D coming down thick as pea soup

From "Distillation" slightly adapted from *The Last Laugh and Other Stories* by Hugo Martínez-Serros. Copyright © 1988 by Hugo Martínez-Serros. Published by **Arte Público Press**—University of Houston, Houston, TX, 1988. Reproduced by permission of the publisher.

Collection 1 Summative Test

_____ 4. Two examples of spheres are —
   F boxes and books
   G tubes and pencils
   H oranges and balls
   J ice-cream cones and pyramids

_____ 5. "Slowly, the rain abated," means the rain —
   A increased
   B decreased
   C rose and fell
   D soothed the listener

COMPREHENSION (25 points; 5 points each)
On the line provided, write the letter of the *best* answer to each of the following items.

_____ 6. While the father and sons are at the dump, a natural disaster occurs when a(n) —
   F earthquake shakes the dump
   G tornado touches down near the dump
   H hailstorm passes over the dump
   J flash flood sweeps through the dump

_____ 7. Who or what is Uñas?
   A The son who tells the story
   B The father
   C A man who lives on the dump
   D A beetle

_____ 8. The father protects his sons from disaster by —
   F removing them from the dump in time to avoid the storm
   G fighting the enemy who appears at the dump
   H telling them to run while he guards the wagon
   J covering them with a tarp and his own body

_____ 9. What does the narrator learn when he sees his father in the bathroom?
   A His father's back and arms are covered with welts.
   B His father is not as tall as the boy had thought he was.
   C The look in his father's eyes is one of love.
   D The shower in the bathroom is broken.

NAME _____ CLASS _____ DATE _____ SCORE _____

_____ 10. When he tells the story, the narrator is —
  F a grown man, so the entire story is a flashback
  G attending his father's funeral, so some of the story is foreshadowing
  H watching his father clean up, so the story is out of chronological order
  J sharing memories with his brothers, so part of the story is new to him

READING SKILLS AND STRATEGIES: CONSTRUCTED RESPONSE *(30 points; 10 points each)*

Making Predictions

11. On a separate sheet of paper, make a prediction about something that will happen to one or more of the characters in "Distillation" after the story ends. Be sure to state which details from the story have influenced your prediction.

Analyzing Cause and Effect

12. On the way home from the dump, the father and his sons are silent. Why? On a separate sheet of paper, give details from the story to support your inference.

Determining an Author's Purpose

13. On a separate sheet of paper, describe what you think the writer of "Distillation" is trying to tell the reader.

LITERARY FOCUS: CONSTRUCTED RESPONSE *(20 points)*

14. The plot of "Distillation" arises from and reflects the father's character. On a separate sheet of paper, describe how the father's character influences the sequence of events in the story. Cite actions the father takes that move the plot forward. Describe an example of foreshadowing or flashback in the story.

Collection 1 Summative Test

COLLECTION 2 DIAGNOSTIC TEST

Character

On the line provided, write the letter of the *best* answer to each of the following items. (100 points; 10 points each)

_____ 1. Which of the following sentences is an example of **direct characterization**?
   A Eva said to her cousin, "My mother thinks that you are talented."
   B Loretta was an ambitious person who set high goals for herself.
   C Carlos talked for two hours straight.
   D Kevin wears a grungy old jacket wherever he goes.

_____ 2. **Dramatic monologue** and **soliloquy** —
   F occur near the end of a play
   G are parts of a dialogue
   H are generally humorous
   J convey the thoughts of only one character

_____ 3. The **main character** in a story is also called —
   A the protagonist
   B a dynamic character
   C a static character
   D the antagonist

_____ 4. Why are some **conflicts** described as *external*?
   F They pit a character against an outside force.
   G They are minor problems in a story.
   H They relate to events that happened in a character's past.
   J They refer to political struggles taking place in a character's world.

_____ 5. A writer has successfully conveyed a character's **motivation** when —
   A the character is completely predictable
   B the reader can identify with the character
   C the reader understands why the character does something
   D the character is respected by the other characters in the story

NAME _____ CLASS _____ DATE _____ SCORE _____

_____ 6. Complex, three-dimensional characters are called —
   F round characters
   G flat characters
   H character foils
   J subordinate characters

_____ 7. Which of the following items is an example of a **secondary source**?
   A Interview
   B Oral history
   C Biography
   D Autobiography

_____ 8. To evaluate the **credibility** of a source, you should —
   F verify that the facts cited by the author are accurate
   G summarize the main idea
   H determine the author's audience
   J elaborate on the author's points by offering your own opinions

_____ 9. In a sentence all of the following words signal **contrast** except —
   A however
   B instead
   C also
   D although

_____ 10. Which of the following sentences uses **restatement** to clarify the meaning of the underlined word?
   F Robert sidled up to his friend from camp.
   G He led an insular life, separated from the rest of the town.
   H When it was her turn to speak, she walked sedately to the stage.
   J We swam in the tepid water, and then we went sailing.

Collection 2 Diagnostic Test

33

| NAME | CLASS | DATE | SCORE |

SELECTION TEST   LITERARY RESPONSE AND ANALYSIS

Everyday Use Alice Walker

COMPREHENSION *(40 points; 4 points each)*
On the line provided, write the letter of the *best* answer to each of the following items.

_____ 1. Maggie's shyness arises *mainly* from —
  A her fear of her sister
  B the sudden attraction she feels toward Hakim-a-barber
  C a trauma she suffered when the house burned down
  D the ridicule her family heaps on her

_____ 2. Dee *probably* changes her name because she —
  F wants to get back at her family
  G wants to connect with her African roots
  H never liked the sound of it
  J thinks a new name will enhance her career

_____ 3. The mother is reluctant to let Dee have the quilts because the mother —
  A has promised them to Maggie
  B distrusts Dee and Hakim-a-barber
  C knows the quilts have great monetary value
  D is angry with Dee for leaving home

_____ 4. Why does the mother finally decide to give the quilts to Maggie instead of to Dee?
  F The mother thinks Dee will sell them.
  G Hakim-a-barber makes insulting remarks about them.
  H Dee changes her mind about wanting them.
  J She is touched by Maggie's vulnerability and deep sense of family.

_____ 5. Dee and Maggie differ in that Maggie is —
  A less practical than Dee
  B closer to her mother than Dee is
  C more educated than Dee
  D better looking than Dee

_____ 6. Which of the following traits does Dee share with her mother?
  F Neither of them likes the family house.
  G Both women are strong-willed.
  H Both of them love their country.
  J Neither of them went to high school.

_____ **7.** Which of the following statements *best* describes the story's main conflict?
  A Dee argues with her mother over the butter churn.
  B The mother wants Maggie to be more like Dee.
  C Dee wants the quilts, but her mother has promised them to Maggie.
  D The mother does not approve of Dee's choice in men.

_____ **8.** What happens at the end of the story?
  F The mother hugs Maggie for the first time.
  G The mother apologizes to Dee for not understanding her.
  H Maggie speaks up for herself for the first time.
  J Dee decides to make quilts herself.

_____ **9.** Who has the quilts at the end of the story?
  A Dee
  B Maggie
  C Hakim-a-barber
  D The mother

_____ **10.** When Dee tells her mother, "You just don't understand," the statement shows the reader that —
  F it's actually Dee who doesn't understand
  G Dee is cleverer than her mother
  H Dee thinks her mother is being mean
  J Dee understands her mother and Maggie

LITERARY FOCUS *(20 points; 5 points each)*
On the line provided, write the letter of the *best* answer to each of the following items.

_____ **11.** We learn about the mother in "Everyday Use" *mainly* through the story's —
  A narration
  B dialogue
  C description
  D soliloquy

_____ **12.** In her own mind the mother —
  F thinks she is a gifted writer
  G feels she has set a bad example for her daughters
  H accepts herself as a strong, capable woman
  J believes that her life lacks meaning and purpose

Everyday Use   **35**

NAME	CLASS	DATE	SCORE

_____ 13. Which of the following lines of dialogue *best* shows how Dee feels about herself?
      A "How do you pronounce this name?"
      B "She did all this stitching by hand. Imagine!"
      C "You know as well as me you was named after your aunt Dicie."
      D "I couldn't bear it any longer, being named after the people who oppress me."

_____ 14. In the mother's dream about appearing on television, she —
      F is tearfully reunited with Dee
      G takes over the role of talk-show host
      H kills a bull calf with a sledgehammer
      J is afraid to look a strange white man in the eye

VOCABULARY DEVELOPMENT *(20 points; 4 points each)*
On the line provided, write the Vocabulary word that *best* completes each sentence.

    doctrines   **rifling**   **furtive**   **oppress**   **cowering**

15. Dee seems to live by _____ that are at odds with her mother's beliefs.

16. There is nothing _____ or sneaky about Dee.

17. Dee begins _____ through the house for the things she wants.

18. Poverty and a lack of education still _____ many people.

19. The mother sees Maggie _____ fearfully in a corner as Dee exclaims over the two quilts.

CONSTRUCTED RESPONSE *(20 points)*

20. Re-read the passage on page 78 beginning with "You've no doubt seen those TV shows" and ending with "Hesitation was no part of her nature." Then, on a separate sheet of paper, describe what this passage tells you about the mother's character. Support your ideas by referring to specific parts of the text.

| NAME | CLASS | DATE | SCORE |

SELECTION TEST **INFORMATIONAL READING**

Interview with Alice Walker Roland L. Freeman
Interview with Nikki Giovanni Roland L. Freeman
"Thinkin' on Marryin'" Patricia Cooper and Norma Bradley Allen
A Baby's Quilt to Sew Up the Generations
Felicia R. Lee

COMPREHENSION *(100 points; 10 points each)*
On the line provided, write the letter of the *best* answer to each of the following items.

_____ 1. What makes the interviews primary sources?
   A The quilters talk about their own experiences.
   B It is an important source of information.
   C Author Roland L. Freeman is a respected authority on the subject.
   D Alice Walker and Nikki Giovanni are well-known writers.

_____ 2. To Alice Walker, quilting is important *mainly* because quilts —
   F are useful and warm
   G can be sold for a lot of money
   H connect people to their heritage
   J can be displayed in museums

_____ 3. It can be inferred from this interview that Alice Walker connects quilting and —
   A the power of creativity
   B poetry
   C medicine
   D education

_____ 4. Nikki Giovanni uses quilts as a —
   F poetic metaphor
   G sleeping aid
   H way to earn money
   J reminder of her childhood

_____ 5. For Nikki Giovanni, quilts symbolize black women's lives because quilts are —
   A soft but durable
   B beautiful but made from scraps
   C cheerful but practical
   D serious but whimsical

Interview with Alice Walker . . . A Baby's Quilt . . .   **37**

_____ 6. Which phrase from "Thinkin' on Marryin'" is a good example of regional dialect?
   F "I made three by myself...."
   G "You won't believe it to look at me now...."
   H "What I was doin' was settin' there...."
   J "That was the longest speech he ever said...."

_____ 7. In "Thinkin' on Marryin'," the speaker meets her husband when he —
   A buys one of her quilts at a fair
   B claims to be a fine quilter himself
   C says that her quilts are the most beautiful he has ever seen
   D watches her quilting and introduces himself

_____ 8. What did each member of the Webb family contribute to the baby's quilt?
   F Money or supplies
   G A square of fabric
   H His or her quilting skills
   J A quotation from *The Little Prince*

_____ 9. For Marilyn Webb, quilting can be an important way to —
   A keep track of a family's past
   B announce a birth
   C make extra money
   D find new subjects to write about

_____ 10. "A Baby's Quilt to Sew Up the Generations" is a secondary source because the writer is *not* —
   F using her own experiences
   G familiar with the topic
   H a reliable source of information
   J getting paid for her work

SELECTION TEST

LITERARY RESPONSE AND ANALYSIS

Two Kinds Amy Tan

COMPREHENSION (40 points; 4 points each)
On the line provided, write the letter of the *best* answer to each of the following items.

_____ 1. Jing-mei's mother's life in China was hard because she —
  A lost her home and family
  B was wounded in war
  C lost her family's vast fortune
  D was not allowed to practice her religion

_____ 2. When first considering the idea of becoming famous, Jing-mei —
  F feels that she does not have the talent to achieve it
  G likes the idea, imagining that it will make her parents love her
  H purposely gets her hair cut badly so that she will not be allowed on TV
  J is sure that she will become a famous writer someday

_____ 3. When Jing-mei sees her "prodigy side" in the mirror, she realizes that she —
  A has successfully become a prodigy
  B has inherited that side of herself from her mother
  C has no right to think so well of herself
  D must resist her mother's efforts to make her a prodigy

_____ 4. Old Chong —
  F mercilessly forces Jing-mei to practice until she is perfect
  G tells Jing-mei that he doesn't care if she learns her lessons or not
  H is easy to fool because his hearing and sight are not good
  J really knows almost nothing about how to play the piano

_____ 5. According to Jing-mei's mother, what are the "two kinds"?
  A Daughters who obey and daughters who do not
  B Great pianists and all other pianists
  C People who try their best and people who are lazy
  D Parents who are proud and loving and parents who are selfish

_____ 6. The *main* source of conflict between Jing-mei and her mother is Jing-mei's —
  F friendship with Waverly
  G dislike for Old Chong
  H feeling that she is not appreciated for who she is
  J desire to be a prodigy

Two Kinds 39

_____ 7. Jing-mei does not apply herself studiously to her piano lessons because she —
   A has no love or respect for her mother
   B dislikes the instructor
   C resents the pressure from her mother
   D wants to play chess like her cousin

_____ 8. The mother immediately gives up on her goals for Jing-mei when —
   F Jing-mei calmly explains her real goals
   G Jing-mei mentions the dead twin girls
   H the school guidance counselor offers sound advice
   J Old Chong raises his fee

_____ 9. When her mother offers to give her the piano, the adult Jing-mei —
   A is angry that her mother still wants her to be a prodigy
   B begins taking piano lessons again
   C refuses the gift but is pleased that her mother offered it
   D takes the piano for her own daughter to play

_____ 10. At college, Jing-mei —
   F gets straight A's
   G changes her major
   H attends Stanford
   J drops out

LITERARY FOCUS *(20 points; 5 points each)*
On the line provided, write the letter of the *best* answer to each of the following items.

_____ 11. A character's **motivation** is his or her —
   A history or background
   B ability to influence the plot
   C acting style
   D reason for behaving in a certain way

_____ 12. Based on Jing-mei's behavior toward her mother, a reader can infer that Jing-mei is —
   F strong-willed
   G hard-working
   H old-fashioned
   J self-conscious

_____ **13.** At first, her mother's ambitions for Jing-mei are motivated by —
   A   the family's extreme poverty
   B   resentment of her sister
   C   a belief that America is the land of opportunity
   D   Old Chong's enthusiastic reports

_____ **14.** How does Jing-mei's mother feel after her daughter's performance?
   F   Devastated
   G   Overjoyed
   H   Terrified
   J   Exhausted

VOCABULARY DEVELOPMENT (20 points; 4 points each)
Match the definition on the left with the Vocabulary word on the right. On the line provided, write the letter of the Vocabulary word that *best* matches each definition.

_____ **15.** without energy or interest   a. betrayal
_____ **16.** complete failure   b. dawdled
_____ **17.** regretted deeply   c. fiasco
_____ **18.** wasted time   d. lamented
_____ **19.** act of disloyalty   e. listlessly

CONSTRUCTED RESPONSE (20 points)

20. At the beginning of "Two Kinds," Jing-mei tries hard to satisfy her mother's high expectations. As the story progresses, Jing-mei's attitude changes. This shift in attitude leads to a **conflict** between mother and daughter. On a separate sheet of paper, write a paragraph describing the conflict and telling how it is resolved. Support your ideas by citing at least two interactions between Jing-mei and her mother.

Two Kinds

| NAME | CLASS | DATE | SCORE |

SELECTION TEST LITERARY RESPONSE AND ANALYSIS

By Any Other Name Santha Rama Rau

COMPREHENSION (40 points; 4 points each)
On the line provided, write the letter of the *best* answer to each of the following items.

_____ 1. Santha and Cynthia are —
   A sisters
   B mother and daughter
   C best friends
   D the same person

_____ 2. You know from the opening lines of the story that —
   F Santha is more cautious than Premila
   G Santha is stronger than Premila
   H Premila is more obedient than Santha
   J Premila is older than Santha

_____ 3. One reason the girls' mother sends them to the Anglo-Indian school is that —
   A they have already learned everything she can teach them
   B she can no longer teach them at home
   C she is legally required to do so
   D the sisters beg to be sent there

_____ 4. How does Santha feel about "Cynthia"?
   F Competitive, envious
   G Detached, uninterested
   H Loving, affectionate
   J Friendly, casual

_____ 5. Why does Santha answer "I don't know" when asked her name?
   A She cannot translate her name.
   B Indian names are hard for her to pronounce.
   C She's not sure what answer to give.
   D First names are kept secret in India.

_____ 6. To the narrator the word *apple* is —
   F unfamiliar
   G silly
   H significant
   J babyish

42 Holt Assessment: Literature, Reading, and Vocabulary

NAME _____ CLASS _____ DATE _____ SCORE _____

_____ 7. How might the interactions between the English and Indian children be *best* characterized?
   A Friendly and open
   B Hostile but polite
   C Playful and mischievous
   D Infrequent and cool

_____ 8. Which aspect of school life does Santha find *hardest* to understand?
   F Reading and writing
   G Tests
   H Sandwiches
   J Sports

_____ 9. Premila wants to leave school because —
   A her teacher insulted Indians
   B she is jealous of Santha's popularity
   C the family is moving to another city
   D the girls' mother told them to

_____ 10. Santha's mother and sister think she is too young to understand —
   F school rules
   G family tradition
   H the importance of a good education
   J anti-Indian sentiment

LITERARY FOCUS (20 points; 5 points each)
On the line provided, write the letter of the *best* answer to each of the following items.

_____ 11. Which of the following characters is a subordinate character in the story?
   A Nalini
   B Premila
   C Santha
   D The mother

_____ 12. In interactions between Santha and her sister, Santha —
   F bosses her sister around
   G gives in to her sister
   H challenges her sister
   J ignores her sister's advice

By Any Other Name   43

_____ **13.** When told why the girls have left school, their mother reacts with —
  A uncontrollable anger
  B utter indifference
  C calm dignity
  D intense fear

_____ **14.** What quality do Premila and her mother share?
  F Ambitiousness
  G Optimism
  H Self-respect
  J Vanity

Vocabulary Development (20 points; 4 points each)
Match the definition on the right with the Vocabulary word on the left. On the line provided, write the letter of the word or phrase that *best* defines each Vocabulary word.

_____ **15.** precarious   a. made afraid
_____ **16.** provincial   b. meeting the required standard
_____ **17.** insular   c. unsophisticated
_____ **18.** intimidated   d. isolated
_____ **19.** valid   e. unstable

Constructed Response (20 points)

20. The conflict in "By Any Other Name" occurs not only between individual characters but between cultures. Analyze one interaction that demonstrates this clash of British and Indian cultures. Then, on a separate sheet of paper, state what happens during the interaction and what is revealed.

COLLECTION 2 SUMMATIVE TEST

Character

This test asks you to use the skills and strategies you have learned in this collection. Read "The Other Wife," and then answer the questions that follow it.

The Other Wife
by Colette
translated by Margaret Crosland

"For two? This way, Monsieur and Madame, there's still a table by the bay window, if Madame and Monsieur would like to enjoy the view."

Alice followed the *maître d'hôtel.*

"Oh, yes, come on, Marc, we'll feel we're having lunch on a boat at sea . . ."

Her husband restrained her, passing his arm through hers.

"We'll be more comfortable there."

"There? In the middle of all those people? I'd much prefer . . ."

"Please, Alice."

He tightened his grip in so emphatic a way that she turned round.

"What's the matter with you?"

He said "sh" very quietly, looking at her intently, and drew her towards the table in the middle.

"What is it, Marc?"

"I'll tell you, darling. Let's order lunch. Would you like shrimp? Or eggs in aspic?"

"Whatever *you* like, as you know."

They smiled at each other, wasting the precious moments of an overworked, perspiring *maître d'hôtel* who stood near them, suffering from a kind of St. Vitus's dance.

"Shrimp," ordered Marc. "And then eggs and bacon. And cold chicken with cos lettuce salad. Cream cheese? *Spécialité de la maison*? We'll settle for the *spécialité*. Two very strong coffees. Please give lunch to my chauffeur, we'll be leaving again at two o'clock? Cider? I don't trust it. . . . Dry champagne."

He sighed as though he had been moving a wardrobe, gazed at the pale noonday sea, the nearly white sky, then at his wife, finding her pretty in her little Mercury-type hat with its long hanging veil.

"You're looking well, darling. And all this sea-blue color gives you green eyes, just imagine! And you put on weight when you travel. . . . It's nice, up to a point, but only up to a point!"

Her rounded bosom swelled proudly as she leaned over the table.

"Why did you stop me taking that place by the bay window?"

It did not occur to Marc Séguy to tell a lie.

"Because you'd have sat next to someone I know."

"And whom I don't know?"

"My ex-wife."

She could not find a word to say and opened her blue eyes wider.

"What of it, darling? It'll happen again. It's not important."

Alice found her tongue again and asked the inevitable questions in their logical sequence.

"Did she see you? Did she know that you'd seen her? Point her out to me."

"Don't turn round at once, I beg you, she must be looking at us. A lady with dark hair, without a hat, she must be staying at this hotel. . . . On her own, behind those children in red . . ."

"Yes, I see."

Sheltered behind broad-brimmed seaside hats, Alice was able to look at the woman who fifteen months earlier had still been her husband's wife.

"Incompatibility," Marc told her. "Oh, it was total incompatibility! We divorced like well-brought-up people, almost like friends, quietly and quickly. And I began to love you, and you were able to be happy with me. How lucky we are that in our happiness there haven't been any guilty parties or victims!"

The woman in white, with her smooth, lustrous hair over which the seaside light played in blue patches, was smoking a cigarette, her eyes half closed. Alice turned back to her husband, took some shrimp and butter and ate composedly.

"Why didn't you ever tell me," she said after a moment's silence, "that she had blue eyes too?"

"But I'd never thought about it!"

He kissed the hand that she stretched out to the bread basket and she blushed with pleasure. Dark-skinned and plump, she might have seemed slightly earthy, but the changing blue of her eyes, and her wavy golden hair, disguised her as a fragile and soulful blond. She showed overwhelming gratitude to her husband. She was immodest without knowing it and her entire person revealed over-conspicuous signs of extreme happiness.

They ate and drank with good appetite and each thought that the other had forgotten the woman in white. However, Alice sometimes laughed too loudly and Marc was careful of his posture, putting his shoulders back and holding his head up. They waited some time for coffee, in silence. An incandescent stream, a narrow reflection of the high and invisible sun, moved slowly over the sea and shone with unbearable brilliance.

"She's still there, you know," Alice whispered suddenly.

"Does she embarrass you? Would you like to have coffee somewhere else?"

"Not at all! It's she who ought to be embarrassed! And she doesn't look as though she having a madly gay time, if you could see her . . ."

"It's not necessary. I know that look of hers."

"Oh, was she like that?"

He breathed smoke through his nostrils and wrinkled his brows.

"Was she like that? No. To be frank, she wasn't happy with me."

"Well, my goodness!"

"You're delightfully generous, darling, madly generous. . . . You're an angel, you're. . . . You love me . . . I'm so proud, when I see that look in your eyes . . . yes, the look you have now. . . . She. . . . No doubt I didn't succeed in making her happy. That's all there is to it, I didn't succeed."

"She's hard to please!"

NAME	CLASS	DATE	SCORE

Alice fanned herself irritably, and cast brief glances at the woman in white who was smoking, her head leaning against the back of the cane chair, her eyes closed with an expression of satisfied lassitude.

Marc shrugged his shoulders modestly.

"That's it," he admitted. "What can one do? We have to be sorry for people who are never happy. As for us, we're so happy.... Aren't we, darling?"

She didn't reply. She was looking with furtive attention at her husband's face, with its good color and regular shape, at his thick hair with its occasional thread of white silk, at his small, well-cared-for hands. She felt dubious for the first time, and asked herself: "What more did she want, then?"

And until they left, while Marc was paying the bill, asking about the chauffeur and the route, she continued to watch, with envious curiosity, the lady in white, that discontented, hard-to-please, superior woman....

VOCABULARY SKILLS *(25 points; 5 points each)*

On the line provided, write the letter of the *best* answer to each item.

_____ 1. The Latin word *compati*, which means "to suffer together" or "to feel pity," is a clue that *incompatibility* means —

   A ability to feel another person's pain

   B cruelty toward the weak and helpless

   C inability to live together without conflict

   D smooth blending of different ingredients

_____ 2. A writer writes "her lustrous hair" but then decides to replace *lustrous* with a similar word. What word might the writer use?

   F glossy

   G curly

   H shapeless

   J long

_____ 3. In "The Other Wife" the woman in white sits back "with an expression of satisfied *lassitude*." Her expression would show her to be —

   A relaxed

   B lazy

   C conceited

   D dull-witted

"The Other Wife" from *The Other Woman* by Colette, translated by Margaret Crosland. Copyright 1951, ©1958 by Flammarion; English translation ©1971 by **Peter Owen Ltd. Publishers, London.** Reproduced by permission of the publisher.

Collection 2 Summative Test

_____ 4. An *incandescent* light bulb casts bright light. An *incandescent* smile is —
   F honest
   G fake
   H brilliant
   J brief

_____ 5. A person who is *dubious* is —
   A ignorant
   B fortunate
   C foolish
   D doubtful

COMPREHENSION *(25 points; 5 points each)*
On the line provided, write the letter of the *best* answer to each item.

_____ 6. Marc insists on sitting in the crowded area of the dining room because —
   F he dislikes the view of the water
   G there are no tables by the bay window
   H Alice wants to sit there
   J he wants to avoid his ex-wife

_____ 7. While dining, Alice sometimes laughs too loudly, and Marc carefully holds his head up. These behaviors are meant to impress —
   A the reader
   B the *maître d'hôtel*
   C the other diners
   D Marc's ex-wife

_____ 8. At the end of the story, Alice —
   F realizes what a wonderful husband Marc is
   G understands why Marc's first marriage failed
   H sees for the first time how good-looking Marc is
   J wonders if there is something lacking in Marc

_____ 9. The story is set in —
   A the United States in the twenty-first century
   B France in the twentieth century
   C France in the twelfth century
   D the United States in the nineteenth century

NAME	CLASS	DATE	SCORE

_____ **10.** According to Marc, why did he and his first wife split up?

    F He didn't make enough money.

    G They were incompatible.

    H His wife fell in love with another man.

    J Marc and Alice fell in love.

READING SKILLS AND STRATEGIES: CONSTRUCTED RESPONSE *(30 points; 10 points each)*

Making Inferences About Motivation

11. Make an inference about why Alice and Marc act the way they do at dinner. Write your answer in a paragraph on a separate sheet of paper.

Making Inferences About Character

12. Make an inference about one or more of the characters in "The Other Wife." Your inference must be based on details from the story. On a separate sheet of paper, explain your inference in a paragraph.

Comparing and Contrasting

13. Compare and contrast two characters in "The Other Wife." How are they alike? How are they different? Write your comparison in a paragraph on a separate sheet of paper.

LITERARY FOCUS: CONSTRUCTED RESPONSE *(20 points)*

14. Not much happens externally in "The Other Wife," but a major change occurs in the wife's attitude toward the husband. In the story map on the next page, write brief descriptions of the basic situation (exposition), significant events, climax, and resolution of "The Other Wife." Keep in mind that in this story an event might be something that a character says, learns, thinks, feels, or remembers, rather than an action.

Collection 2 Summative Test

| NAME | CLASS | DATE | SCORE |

Story Map for "The Other Wife"

Basic situation:

↓

Event:

↓

Event:

↓

Event:

↓

Event:

↓

Climax:

↓

Resolution:

Holt Assessment: Literature, Reading, and Vocabulary

| NAME | CLASS | DATE | SCORE |

COLLECTION 3 DIAGNOSTIC TEST

Narrator and Voice

LITERATURE
INFORMATIONAL TEXT
VOCABULARY

On the line provided, write the letter of the *best* answer to each of the following items.
(100 points; 10 points each)

_____ 1. Which of the following items is told from the **omniscient point of view**?

    A I followed the stranger into the dark library.

    B The stranger entered the dark library, unaware that someone was following him.

    C I was aware that someone was following me into the dark library, so I decided to hide.

    D She sensed the stranger's presence instantly, but where was he hiding? She looked around frantically until she saw that he had fled.

_____ 2. In analyzing the story's **point of view**, the reader should consider all of the following factors *except* —

    F how the story would differ if someone else were telling it

    G the narrator's knowledge and understanding

    H the universal appeal of the theme

    J whether the narrator is trustworthy

_____ 3. One of the key elements contributing to a writer's **voice** is —

    A word choice

    B alliteration

    C character

    D dialogue

_____ 4. A writer's attitude toward the reader, a subject, or a character is called —

    F mood

    G style

    H irony

    J tone

_____ 5. A reference to a well-known person or event from literature, history, or religion is a(n) —

    A flashback

    B allegory

    C analogy

    D allusion

Collection 3 Diagnostic Test   **51**

_____ 6. What is the *first* step you should take when setting out to write a **research report**?
   F Write a good opening sentence to catch the reader's attention.
   G Create a detailed outline.
   H Generate research questions that you plan to answer.
   J Cite sources in a *Works Cited* list.

_____ 7. You would probably find the *most* reliable information on a Web site maintained by a —
   A government agency
   B fellow high school student
   C corporation
   D political organization

_____ 8. If you wanted to use a **search engine** to research the life of Irish immigrants in the United States, the **search term** *immigrants* would be —
   F out-of-date
   G too broad
   H too narrow
   J irrelevant

_____ 9. Adding a **suffix** to a word can change its —
   A connotation
   B root
   C part of speech
   D prefix

_____ 10. A **thesaurus** contains —
   F word histories
   G synonyms
   H famous quotations
   J definitions

NAME	CLASS	DATE	SCORE

SELECTION TEST LITERARY RESPONSE AND ANALYSIS

By the Waters of Babylon Stephen Vincent Benét

COMPREHENSION *(60 points; 6 points each)*
On the line provided, write the letter of the *best* answer to each of the following items.

_____ 1. John encounters all of the following in the Place of the Gods *except* —
   A paintings
   B books
   C a pistol
   D a dead man

_____ 2. Based on clues in the story, readers can conclude that the rituals surrounding touching the metal developed —
   F because the metal is rare and valuable
   G to keep the metal out of the hands of robbers
   H because the metal stayed blazingly hot
   J because the metal has little real value

_____ 3. The statue with the cracked name ASHING is probably a sculpture of —
   A a man burned at the stake
   B a laundromat
   C Washington, D.C.
   D George Washington

_____ 4. Based on story clues, readers can conclude that John's father punishes John for eating the gods' food because —
   F the gods forbid people from eating it
   G the food is sometimes deadly
   H the food is specially blessed
   J only priests are allowed to eat it

_____ 5. The many lights that John sees in his dream of the Place of the Gods are probably —
   A cooking fires
   B electrical lights
   C television sets
   D rays of the sun

_____ 6. John loses his fear of the Place of the Gods because —
   F the wild dogs stop chasing him
   G he enjoys the foods the gods used to eat
   H he realizes that the gods were mortals
   J a voice in the dream explained the city to him

By the Waters of Babylon   53

NAME	CLASS	DATE	SCORE

_____ 7. Based on clues in the story, readers can reasonably conclude that the roaming cats —
  A are descended from people's pets
  B are wild cougars from nearby woods
  C are far more dangerous than the dogs
  D were used for sacrifices at the temples

_____ 8. Readers can conclude that John and his people are —
  F descended from the survivors of some catastrophe
  G visitors from outer space
  H barbarians who do not understand their world
  J the gods themselves

_____ 9. John's father wants John to withhold the complete truth because the father —
  A thinks that his son imagined the entire journey
  B worries that people will steal the metal from the Place of the Gods
  C is concerned that people will think his son is crazy
  D is afraid that people cannot accept the entire truth at once

_____ 10. From his experiences, John learns that the gods are —
  F hiding in their palaces waiting to be reborn
  G gods no one believes in anymore
  H victims of mass destruction
  J fierce demons

LITERARY FOCUS *(20 points; 5 points each)*
On the line provided, write the letter of the *best* answer to each of the following items.

_____ 11. The story's first-person point of view can *best* be described as —
  A universal
  B philosophical
  C metaphorical
  D restricted

_____ 12. The author selected this viewpoint to —
  F see inside the minds of the living characters and the gods at the same time
  G limit our knowledge and increase the story's suspense
  H understand how the gods live and die
  J give readers the widest possible vantage point

NAME	CLASS	DATE	SCORE

_____ **13.** The narrator's voice is *best* described as —
   A   self-assured but inexperienced
   B   weary and worldly-wise
   C   young but all-knowing
   D   cynical and experienced

_____ **14.** What tone is created by the narrator's voice?
   F   Fearful and amazed
   G   Ironical and amazed
   H   Terrified and hostile
   J   Hostile and ironical

CONSTRUCTED RESPONSE *(20 points)*
15. On a separate sheet of paper, write a paragraph that explains why Benét selected John to be the story's narrator and why he chose to relate the events through John's eyes. Support your ideas with details from the story.

By the Waters of Babylon   55

| NAME | CLASS | DATE | SCORE |

SELECTION TEST

LITERARY RESPONSE AND ANALYSIS

The Storyteller Saki

COMPREHENSION *(40 points; 4 points each)*
On the line provided, write the letter of the *best* answer to each of the following items.

_____ 1. The aunt is *best* described as —
   A poor and mistreated
   B ordinary and unimaginative
   C creative but overworked
   D clever and determined

_____ 2. All of the following factors make the train ride unbearable for everyone involved *except* —
   F sorrow
   G lack of things to do
   H boredom
   J the humidity and heat

_____ 3. The children consider the aunt's story unsatisfactory because the —
   A girl is dreadfully wicked
   B story is too long
   C story teaches a boring moral lesson
   D children have heard the same story before

_____ 4. Readers can infer that the bachelor tells the children a story because he —
   F feels sorry for the aunt and wants some peace for the both of them
   G is really very fond of children
   H rises to the aunt's challenge and wishes to show her up
   J is a professional storyteller

_____ 5. The children are especially pleased with the bachelor's story because —
   A there is a wolf in it
   B the Prince is foolish
   C the park is filled with beautiful talking parrots
   D Bertha is "horribly good"

_____ 6. Readers can conclude that the children liked the bachelor's story a great deal because —
   F the little girl is saved at the end
   G they can predict what will happen
   H they prefer pigs to sheep
   J good is not rewarded at the end

56 Holt Assessment: Literature, Reading, and Vocabulary

_____ 7. Saki's story is similar to the bachelor's story in that both —
   A reverse the reader's expectations
   B teach moral lessons
   C have happy endings
   D please the aunt very much

_____ 8. At the end of the story, the bachelor's mood is *best* described as —
   F self-satisfied
   G apologetic
   H thrilled
   J unhappy

_____ 9. In this story the author is satirizing —
   A people who take children on long journeys
   B spoiled children who bother other people
   C arrogant people who impose their ideas on others
   D sentimental and idealistic children's stories

_____ 10. All of the following details from the story are humorous *except* —
   F Cyril's constant questions
   G the girl reciting "On the Road to Mandalay"
   H the train's clicking wheels
   J Bertha's conceited attitude

LITERARY FOCUS (20 points; 5 points each)
On the line provided, write the letter of the *best* answer to each of the following items.

_____ 11. The **omniscient** point of view can *best* be described as —
   A inclusive
   B one-sided
   C symbolic
   D reflective

_____ 12. Using the omniscient point of view allows Saki to —
   F unfold events from the bachelor's viewpoint
   G comment directly on each character
   H make the bachelor's persona dominant
   J slant the perspective and withhold specific information

The Storyteller

_____ 13. The tone of this story is *best* described as —
    A moralistic and rigid
    B anxious and tense
    C humorous and ironic
    D serious and instructive

_____ 14. If the story had been told from the aunt's point of view *only*, the tone would likely have been —
    F less humorous
    G more humorous
    H less serious
    J the same as it is now

VOCABULARY DEVELOPMENT *(20 points; 4 points each)*

Match the definition on the right with the Vocabulary word on the left. On the line provided, write the letter of the word or phrase that *best* defines each Vocabulary word.

_____ 15. persistent   a. something that distracts attention

_____ 16. resolute   b. hot and humid

_____ 17. sultry   c. continuing

_____ 18. assail   d. determined

_____ 19. diversion   e. attack

CONSTRUCTED RESPONSE *(20 points)*

20. What do we learn from each character through the omniscient point of view? How does this choice of narrator affect the plot? On a separate sheet of paper, write a paragraph that explains your answer. Support your ideas with details from the story.

| NAME | CLASS | DATE | SCORE |

SELECTION TEST LITERARY RESPONSE AND ANALYSIS

The Cold Equations Tom Godwin

Comprehension *(40 points; 4 points each)*
On the line provided, write the letter of the *best* answer to each of the following items.

_____ 1. Barton is on a mission to —
   A take fever serum to a group of settlers
   B rescue a group of settlers stranded by a tornado
   C repair a disabled space cruiser
   D reunite a war hero and his sister

_____ 2. Which of the following characterizations *best* describes Marilyn?
   F Crafty and inventive
   G Professional and competent
   H Naive and innocent
   J Compassionate but unbending

_____ 3. The rule regarding EDS stowaways is based on —
   A the importance of stressing discipline
   B past experiences with renegades and hijackers
   C physical laws regarding fuel and weight
   D the need to maintain the secrecy of space missions

_____ 4. On first discovering the identity of the stowaway, Barton is shocked because —
   F he has never had to use the stowaway rule
   G he had expected to find a male stowaway
   H the gauge had indicated a much heavier person
   J he is a friend of Marilyn's brother Gerry

_____ 5. When Marilyn first realizes the seriousness of her situation, she —
   A bursts into tears
   B asks Barton a series of questions, seeking hope
   C attempts to take command of the EDS
   D lashes out at Barton

_____ 6. Barton chooses to jettison Marilyn because —
   F not doing so means death for both of them and others as well
   G he will lose his job if he disobeys the rules
   H her life is not as significant as that of a space explorer
   J she has risked her life and those of others for selfish reasons

The Cold Equations   59

| NAME | CLASS | DATE | SCORE |

_____ 7. While waiting to be jettisoned, Marilyn experiences all of the following emotions *except* —

   A   fear
   B   guilt
   C   disbelief
   D   hatred

_____ 8. Barton waits until the last possible minute to jettison Marilyn because he —

   F   wants to know why she has taken such a risk
   G   thinks she's attractive and enjoys her company
   H   thinks another EDS will rescue her
   J   is trying to give her time to accept the situation

_____ 9. The author increases the suspense by repeatedly referring to —

   A   the time kept on the chronometer
   B   the letters that Marilyn writes to her family
   C   Marilyn's appearance
   D   Barton's emotions

_____ 10. The story's theme is *best* described as —

   F   people never get away with being selfish
   G   space is merciless
   H   survival can demand hard choices
   J   the future of humanity is cold and grim

LITERARY FOCUS (20 points; 5 points each)
On the line provided, write the letter of the *best* answer to each of the following items.

_____ 11. The story is told from which point of view?

   A   Omniscient
   B   Third person limited
   C   First person
   D   A combination of first person and third person limited

_____ 12. The narrator's voice is *best* described as —

   F   hysterical
   G   uncaring
   H   calm
   J   light

| NAME | CLASS | DATE | SCORE |

_____ 13. The narrator's voice serves to —
  A echo the tone
  B provide an ironic counterpoint to the plot
  C increase the story's horror
  D decrease the emotion of Marilyn's fate

_____ 14. As a result of the point of view, Barton emerges as —
  F compassionate
  G unyielding
  H stern
  J foolish

VOCABULARY DEVELOPMENT *(20 points; 4 points each)*
On the lines provided, match each boldface Vocabulary word with its antonym.

annihilate   **recoiled**   **increments**   **paramount**   **irrevocable**

15. large increases _____

16. embraced _____

17. minor _____

18. build _____

19. changeable _____

CONSTRUCTED RESPONSE *(20 points)*

20. How might the story have changed if Marilyn had been the narrator? Consider the story's voice and tone in your response. On a separate sheet of paper, write a paragraph that explains your answer. Support your ideas with details from the story.

The Cold Equations

SELECTION TEST
INFORMATIONAL READING

Taste—The Final Frontier Esther Addley

COMPREHENSION *(50 points; 10 points each)*
On the line provided, write the letter of the *best* answer to each of the following items.

_____ 1. What is the *main* challenge in cooking for astronauts who are in space for a long time?
   A Keeping food fresh
   B Making food taste good
   C Balancing vitamins and minerals
   D Supplying sufficient nourishment

_____ 2. "Gastronautics" is a —
   F new way of growing food in space
   G special way of cooking good food for astronauts
   H French scientist and chef
   J new type of French food for astronauts

_____ 3. Scientists are working on providing good food for space flights by —
   A cooking food onboard
   B raising chickens onboard
   C packaging food in tubes
   D growing food in space

_____ 4. Hydroponic plants are grown —
   F on Mars
   G without air
   H in soil
   J in water

_____ 5. In this article the author's purpose is to —
   A convince readers to become astronauts
   B narrate a story about astronauts and food
   C inform and entertain readers
   D persuade readers to eat properly on earth

NAME _____ CLASS _____ DATE _____ SCORE _____

VOCABULARY DEVELOPMENT *(50 points; 10 points each)*
Complete each of the following analogies with the Vocabulary word that fits *best*. Select the Vocabulary words from the list below.

    judicious   habitat   mutiny   rancid   palatable

6. DELECTABLE : DELICIOUS :: tasty : _____

7. SOLDIERS : REBEL :: sailors : _____

8. SENSIBLE : WISE :: rational : _____

9. PURE : SPOILED :: fresh : _____

10. CITY : COLONY :: home : _____

Taste—The Final Frontier

63

| NAME | CLASS | DATE | SCORE |

SELECTION TEST

LITERARY RESPONSE AND ANALYSIS

Typhoid Fever *from* Angela's Ashes   Frank McCourt

COMPREHENSION *(40 points; 4 points each)*
On the line provided, write the letter of the *best* answer to each of the following items.

_____ 1. What gift does Patricia give Frankie?
   A A book of English poems
   B Several chocolate bars
   C A short history of England
   D A lock of her hair

_____ 2. What poem does Patricia read to Frankie?
   F "Annabel Lee"
   G "The Highwayman"
   H "The Tale of Typhoid Mary"
   J *The Little Messenger of the Sacred Heart*

_____ 3. The poem Patricia reads symbolizes —
   A Patricia's own tragic death
   B Frankie's terrible illness
   C the problems in the McCourt household
   D the continuing strife between the English and the Irish

_____ 4. The Kerry nurse has all the following character traits *except* —
   F coldness
   G sympathy
   H dullness
   J dedication

_____ 5. When Frankie is moved upstairs, he most fears —
   A the English
   B Seamus and the Kerry nurse
   C Patricia's ghost
   D the spirits of patients who died there

_____ 6. Most adults in the story attempt to make Frankie behave by —
   F giving him chocolate bars
   G telling him about former patients
   H making him feel guilty
   J threatening him

64 Holt Assessment: Literature, Reading, and Vocabulary

_____ 7. Which of the following words *best* describes the narrator's attitude toward the fever ward?
    A astonished
    B bittersweet
    C respectful
    D grateful

_____ 8. Which of the following situations might *best* be seen as an example of comic relief in the memoir?
    F Sister Rita separates the two young patients.
    G Frankie is ten, and Patricia is thirteen.
    H Seamus completes the poem for Frankie.
    J Frankie worries about phantoms eating his chocolate.

_____ 9. Which of the following characters is *not* a source of comic relief in this memoir?
    A Patricia
    B Frankie's mother
    C Seamus
    D The Kerry nurse

_____ 10. Frankie's parents emerge as —
    F kind and attentive
    G weak and distant
    H sick and dispirited
    J powerful and effective

LITERARY FOCUS *(20 points; 5 points each)*
On the line provided, write the letter of the *best* answer to each of the following items.

_____ 11. Who is the narrator of this story?
    A An unnamed omniscient narrator
    B Patricia Madigan
    C Frank McCourt
    D Seamus

_____ 12. The voice in this memoir is that of a(n) —
    F strict, demanding nun
    G kindhearted, clever girl
    H intelligent, sensitive boy
    J worried, caring mother

Typhoid Fever

NAME	CLASS	DATE	SCORE

_____ 13. Which of the following words *best* describes the voice in this memoir?
   A poetic
   B unemotional
   C angry
   D instructive

_____ 14. The author selected this narrator, voice, and persona to —
   F show how the past shaped his present
   G persuade people to take better care of their children
   H argue in favor of better social programs for the poor
   J compare and contrast America with Ireland

VOCABULARY DEVELOPMENT (20 points; 4 points each)
On the lines provided, match each boldface Vocabulary word with its synonym or antonym, as directed. One Vocabulary word will be used twice.

clamoring   induced   potent   torrent

15. persuaded   synonym: _____

16. powerless   antonym: _____

17. trickle   antonym: _____

18. crying out; asking synonym: _____

19. prevented   antonym: _____

CONSTRUCTED RESPONSE (20 points)

20. In what ways is the poem about the highwayman similar to the story of Patricia and Frankie? To support your conclusions, include at least two references to specific details in the selection. On a separate sheet of paper, write a paragraph that explains your answer. Support your ideas with details from the story.

NAME	CLASS	DATE	SCORE

SELECTION TEST **INFORMATIONAL READING**

An Ancient Enemy Gets Tougher Karen Watson

COMPREHENSION *(100 points; 10 points each)*
On the line provided, write the letter of the *best* answer to each of the following items.

_____ 1. You can infer from the title that tuberculosis is —
   A becoming even more dangerous
   B a disease that will soon be cured by medicine
   C a disease that leaves a trail that scientists can follow
   D a disease that once killed millions

_____ 2. The author compares tuberculosis to David in the biblical story of David and Goliath to show that —
   F tuberculosis has been around since biblical times
   G one tiny bacterium can kill a person
   H even little people can fight this disease
   J one tiny pill can defeat this deadly disease

_____ 3. According to the information in this article, scientists have found evidence of tuberculosis in all of the following cultures *except* the —
   A ancient Egyptians
   B ancient Hindus
   C modern Inuit
   D modern Chinese

_____ 4. Tuberculosis is also called —
   F the mummy disease
   G the biblical illness
   H AIDS
   J consumption

_____ 5. The World Health Organization has announced that —
   A tuberculosis has ceased to be a major threat
   B tuberculosis still causes millions of deaths
   C everyone should get vaccinated against tuberculosis
   D tuberculosis is both a virus and a bacteria

_____ 6. The article states that tuberculosis attacks many animals. Which of the following creatures is *not* mentioned?
   F Birds
   G Lions and tigers
   H Dogs and cats
   J Sheep

An Ancient Enemy Gets Tougher 67

_____ 7. According to the article, tuberculosis usually enters the body through —
   A a cut or a wound
   B the eyes
   C the lungs
   D the transmission of bodily fluids

_____ 8. The method of transmission suggests that tuberculosis is —
   F not very contagious
   G rarely passed among people who live or work together
   H easily cured
   J highly contagious

_____ 9. Which of the following statements is *true*?
   A Scientists still do not clearly understand how tuberculosis works.
   B Tuberculosis can only be contracted by people whose immune systems are already weakened.
   C Scientists have an effective vaccine against tuberculosis, but the vaccine is very expensive.
   D Tuberculosis always develops very quickly.

_____ 10. Of the following choices the source with the *most* up-to-date information about tuberculosis would be a(n) —
   F Web page
   G museum exhibition
   H encyclopedia article
   J science textbook

| NAME | CLASS | DATE | SCORE |

COLLECTION 3 SUMMATIVE TEST

Narrator and Voice

This test asks you to use the skills and strategies you have learned in this collection. The passage you are about to read is from the book *Sacajawea* by Joseph Bruchac. Sacajawea was the famous American Indian woman who helped Lewis and Clark explore the West. This passage takes place before Sacajawea met the famous explorers. Read the passage. Then, answer the questions that follow it.

Stories Up the River
FROM **Sacajawea**
by Joseph Bruchac

When the world was new, Wolf made it so that it was easy to travel the rivers. Wolf made it so the rivers flowed both ways. On one side of the river, the water flowed upstream. On the other side, it flowed downstream. To go one way or the other, you had only to paddle over to whichever side you wished and the river would carry you.

The Coyote came along. "This is too easy for everyone," he said. "This is not interesting."

So Coyote made things more interesting. He made all the rivers flow in just one direction. He threw in rocks so that the rivers would be rough in some places, and made waterfalls so the rivers would be dangerous in others.

Why did he do that? Because he was Coyote.

Still, things come upstream: fish, water creatures, and people in boats.

And another thing that cannot be seen but is even stronger than fish and water creatures and the boats of people always comes up the river, too. What is that? It is stories.

If you look at the river, Firstborn Son, you might think that everything in it always goes downstream. You see how the river's strength pushes down the limbs of trees and the small islands of grass that are torn from the banks. You see how its waters move so swiftly. But just as some things go downriver with the current, so do other things push up against it. You see how people take their boats upstream—how they paddle and push them or how they spread sails like the big white wings of birds, and then the wind helps them travel upstream. It is not easy for people to go upstream. They must work hard.

That fourth summer since I had been taken captive, as the captains made their way up the Great Muddy River, the stories about them traveled ahead of them. Those stories even reached the place where we lived among the Mandans and the Minnetarees. What were those stories? Curious stories. Stories of a huge war boat that had guns on it so big that when they were fired it was like the crack of thunder. Stories of soldiers who came and told the nations along the river that they were no longer the children of the Spanish king. Now the Great White Father of the new nation to the east was their father. Now there must be a new way among their people, the white warrior chiefs said. Now it was wrong for the Indian nations to fight one another. Think of that, warriors telling other warriors not to fight. They actually ordered the people to stop fighting and said if they did not stop, they would punish them.

Collection 3 Summative Test **69**

People laughed when they heard that. It was amusing. If the young men of one tribe could not go and raid another tribe, then how would they be able to earn names of honor? How could any young man of one tribe become a leader if he could not prove himself in battle? It was curious that a few handfuls of white men thought they could punish whole villages of Indians. These white men coming up the river were brave, but they were also foolish.

Other strange stories were told about them, too. It was said that their boats were filled with trade goods, with guns and powder and useful things. Everyone wanted to trade for these things, especially for the weapons. People understood trading. Even those tribes that fought with each other one season would meet together in peace to trade the next. For many winters other white men, British and Spanish and French, had gone up and down the rivers trading. But these strangers said they did not want to trade. They would not sell their guns or powder to anyone. They said they had brought all the other things to give away as gifts. But even though they gave gifts, the gifts they gave were very small. It was as if they were crazy.

When those stories came to us, we were not sure that those crazy white soldiers would reach the Mandans and Minnetarees. First they would have to pass by the Brule, the people the whites call the Tetons. If the white men would not trade with them, if they just gave the Brule a handful of little presents, the Brule would be insulted. Then those stories of the white men would stop coming up the river. They would float back down with the same current that would carry the burned remains of their war boat and the dead bodies of those brave but foolish white men, and their story would be at an end.

But the ways of stories are mysterious, Firstborn Son. And I will end this part of our story for now.

VOCABULARY SKILLS *(25 points; 5 points each)*

Each of the underlined words below has also been underlined in the selection. Re-read those passages in which the underlined words appear, and then use context clues and your prior knowledge to select an answer. On the line provided, write the letter of the word that *best* answers each question.

_____ 1. Which synonym of current has the closest meaning to how it is used in the following sentence?

"But just as some things go downriver with the current, so do other things push up against it."

A recent

B accepted

C stylish

D flow

"Sacajawea: Stories up the River" from *Sacajawea: The Story of Bird Woman and the Lewis and Clark Expedition* by Joseph Bruchac. Copyright © 2000 by Joseph Bruchac. Reproduced by permission of **Harcourt, Inc.** This material may not be reproduced in any form or by any means without the prior written permission of the publisher.

_____ 2. Which synonym of curious has the closest meaning to how it is used in the following sentence?

"It was curious that a few handfuls of white men thought they could punish whole villages of Indians."

F unusual
G prominent
H visible
J inquisitive

_____ 3. Which synonym of prove has the closest meaning to how it is used in the following sentence?

"How could any young man of one tribe become a leader if he could not prove himself in battle?"

A establish
B examine
C demonstrate
D settle

_____ 4. Which synonym of remains has the closest meaning to how it is used in the following sentence?

"They would float back down with the same current that would carry the burned remains of their war boat and the dead bodies of those brave but foolish white men. . . ."

F crumbs
G corpse
H refuse
J leavings

_____ 5. Which synonym of mysterious has the closest meaning to how it is used in the following sentence?

"But the ways of stories are mysterious, Firstborn Son."

A puzzling
B dark
C secret
D shrouded

Collection 3 Summative Test

71

COMPREHENSION *(25 points; 5 points each)*
On the line provided, write the letter of the *best* answer to each of the following items.

_____ 6. In the myth that begins this selection, Coyote makes the rivers flow in just one direction because he —
   F believes that a single direction will make river traffic more efficient
   G wants to get even with Wolf
   H wants to help human beings
   J wants to have some fun by causing difficulty

_____ 7. According to the myth, which of the following items is the strongest thing that travels up the river?
   A Fish
   B Stories
   C Other water
   D Boats of people

_____ 8. The message delivered by the people on the war boat traveling up the river is that —
   F the Indians are now under the control of the Great White Father
   G there is no longer a king of Spain
   H Indian nations should fight one another to show their bravery
   J the Indian people would be treated as equals to other Americans

_____ 9. Sacajawea is living among the Mandans and the Minnetarees because she —
   A is a warrior princess
   B has married a Mandan
   C has been taken captive
   D is traveling with Lewis and Clark

_____ 10. Sacajawea thinks the Brule will react to the gifts of the white men by —
   F being insulted and killing the white men
   G welcoming the white men into their camps
   H sending the white men back down the river to find better gifts
   J holding the white men hostage

NAME	CLASS	DATE	SCORE

READING SKILLS AND STRATEGIES *(20 points; 10 points each)*
Drawing Conclusions
On the line provided, write the letter of the *best* answer to each of the following items.

_____ 11. Based on this selection, you can conclude that the members of the Indian nations —
   A   do not like the Spanish king
   B   like the gifts Lewis and Clark bring
   C   consider fighting battles indispensable
   D   prefer small gift to elaborate ones

_____ 12. The white men think that they can punish whole groups of Indians for fighting. With this fact in mind, you might conclude that the white men —
   F   fear and respect the courage of the Indians
   G   do not understand the ways of the Indians and underestimate them
   H   think the Indians want their help in making peace with each other
   J   think the Indians fear the Spanish king and so will not put up a fight

LITERARY FOCUS: CONSTRUCTED RESPONSE *(30 points; 10 points each)*
On the line provided, write the letter of the *best* answer to each of the following items.

_____ 13. The myth that begins this selection is told from a(n) —
   A   first-person point of view
   B   second-person point of view
   C   third-person-limited point of view
   D   omniscient point of view

_____ 14. The second part of this selection is told —
   F   in the first person by Sacajawea
   G   by an omniscient narrator
   H   in the third person but limited to Firstborn Son
   J   in the first person by the explorer Meriwether Lewis

15. The author's voice, persona, and choice of a **narrator** affect characterization and the tone, plot, and credibility of a text. Suppose the explorer William Clark had narrated this selection. On a separate sheet of paper, explain how it would be different.

Collection 3 Summative Test

COLLECTION 4 DIAGNOSTIC TEST

Comparing Themes

LITERATURE
INFORMATIONAL TEXT
VOCABULARY

On the line provided, write the letter of the *best* answer to each of the following items.
(100 points; 10 points each)

_____ 1. Which of the following statements is the *best* example of a **theme** in a story?

   A People's taste in music sometimes changes over the years.
   B The oceans are filled with many different species of fish.
   C A great weakness may also be a strength.
   D The main character constantly seeks adventure.

_____ 2. One of the *best* ways to figure out a story's **theme** is to examine —

   F elements of the author's style
   G the setting
   H the writer's life
   J how the main character changes

_____ 3. Which of the following statements about **theme** is *false*?

   A Some themes are universal.
   B The theme is usually not stated directly.
   C There are many ways to express a single theme.
   D A story can have only one theme.

_____ 4. Which of the following sentences provides an example of an **internal conflict**?

   F A boy confronts a friend about being disloyal.
   G A woman struggles to stay alive in a boat on the ocean.
   H A man feels guilty because he committed a crime.
   J A woman argues with her mother about her choice of a career.

_____ 5. **Genres** are —

   A categories, or types, of literary works
   B ways of speaking that are characteristic of a particular region
   C turning points in a story
   D traditional plots that have been used in stories throughout the years

_____ 6. Good **persuasive writing** —
   F criticizes the reader to make a point
   G uses evidence to support an argument
   H relies mainly on emotional appeals
   J is based mostly on opinions

_____ 7. Which of the following sentences is an example of a **generalization**?
   A When people get angry, they often act thoughtlessly.
   B America is made up of fifty states.
   C My dog likes to go to the park all year round.
   D In 1968, my grandfather came to the United States.

_____ 8. An author's **intent** is —
   F his or her purpose for writing
   G a claim stated in an argument
   H his or her attitude toward a subject
   J the topic of a persuasive text

_____ 9. Which of the following sentences contains an example of an **idiom**?
   A Nancy sings like a bird.
   B It was raining cats and dogs outside.
   C The sun was a flaming orange ball in the sky.
   D His hair resembled straw.

_____ 10. What is **jargon**?
   F Words that are no longer in use
   G Words with multiple meanings
   H Vocabulary specific to a particular profession
   J Slang, or informal language

Collection 4 Diagnostic Test

| NAME _____ | CLASS _____ | DATE _____ | SCORE _____ |

SELECTION TEST　　　　　　　　　　　　　　　　　　　　**LITERARY RESPONSE AND ANALYSIS**

Catch the Moon Judith Ortiz Cofer

COMPREHENSION *(40 points; 4 points each)*
On the line provided, write the letter of the *best* answer to each of the following items.

_____ 1. Luis is sent to juvenile hall for six months because he —
   A was framed by his friends
   B breaks into an elderly woman's house
   C tries to destroy his father's junkyard
   D brings a giant snake to school

_____ 2. At first, Luis wonders whether he should do his full sentence in juvenile hall because —
   F his father won't let him forget his crime
   G he doesn't like working for his father
   H he committed three other crimes
   J all his friends are in juvenile hall

_____ 3. Approximately how long ago did Luis begin to get into trouble in school?
   A Six months ago
   B One year ago
   C Two years ago
   D Five years ago

_____ 4. Luis's problems start soon after —
   F his parents divorce
   G he stops going out with Naomi
   H his mother dies
   J he enters junior high school

_____ 5. The Tiburones are a —
   A gang
   B school band
   C family
   D business

_____ 6. Mr. Cintrón is *best* described as —
   F depressed and mean
   G well-meaning and hard-working
   H careless but strict
   J angry and bitter

76　　　　　　　　　　　　　　　Holt Assessment: Literature, Reading, and Vocabulary

NAME _____ CLASS _____ DATE _____ SCORE _____

_____ **7.** Luis likes Naomi because she is —
   A wild and fun loving
   B kind and beautiful
   C a friend of his mother's
   D wealthy and generous

_____ **8.** Luis tries hard to find the hubcap for Naomi because he —
   F wants to make the sale
   G wants to upstage his father
   H takes his friend's dare
   J wants to do something nice for Naomi

_____ **9.** Mr. Cintrón polishes everything that belonged to his wife because —
   A he is too poor to afford new things
   B he is too stingy to buy new things
   C it is a way to show his love for her
   D he wants to sell the things

_____ **10.** At one point in the story, Luis cries "a flood of tears" —
   F because he is embarrassed about his criminal record
   G because he is sad at his mother's funeral
   H when he acknowledges how much he misses his mother
   J because he is badly injured by a flying hubcap

LITERARY FOCUS *(20 points; 5 points each)*
On the line provided, write the letter of the *best* answer to each of the following items.

_____ **11.** One way in which Luis does *not* change is that he does *not* —
   A grow closer to his father
   B acknowledge his feelings about his mother
   C decide to get better grades in school
   D begin to understand the value of hard work

_____ **12.** The story's title refers to —
   F the hubcap Luis gives to Naomi
   G looking for something you can never get
   H learning about the moon and the planets
   J working day and night

Catch the Moon   **77**

_____ 13. Luis's internal conflict is that he —
    A cannot express his grief about his mother
    B clashes with his father about work
    C gets in trouble with the school authorities
    D makes a fool of himself in front of Naomi

_____ 14. The theme of this story is *best* stated as —
    F everyone should work hard
    G you cannot escape your past problems
    H we all have one true love
    J involvement in life can ease painful losses

VOCABULARY DEVELOPMENT (20 points; 4 points each)

Complete each of the following analogies with the Vocabulary word that fits *best*. Select the Vocabulary words from the list below.

dismantled   vintage   ebony   sarcastic   relics

15. ANTIQUES : ARTIFACTS :: heirlooms : _____

16. RESPECTFUL : MOCKING :: polite : _____

17. WHITE : BLACK :: ivory : _____

18. NEW : CLASSIC :: modern : _____

19. CONSTRUCTED : TOOK APART :: assembled : _____

CONSTRUCTED RESPONSE (20 points)

20. How would this story be different if Judith Ortiz Cofer had written it as a poem? How would it be the same? On a separate sheet of paper, write a paragraph that explains your answer. Support your ideas with details from the story.

SELECTION TEST

LITERARY RESPONSE AND ANALYSIS

The Bass, the River, and Sheila Mant W. D. Wetherell

COMPREHENSION *(40 points; 4 points each)*
On the line provided, write the letter of the *best* answer to each of the following items.

_____ 1. How old is the narrator?
   A Twelve years old
   B Thirteen years old
   C Fourteen years old
   D Sixteen years old

_____ 2. How old is Sheila Mant?
   F Fourteen years old
   G Fifteen years old
   H Sixteen years old
   J Seventeen years old

_____ 3. The narrator loves Sheila because she —
   A is beautiful and unattainable
   B is kind and intelligent
   C is sensitive and emotional
   D shares his interest in fishing

_____ 4. When the narrator asks Sheila go to Dixford, she —
   F responds with an enthusiastic yes
   G responds with a clear no
   H asks him if he has a car
   J says that she is going to a dance with Eric

_____ 5. The narrator sets up his fishing rod on the canoe because —
   A he wants to have something to do if Sheila leaves
   B the fish bite best at night
   C he knows that Sheila likes to fish
   D he never goes anywhere without his fishing rod.

_____ 6. The narrator won't tell Sheila that he has caught a huge bass because —
   F he has never caught a bass before
   G she is terrified of fish
   H he knows that she will want the fish for herself
   J he doesn't want to embarrass himself

The Bass, the River, and Sheila Mant

NAME	CLASS	DATE	SCORE

_____ 7. The narrator is distracted by the tugging of the bass and —
   A   Sheila's conversation
   B   his struggle to grow up
   C   his social failures
   D   the sound of the music in the background

_____ 8. What does the narrator eventually do?
   F   Tell Sheila about the huge fish
   G   Reel in the bass
   H   Cut the bass loose
   J   Dump Sheila overboard

_____ 9. The narrator takes this action because he —
   A   feels a strong emotional bond with Sheila
   B   knows that Sheila does not like fishing
   C   does not like to fish at night
   D   is very clumsy

_____ 10. The *best* example of an external conflict is the narrator's —
   F   struggle to hide the fishing rod from Sheila
   G   mental anguish while riding in the canoe
   H   wistful memories and his regrets later in life
   J   struggle to compete with Eric

LITERARY FOCUS *(20 points; 5 points each)*
On the line provided, write the letter of the *best* answer to each of the following items.

_____ 11. Sheila is *best* described as —
   A   self-centered
   B   sensitive to other people's feelings
   C   mature and sophisticated
   D   a role model for the narrator

_____ 12. The central conflict in this story is revealed when the narrator —
   F   considers whether to reel in the fish or let it go
   G   catches his first fish
   H   asks Sheila to go on a date
   J   realizes that he has no hope of dating Sheila

| NAME | CLASS | DATE | SCORE |

_____ **13.** After the narrator resolves this conflict, he —
  A is angry with Sheila
  B is filled with regret
  C decides to give up fishing
  D decides to give up dating

_____ **14.** The story's theme is *best* expressed as —
  F fishing is more important than dating
  G it is important to have a hobby you like
  H dating is difficult and often painful
  J enduring values, not superficial values, guide the best choices

VOCABULARY DEVELOPMENT (20 points; 4 points each)
Match the definition on the right with the Vocabulary word on the left. On the line provided, write the letter of the word or words that *best* define each Vocabulary word.

_____ **15.** denizens   **a.** pertaining to a son or daughter
_____ **16.** pensive   **b.** doubtful; not sure
_____ **17.** dubious   **c.** inhabitants
_____ **18.** antipathy   **d.** dreamily thoughtful
_____ **19.** filial   **e.** strong dislike

CONSTRUCTED RESPONSE (20 points)

20. Each of the title's elements—the bass, the river, and Sheila Mant—is important to the narrator. Choose one of these elements, and, on a separate sheet of paper, write a paragraph explaining what the element represents in terms of the story's theme. Support your ideas with details from the story.

The Bass, the River, and Sheila Mant

| NAME | CLASS | DATE | SCORE |

SELECTION TEST   LITERARY RESPONSE AND ANALYSIS

And of Clay Are We Created Isabel Allende
translated by Margaret Sayers Peden
Ill-Equipped Rescuers Dig Out Volcano Victims
Bradley Graham

COMPREHENSION (40 points; 4 points each)
On the line provided, write the letter of the *best* answer to each of the following items.

_____ 1. Rolf Carlé is —
   A the narrator
   B a public official
   C a little girl trapped in the mud
   D a reporter

_____ 2. The village is destroyed when —
   F an avalanche buries it
   G war breaks out
   H a great hurricane sweeps everything away
   J mud bubbles up from underground hot springs

_____ 3. Azucena is —
   A a little girl trapped in the mud
   B Rolf Carlé's life partner
   C Rolf Carlé's co-worker
   D a young boy trapped in the mud

_____ 4. You can infer that Rolf tries to save Azucena for all of the following reasons *except* that he —
   F associates her with his dead sister
   G is a brave man
   H wants to win a prize for his TV show
   J is kind and decent

_____ 5. The narrator notes that the reporters keep broadcasting Azucena's face around the world. In this way the narrator shows —
   A how hard the media works
   B how difficult it is to gather news
   C how the media can prey on victims
   D that we can prevent tragedies with information

_____ 6. Rolf keeps promising Azucena that he will save her because he —
   F wants to see her reaction
   G believes that he can save her
   H knows that they will both die
   J thinks this lie will protect her from fear

_____ 7. After Rolf stays, and they talk, sing, and pray, he —
   A is filled with hope
   B hears birds singing
   C panics when he sinks deeper and deeper
   D confronts his painful past

_____ 8. Rolf and Azucena are similar in that they both are —
   F trapped by circumstances beyond their control
   G young teenagers who have made mistakes
   H careless and have gotten into dangerous situations
   J dying and have given up hope

_____ 9. Azucena comes to represent all —
   A children
   B victims of tragedy
   C Colombians
   D poor people

_____ 10. Rolf does not save Azucena because —
   F he dies before she does
   G he gives up hope and leaves
   H she does not want to be saved
   J the pump does not arrive in time

LITERARY FOCUS (20 points; 5 points each)
On the line provided, write the letter of the *best* answer to each of the following items.

_____ 11. As the story progresses, Rolf changes, and he —
   A becomes hardened to suffering
   B no longer loves the narrator
   C becomes fearful and timid
   D learns to accept death and tragedy

And of Clay Are We Created / Ill-Equipped Rescuers . . .

NAME	CLASS	DATE	SCORE

_____ 12. How is the conflict resolved?

    F Azucena dies.

    G The pump arrives.

    H The mud recedes.

    J Azucena is rescued.

_____ 13. What does the "clay" in the title represent?

    A Life and death

    B The earth

    C Childhood

    D Birth

_____ 14. The theme of both the story and the article may be best expressed as —

    F no pain, no gain

    G the media creates reality

    H nature's kindness can be disguised as cruelty

    J some things must simply be accepted

VOCABULARY DEVELOPMENT *(20 points; 4 points each)*
Complete each sentence with the Vocabulary word from the list below that *best* fits the context.

commiserate	**magnitude**	**tenacity**	**pandemonium**	**ingenuity**

15. The great _____ of the eruptions sends tons of mud down into the village.

16. If not for the stubborn _____ of the workers, many more people would have died.

17. _____ breaks out as everyone starts screaming, crying, and moaning.

18. The rescue team shows great _____ in finding ways to help people.

19. As the news crews stood by, they could only _____ with the relatives of the victims and offer sympathy.

84   Holt Assessment: Literature, Reading, and Vocabulary

CONSTRUCTED RESPONSE (20 points)

20. The newspaper article and Allende's story both tell of a tragedy. How are the newspaper article and Allende's story the same? How are they different? Explain how the focus and concerns of the narrator differ in the story and the newspaper article. How do the narrators view the plot, theme, and main idea in the two works? On a separate sheet of paper, write a paragraph that explains your answer. Support your ideas with details from the story and the newspaper article.

| NAME | CLASS | DATE | SCORE |

SELECTION TEST LITERARY RESPONSE AND ANALYSIS

The Man in the Water Roger Rosenblatt
The Parable of the Good Samaritan King James Bible
A State Championship Versus Runner's Conscience John Christian Hoyle

COMPREHENSION (40 points; 4 points each)
On the line provided, write the letter of the *best* answer to each of the following items.

_____ 1. Which of the following factors made the crash of Flight 90 unusual?
   A The ice on the plane's wings caused the crash.
   B The crash occurred in January.
   C The plane struck a bridge.
   D Few passengers survived.

_____ 2. What did "the man in the water" do that was so special?
   F Talk to the rescuers
   G Repeatedly pass the lifeline to others
   H Swim to safety
   J Refuse to cooperate

_____ 3. According to the essay, the man in the water was —
   A Donald Usher
   B never identified
   C probably Lenny Skutnik
   D the author

_____ 4. The author contradicts Lenny Skutnik's assertion that "somebody had to go in the water" because the author thinks Skutnik is —
   F foolish
   G cowardly
   H modest
   J dishonest

_____ 5. Which word *best* describes how Rosenblatt views nature?
   A impersonal
   B life-giving
   C hostile
   D good

Holt Assessment: Literature, Reading, and Vocabulary

NAME	CLASS	DATE	SCORE

_____ **6.** According to Rosenblatt, what two elements are in conflict?

    F Humanity and nature

    G Nature and God

    H Humanity and God

    J Good and evil

_____ **7.** What sets the man in the water apart from others?

    A Endurance

    B Intelligence

    C Sense of humor

    D Selflessness

_____ **8.** The author's *main* purpose in writing this article is to —

    F report the crash of Flight 90

    G explain the cause of the crash

    H think about how he would act in the same situation

    J praise the heroes of the crash

_____ **9.** What lesson does "The Parable of the Good Samaritan" teach?

    A Flying is risky.

    B Helping others is important.

    C Strangers can pose dangers.

    D Everyone needs help sometime.

_____ **10.** What happens to John Christian Hoyle when he stops to help an injured runner?

    F He wins the race anyway.

    G His coach is furious at him for losing the race.

    H His coach is proud of his unselfish action.

    J He receives a special award.

LITERARY FOCUS (20 points; 5 points each)
On the line provided, write the letter of the *best* answer to each of the following items.

_____ **11.** Donald Usher, Lenny Skutnik, and the man in the water have in common the fact that they all —

    A saved lives

    B survived

    C are trained rescue workers

    D are passengers on the airplane

The Man in the Water . . . Runner's Conscience

_____ 12. Which statement *best* summarizes Rosenblatt's main idea?
    F The man in the water is a hero and a rare human being.
    G Humans do not have to be powerless against nature.
    H No ordinary person could do what the man in the water did.
    J Nature has total power over humanity.

_____ 13. Which of the following details *most* strongly supports Rosenblatt's main idea?
    A A mechanical failure caused the crash of Flight 90.
    B The man in the water was middle-aged.
    C The man in the water did not reveal his identity.
    D Five people were saved because of the man in the water.

_____ 14. These three selections are *mainly* about —
    F helping others
    G not getting the credit you deserve
    H rescue workers
    J unexpected problems

VOCABULARY DEVELOPMENT *(20 points; 4 points each)*
Write a synonym or antonym for each Vocabulary word, as directed.

15. flailing   *synonym:* _____

16. extravagant   *antonym:* _____

17. abiding   *synonym:* _____

18. pitted   *synonym:* _____

19. implacable   *antonym:* _____

CONSTRUCTED RESPONSE *(20 points)*

20. "The Man in the Water," "The Parable of the Good Samaritan," and "A State Championship Versus Runner's Conscience" all explore the topic of heroism. How does the purpose of each selection determine the way it gets its point across? On a separate sheet of paper, write a paragraph that explains your answer. Support your ideas with details from the selections.

| NAME | CLASS | DATE | SCORE |

SELECTION TEST INFORMATIONAL READING

If Decency Doesn't, Law Should Make Us Samaritans Gloria Allred *and* Lisa Bloom
Good Samaritans U.S.A. Are Afraid to Act
Ann Sjoerdsma

COMPREHENSION *(50 points; 10 points each)*
On the line provided, write the letter of the *best* answer to each of the following items.

_____ 1. According to France's "Good Samaritan" law, —
  A people who help others must be rewarded
  B heroes are celebrated for their unselfish deeds
  C the pictures of Princess Diana's car crash could not be published
  D people must help others in distress

_____ 2. According to the authors of "If Decency Doesn't, Law Should Make Us Samaritans," —
  F the United States has a "Good Samaritan" law
  G the United States needs a "Good Samaritan" law
  H Princess Diana would not have died if there had been a "Good Samaritan" law
  J no one should be forced to help someone else

_____ 3. According to current United States laws, if you see someone choking in a restaurant, you —
  A must try to help the victim yourself
  B must call for help at once
  C are not required to do anything
  D are not allowed to help in any way

_____ 4. According to the authors, people ignore the needs of victims for all of the following reasons *except* —
  F malicious enjoyment
  G fear of getting involved
  H feeling disconnected from strangers in need
  J worrying that it will take too much time

_____ 5. The authors' arguments are effective because they —
  A use convincing evidence to support generalizations
  B appeal only to emotion
  C appeal only to reason
  D use loaded words, generalizations, and opinions

If Decency Doesn't, . . . / Good Samaritans . . .   **89**

VOCABULARY DEVELOPMENT *(50 points; 10 points each)*
Match the definition on the right with the Vocabulary word on the left. On the line provided, write the letter of the word or phrase that *best* defines each Vocabulary word.

_____ 6. allegations   a. legal responsibility to make good a loss
_____ 7. depraved   b. interpreted
_____ 8. liability   c. assertions made without proof
_____ 9. callous   d. morally wrong
_____10. construed   e. unfeeling

Comparing Themes

This test asks you to use the skills and strategies you have learned in this collection. Read the following passage from a nonfiction book, and then answer the questions that follow it.

FROM **Another Writer's Beginnings**
by R. A. Sasaki

I was an ugly child. I had a long horse face, not much of a nose, and two front teeth that got in the way no matter what I tried to do and made my expressions for surprise, friendliness, confusion, and anger all look the same. On top of that, my hair, lopped straight across the front above the eyebrows and straight around from side to side just above the earlobes, looked like a lumberjack had taken a buzz saw to it. Actually, my father was not a lumberjack. Neither was he a barber; but for some reason it always fell to him to do the job. As if that weren't enough, I had glasses that winged up like the back fins of a Cadillac—white, speckled with silver.

I was sheltered from the crushing reality of my own plainness by the reassurances of a loving family. I was no different from other little girls in that I spent long hours before my mother's looking glass trying out different expressions, poses, angles, looking for that glimmer of beauty that could make me a Mouseketeer. My sister had a much better sense of reality. She knew, at the age of eight, that there was no such thing as a Japanese Mouseketeer. Reality never stopped *me* from hoping. Had I been aware of it, it might have. But I was oblivious. That was the source of my confidence.

My first inkling of my ugliness was when I brought home my fifth-grade school picture. There I was in a pink dress with a white collar, bangs cut straight across my face, their line marred only by the Cad fins winging up to each corner. It looked like I had a mouth full of marbles. (It was just my teeth.) I dutifully delivered the picture over to my mother, without pride, without apology, in the same way I'd hand over a report card—impersonally, dissociating myself from it so that whatever the reaction, I would not be culpable. Then I retired to the stairway as my mother studied the picture.

There was a rather long silence, followed by a sigh.

You have to know my mother in order to understand just how devastating this reaction was, even in my dissociated state. My mother believes in being positive. One summer when we went to Yosemite, the waterfalls were dry. My sister expressed her disappointment in a postcard to a friend: "There is no water in Yosemite Falls." My mother was horrified. "You shouldn't write a thing like that," she chided. "You should say Yosemite is beautiful and you're having a wonderful time."

Well, when my mother saw my fifth-grade picture, I knew that there was no water in Yosemite Falls; but I expected some encouraging remark. I realized the extent of my plainness when even my mother could find absolutely nothing to say. I was sorry for her and thought she deserved better: a daughter like my friend Marilyn, for example, who was cute and sweet and always took Shirley Temple pictures full of personality. Instead, she had this horse-faced daughter, whose picture was full of teeth. Teeth and wings.

Collection 4 Summative Test 91

So for the first time I considered the possibility that I might not make it as a Mouseketeer after all. Looks would never be my meal ticket. I would have to develop other talents.

VOCABULARY SKILLS *(25 points; 5 points each)*
Each of the underlined words below has also been underlined in the selection. Re-read those passages in which the underlined words appear, and then use context clues and your prior knowledge to help you select an answer. On the line provided, write the letter of the word or phrase that *best* completes each statement.

_____ 1. Reassurances are meant to make you feel —
   A   attractive
   B   better
   C   bad
   D   ashamed

_____ 2. Someone who is oblivious is *not* —
   F   nasty
   G   comfortable
   H   attractive
   J   paying attention

_____ 3. Dissociating oneself from something means —
   A   keeping distant from it
   B   liking it
   C   understanding it
   D   creating it

_____ 4. If you are culpable, you could be —
   F   blamed
   G   overlooked
   H   praised
   J   rewarded

_____ 5. An example of devastating news is the report of —
   A   sunny weather
   B   an award
   C   the death of someone you love
   D   an overdue bill

From "Another Writer's Beginnings" from *The Loom and Other Stories* by R. A. Sasaki. Copyright © 1991 by R. A. Sasaki. Reproduced by permission of **Graywolf Press, Saint Paul, Minnesota.**

NAME _____ CLASS _____ DATE _____ SCORE _____

COMPREHENSION *(25 points; 5 points each)*
On the line provided, write the letter of the *best* answer to each of the following items.

_____ **6.** To what does the author compare her glasses?
   F   A bird's wings
   G   A car's fins
   H   Shark's fins
   J   Goggles

_____ **7.** The author dreams of becoming a —
   A   Mouseketeer
   B   lumberjack
   C   hairdresser
   D   Japanese Shirley Temple

_____ **8.** The author implies that she developed her writing talent because —
   F   she could not rely on beauty for recognition
   G   she was naturally good with words
   H   beauty is a drawback for a writer
   J   her sister encouraged her to write

_____ **9.** When the author shows her mother the school picture, the author —
   A   tries to show pride in her looks
   B   pretends to be unconcerned about her mother's reaction
   C   tries to prevent her mother from seeing the picture
   D   laughs and makes a joke about the picture

_____ **10.** As a result of her mother's reaction to the picture, the author realizes that her mother —
   F   thinks the author is beautiful
   G   wants to change the subject
   H   was looking at the wrong picture
   J   thinks her daughter is unattractive

READING SKILLS AND STRATEGIES: CONSTRUCTED RESPONSE *(30 points; 10 points each)*
Determining an Author's Purpose

11. On a separate sheet of paper, describe R. A. Sasaki's purpose in this passage from *Another Writer's Beginnings*. Consider why the subject was important to her and what she wants us to think about it.

Collection 4 Summative Test

93

Making Inferences About Character

12. What motivated the writer to act the way she did? Complete the following chart to make inferences about her motivation.

▶ Goal	▶ Motivation	▶ Outcome
Wanting to become a Mouseketeer		
Showing her mother the school picture		
Deciding to become a writer		

Summarizing the Main Idea

13. What insight or message does R. A. Sasaki want to communicate? Consider her appearance, personality, and family. On a separate sheet of paper, state the main idea in your own words. Include at least two supporting details.

LITERARY FOCUS: CONSTRUCTED RESPONSE *(20 points)*

14. Imagine that this passage from *Another Writer's Beginnings* had been written as a novel rather than an essay. Complete the following chart to analyze how the selection would change.

▶ Literary Element	▶ As a novel	▶ As an essay
Form		
Length		
Content		
Purpose		
Statement about life		

COLLECTION 5 DIAGNOSTIC TEST

LITERATURE
INFORMATIONAL TEXT
VOCABULARY

Irony and Ambiguity

On the line provided, write the letter of the *best* answer to each of the following items.
(100 points; 10 points each)

_____ 1. A story contains **situational irony** when —
   A something humorous or ridiculous happens
   B what a character means contrasts with what he or she actually says
   C something happens that is the opposite of what is expected
   D events in a story do not seem related

_____ 2. **Dramatic irony** occurs when —
   F there is a surprising plot twist in a play
   G the truth about something is not revealed until the end of a play
   H the narrator of a story is unreliable
   J the reader or audience knows something that a character does not know

_____ 3. What is a **contradiction**?
   A Two statements that have opposite meanings
   B An illogical outcome or resolution
   C An argument against something
   D An action taken against a character

_____ 4. When a text is **ambiguous,** —
   F the characters are unbelievable
   G it is open to several interpretations
   H it does not rely on a traditional structure
   J the plot does not follow chronological order

_____ 5. **Subtleties** in a literary work are —
   A complex themes
   B sensory details
   C fine distinctions
   D implied opinions

| NAME | CLASS | DATE | SCORE |

_____ **6.** Writers use **mood** to —
    F make a story autobiographical
    G evoke an overall feeling in a literary work
    H define the time and place when a story occurs
    J express a character's thoughts

_____ **7.** The **reliability** of a source is *not* affected by —
    A the writer's professional background
    B the source's publication date
    C the source's authoritativeness
    D the organization of information in the source

_____ **8.** When writers display **bias** in sources, —
    F their opinions are based on prejudice
    G their views are objective
    H they do not quote other sources or experts
    J they do not present facts in their texts

_____ **9.** To complete a **word analogy,** you —
    A consider a word's connotations
    B determine the relationship between words in a pair
    C make inferences about a word's meaning based on context clues
    D list words with similar definitions

_____ **10.** *Respectful* and *inspection* share the same —
    F prefix
    G suffix
    H root
    J denotation

| NAME | CLASS | DATE | SCORE |

SELECTION TEST LITERARY RESPONSE AND ANALYSIS

Lamb to the Slaughter Roald Dahl

COMPREHENSION *(40 points; 4 points each)*
On the line provided, write the letter of the *best* answer to each of the following items.

_____ 1. At the beginning of the story, Mary Maloney is —
   A plotting to kill her husband
   B thinking about what to make for dinner
   C happily waiting for her husband
   D worried that her husband has betrayed her

_____ 2. From Mary Maloney's dialogue you know that her husband —
   F is unemployed
   G is a police officer
   H works for a butcher
   J sells life insurance

_____ 3. The fact that the lamb is frozen is significant because —
   A thawing it will take time
   B it mirrors the couple's icy relationship
   C eating improperly thawed meat can make a person ill
   D it could be used as a murder weapon

_____ 4. Whom do the police *first* suspect when they arrive on the scene?
   F Mrs. Maloney
   G The husband's co-workers
   H An intruder
   J The grocer

_____ 5. The real reason Mary goes to the store is that she needs —
   A food for dinner
   B an alibi
   C some time to think
   D something to distract her

_____ 6. Mary attempts to put the police officers at ease by —
   F offering them drinks
   G confessing to the crime
   H making idle chitchat
   J hiding the murder weapon

Lamb to the Slaughter   **97**

_____ 7. One of the police officers thinks the murder weapon was a —
   A kitchen knife
   B leg of lamb
   C wrench, or spanner
   D pistol

_____ 8. Mary refuses to lie down because she —
   F feels too nervous to relax
   G needs to make dinner for the officers
   H wants the officers to feel sorry for her
   J wants to keep an eye on the investigation

_____ 9. Sergeant Noonan probably refuses to eat the lamb at first because he —
   A works better on an empty stomach
   B thinks it is unprofessional to eat on duty
   C suspects that the lamb has been used as a murder weapon
   D doesn't want to take time away from the investigation

_____ 10. Mary probably giggles at the end of the story because —
   F the officers have eaten the murder weapon
   G her mind has snapped
   H she is glad her husband is dead
   J she wants to charm the officers

LITERARY FOCUS *(20 points; 5 points each)*
On the line provided, write the letter of the *best* answer to each of the following items.

_____ 11. The types of irony found in "Lamb to the Slaughter" are —
   A dramatic irony and situational irony
   B verbal irony and ambiguity
   C dramatic irony but no situational irony
   D situational irony but no dramatic irony

_____ 12. Which of the following statements *best* express the irony of the story's title?
   F A lamb generally symbolizes innocence.
   G It was the husband who was slaughtered.
   H The lamb and the husband were both Mary's victims.
   J The lamb is the murder weapon.

NAME	CLASS	DATE	SCORE

_____ 13. The dramatic irony of the officer's comment that the murder weapon is "Probably right under our very noses" comes from the fact that —

    A it really *is* under their noses

    B Mary is giggling uncontrollably

    C it is not what we expected him to say

    D the situation is far worse than he thinks

_____ 14. Which of the following choices is the *best* description of the mood the author creates in "Lamb to the Slaughter"?

    F Darkly comic

    G Light and breezy

    H Neutral

    J Eerie and menacing

VOCABULARY DEVELOPMENT *(20 points; 4 points each)*

Match the definition on the left with the Vocabulary word on the right. On the line provided, write the letter of the Vocabulary word.

_____ 15. comforting   a. anxiety

_____ 16. state of being worried or uneasy   b. hospitality

_____ 17. friendly treatment of guests   c. placid

_____ 18. calm; tranquil   d. consoling

_____ 19. take pleasure in   e. luxuriate

CONSTRUCTED RESPONSE *(20 points)*

20. "Lamb to the Slaughter" is full of irony. On a separate sheet of paper, write a paragraph identifying one example of dramatic irony and one example of situational irony in the story. Tell how each example is used in the story.

Lamb to the Slaughter

SELECTION TEST

LITERARY RESPONSE AND ANALYSIS

R.M.S. Titanic Hanson W. Baldwin
A Fireman's Story Harry Senior
From a Lifeboat Mrs. D. H. Bishop

COMPREHENSION *(40 points; 4 points each)*
On the line provided, write the letter of the *best* answer to each of the following items.

_____ 1. Which of the following actions did *not* contribute to the *Titanic* disaster?
  A None of the men in charge gave much credence to the warnings about ice.
  B The lifeboats were not full when lowered.
  C The *Carpathia* did not pick up the first boats until 4:10.
  D The *Californian* did not respond to the *Titanic*'s CQD.

_____ 2. To prevent the disaster, First Operator Phillips could have —
  F talked more to Cape Race
  G listened to the message from the *Californian*
  H spent more time with the captain
  J played in the band

_____ 3. The *Titanic* was considered unsinkable *mainly* because it was equipped with —
  A modern radio sets
  B triple propellers
  C watertight compartments
  D plenty of lifeboats

_____ 4. The "dancing spark" that appears throughout "R.M.S. Titanic" symbolizes —
  F lightning
  G life
  H the radio transmission
  J the sea

_____ 5. The court ruled that the *Titanic* had —
  A been captained poorly
  B more than enough lifeboats
  C received adequate warning about icebergs
  D been sabotaged

NAME	CLASS	DATE	SCORE

_____ **6.** Of the following events, which one happens *first*?

    F The *Californian* warns the *Titanic* about ice.
    G First Operator Phillips learns that the *Californian* is stuck in an ice field.
    H The *Californian*'s radio operator learns of the disaster nearby.
    J The *Carpathia* comes to the aid of the *Titanic* survivors.

_____ **7.** Of the following events, which one happens *last*?

    A Most of the *Titanic*'s lifeboats are lowered partially empty.
    B The *Carpathia* steams into the North River and brings in the survivors.
    C A passenger chooses to die rather than board a lifeboat without her dog.
    D Captain Smith gives Mr. Ismay the radio message about icebergs ahead.

_____ **8.** In "A Fireman's Story," Harry Senior tries to help an Italian woman by —

    F trying to save one of her babies
    G helping to free up a collapsible boat
    H getting her into a lifeboat
    J carrying her to safety

_____ **9.** In Harry Senior's account the captain threatens to shoot anyone who goes above the well deck because he —

    A thinks the firemen want revenge for the sinking
    B doesn't want the firemen taking up space on the lifeboats
    C believes the area above the well deck is dangerous
    D blames the firemen for the sinking

_____ **10.** In "From a Lifeboat," Mrs. D. H. Bishop explains that she could tell that a mass of people were running on the decks because —

    F the ship was rocking back and forth
    G she could see people's hats moving above the rails
    H the deck lights kept appearing and disappearing
    J the light from the moon made everything visible

LITERARY FOCUS *(20 points; 5 points each)*
On the line provided, write the letter of the *best* answer to each of the following items.

_____ **11.** When Colonel John Jacob Astor helps his wife into a lifeboat and says that he will join her later, his words are an example of —

    A verbal irony
    B confusion
    C poetic irony
    D cowardice

R.M.S. Titanic / A Fireman's Story / From a Lifeboat

_____ 12. When the *Titanic* nearly crashes into the steamer *New York*, the event is an example of —
   F foreshadowing
   G verbal irony
   H characterization
   J climax

_____ 13. Which of the following events in "A Fireman's Story" is an example of dramatic irony?
   A The millionaires escape in a half-filled boat while a poor woman and her babies drown.
   B Harry Senior is hit on the head with an oar but still manages to get in a boat.
   C The woman escapes with her baby but is overtaken by a huge wave.
   D The firemen finally get their hands on a collapsible boat.

_____ 14. In "From a Lifeboat" the rescuers cannot save survivors because the rescuers would be drowned as well. This predicament is a kind of —
   F resolution
   G foreshadowing
   H situational irony
   J verbal irony

VOCABULARY DEVELOPMENT (20 points; 4 points each)
Match the definition on the left with the Vocabulary word on the right. On the line provided, write the letter of the Vocabulary word.

_____ 15. better than all others   a. poised
_____ 16. supported   b. corroborated
_____ 17. determine   c. ascertain
_____ 18. quieted   d. quelled
_____ 19. balanced; in position   e. superlative

CONSTRUCTED RESPONSE (20 points)

20. On a separate sheet of paper, write a paragraph explaining how Baldwin's account illustrates the situational and dramatic irony of the events he describes. Give three examples that show the two types of irony in the selection.

| NAME | CLASS | DATE | SCORE |

SELECTION TEST LITERARY RESPONSE AND ANALYSIS

from Into Thin Air Jon Krakauer

COMPREHENSION (25 points; 5 points each)
On the line provided, write the letter of the *best* answer to each of the following items.

_____ 1. Which word *best* describes the way Jon Krakauer feels standing atop Mount Everest?
   A regret
   B happiness
   C detachment
   D nostalgia

_____ 2. Which of the following items is an example of foreshadowing?
   F Krakauer eating noodle soup and candy
   G Krakauer's early mention of the number of people who died
   H The blanket of clouds Krakauer sees when he turns to take photographs
   J Krakauer's reference to the money that people paid to be guided on the climb

_____ 3. Why does Krakauer feel better after Harris turns the valve on the regulator?
   A Krakauer is happy to see another climber.
   B Harris gives Krakauer a pep talk.
   C Krakauer's thinking improves when he breathes more deeply.
   D Harris accidentally increases the oxygen flow.

_____ 4. Which of the following words *best* summarizes Krakauer's attitude about what happens on the mountain?
   F horrified
   G impressed
   H disinterested
   J enchanted

_____ 5. Krakauer suggests that most tragic events on the mountain are caused by a lack of —
   A skill
   B teamwork
   C fear
   D common sense

Into Thin Air

103

NAME _____ CLASS _____ DATE _____ SCORE _____

LITERARY FOCUS *(20 points; 5 points each)*
On the line provided, write the letter of the *best* answer to each of the following items.

_____ 6. The feeling Krakauer has when he finally stands atop Everest is incongruous because —
   F he feels alive and excited
   G his feet hurt
   H it is extremely cold
   J he doesn't care

_____ 7. According to Krakauer, after the clouds are sighted, the guides do something incongruous: They —
   A keep telling everyone to go up the mountain
   B start to take people back to Base Camp
   C act as if the weather were not serious
   D check their oxygen regulators

_____ 8. When Krakauer sees Fischer on his way down, Fischer's appearance seems to contradict his reputation in that he —
   F looks strong and determined
   G appears to be "hammered"
   H has his oxygen mask on
   J is not leading anyone

_____ 9. In his conclusion, Krakauer ironically suggests that despite what happened, people will die on Everest again because —
   A today's climbing equipment is shoddy
   B most of the guides are inadequately trained
   C the challenge causes people to abandon common sense
   D they are lured by the promise of fame and fortune

VOCABULARY DEVELOPMENT *(25 points; 5 points each)*
Match the definition on the left with the Vocabulary word on the right. On the line provided, write the letter of the Vocabulary word.

_____ 10. harmless   a. jeopardize
_____ 11. worsen   b. deteriorate
_____ 12. cross   c. speculate
_____ 13. endanger   d. benign
_____ 14. think; guess   e. traverse

104   Holt Assessment: Literature, Reading, and Vocabulary

| NAME | CLASS | DATE | SCORE |

CONSTRUCTED RESPONSE *(30 points)*

15. On a separate sheet of paper, write a paragraph identifying examples of situational irony and contradiction in the real-life disaster Krakauer describes. Make at least two references to specific details in the selection to support your ideas.

Into Thin Air

105

| NAME | CLASS | DATE | SCORE |

SELECTION TEST   INFORMATIONAL READING

Explorers Say There's Still Lots to Look For
Helen O'Neill

COMPREHENSION *(50 points; 10 points each)*
On the line provided, write the letter of the *best* answer to each of the following items.

_____ 1. What is the opening setting of this news story?
   A An archaeological site in the Andes
   B A research vessel in the Pacific Ocean
   C The Explorer's Club in New York
   D A balloon high above the surface of the earth

_____ 2. Instead of attending the banquet, what would Sylvia Earle rather have been doing?
   F Deep-sea exploration
   G Circumnavigating the earth
   H Discovering mummies
   J Writing about her adventures

_____ 3. According to Sylvia Earle, it is a popular myth that —
   A explorers search for treasure
   B all corners of the earth have been explored
   C exploration is a dangerous activity
   D all explorers are men

_____ 4. What discovery did Robert Ballard make that could be used to prove the accuracy of a story in the Bible?
   F The remains of Noah's ark
   G Signs of Egypt's seven plagues
   H The tomb of Moses
   J Evidence of a giant flood

_____ 5. Explorer Ernest Shackleton is remembered for —
   A reaching the South Pole first
   B saving his marooned men
   C mapping the North Pole
   D vanishing in the Arctic

106   Holt Assessment: Literature, Reading, and Vocabulary

NAME	CLASS	DATE	SCORE

VOCABULARY DEVELOPMENT *(50 points; 10 each)*

Match the definition on the left with the Vocabulary word on the right. On the line provided, write the letter of the Vocabulary word.

_____ 6. quaint or odd humor   **a.** marooned

_____ 7. person who plots a course   **b.** whimsy

_____ 8. stranded; helpless   **c.** nudged

_____ 9. pushed; bumped   **d.** navigator

_____ 10. misleading or inaccurate idea   **e.** illusion

Explorers Say There's Still Lots to Look For

| NAME | CLASS | DATE | SCORE |

SELECTION TEST LITERARY RESPONSE AND ANALYSIS

Notes from a Bottle James Stevenson

COMPREHENSION *(40 points; 4 points each)*
On the line provided, write the letter of the *best* answer to each of the following items.

_____ 1. What seemingly important information does the narrator of this story fail to provide at the beginning?

　A How high the water will go
　B What year the story is set in
　C Why there is a flood in the first place
　D What time of day it is

_____ 2. What structural elements in the text tell you these notes are a kind of diary?

　F The story is set in the first person.
　G Dates and times are recorded before each entry.
　H The story is set in the present tense.
　J The writer concentrates on everyday details.

_____ 3. What device does Stevenson use to frame the entire story?

　A The story is supposed to be notes found in a bottle.
　B The story begins with the flood at the second floor and ends at the ninth floor.
　C People go from a state of chaos to a state of calm.
　D The story is told as if from one friend to another.

_____ 4. What reason does the writer give for the lack of phones and other services?

　F The flood has destroyed them.
　G The mayor has suspended all services.
　H Nobody has the need for them anymore.
　J The workers are on strike.

_____ 5. The shift in the mood of the people might be *best* described as changing from —

　A sad to delighted
　B carefree to grim
　C pessimistic to optimistic
　D self-centered to spiritual

_____ 6. What item in the story gets moved from the fourth floor to the sixth floor?

　F A sack of flour
　G A bed
　H A piano
　J Food

108 Holt Assessment: Literature, Reading, and Vocabulary

NAME	CLASS	DATE	SCORE

_____ 7. Who moves into the Wenkers's apartment?
    A The narrator
    B The Carsons
    C Martin, the doorman
    D Ed Shea

_____ 8. Which of the following actions is *not* a prank played by the characters in the story?
    F Skipping LPs through the air
    G Dropping bags filled with flour
    H Throwing burning paper out of the windows
    J Setting buckets of water above doors

_____ 9. Which of the following statements explains why people *probably* slip out of the narrator's apartment during the party?
    A Another party is going on down the hall.
    B They see that the water is rising to his floor.
    C They realize they don't like him very much.
    D The food has run out.

_____ 10. Langford *probably* moves to the tallest TV antenna because —
    F he hopes to survive from that position
    G the antenna is his property
    H he wants to tie on a distress signal
    J he thinks it is something to lean on

LITERARY FOCUS *(20 points; 5 points each)*
On the line provided, write the letter of the *best* answer to each of the following items.

_____ 11. What is ambiguous about the way in which the flood is dealt with?
    A There is no clear cause given.
    B The water keeps rising.
    C The cause was an atomic explosion.
    D It happens in a major city.

_____ 12. Which of the following events is *not* an example of subtlety or ambiguity in "Notes from a Bottle"?
    F The people are celebrating for no clear reason.
    G Services have ended not because of the flood but because of strikes.
    H Boats cruise by, but no one tries to escape.
    J The water eventually covers the narrator's floor.

Notes from a Bottle

NAME _____ CLASS _____ DATE _____ SCORE _____

_____ **13.** Considering what you read in "R.M.S. Titanic," what is subtly ironic about the woman wanting to hear "Nearer My God to Thee" at the end of "Notes from a Bottle"?

    A It is the same song that was played as the *Titanic* sank.

    B It expresses the same arrogance demonstrated by the *Titanic*'s builders.

    C In his account, Baldwin tells about his experience as a choirboy.

    D The woman could have saved herself but chose not to.

_____ **14.** The reasons for the celebration at the beginning of the story are ambiguous. What mood does this create?

    F Dark humor

    G Stark terror

    H Cold formality

    J Everyday reality

Vocabulary Development *(20 points; 4 points each)*

Match the definition on the left with the Vocabulary word on the right. On the line provided, write the letter of the Vocabulary word.

_____ **15.** thought; guesswork   **a.** portable

_____ **16.** covered with water   **b.** recede

_____ **17.** move back or away   **c.** speculation

_____ **18.** probably   **d.** presumably

_____ **19.** able to be carried   **e.** submerged

Constructed Response *(20 points)*

20. On a separate sheet of paper, write a paragraph explaining how the author's use of subtlety and ambiguity creates a change in mood from the beginning to the end of the story. Note specific examples of subtlety and ambiguity and how they affect you as a reader.

COLLECTION 5 SUMMATIVE TEST

Irony and Ambiguity

This test asks you to use the skills and strategies you have learned in this collection. Read this Nigerian folk tale, and then answer the questions that follow it.

The Talking Skull
a Nigerian folk tale
translated by
Leo Frobenius and Douglas G. Fox

A hunter goes into the bush. He finds an old human skull. The hunter says: "What brought you here?" The skull answers: "Talking brought me here." The hunter runs off. He runs to the king. He tells the king: "I found a dry human skull in the bush. It asks you how its father and mother are."

The king says: "Never since my mother bore me have I heard that a dead skull can speak." The king summons the Alkali, the Saba, and the Degi and asks them if they have ever heard the like. None of the wise men has heard the like, and they decide to send guards out with the hunter into the bush to find out if his story is true and, if so, to learn the reason for it. The guards accompany the hunter into the bush with the order to kill him on the spot should he have lied.

The guards and the hunter come to the skull. The hunter addresses the skull: "Skull, speak." The skull is silent. The hunter asks as before: "What brought you here?" The skull does not answer. The whole day long the hunter begs the skull to speak, but it does not answer. In the evening the guards tell the hunter to make the skull speak, and when he cannot, the guards kill the hunter in accordance with the king's command.

When the guards are gone, the skull opens its jaws and asks the dead hunter's head: "What brought you here?" The dead hunter's head replies: "Talking brought me here!"

VOCABULARY SKILLS (20 points; 4 points each)
On the line provided, write the letter of the word or phrase that *best* matches the definition of the underlined word.

_____ 1. The bush referred to in this story is —

    A the countryside

    B a shrub

    C a magical land

    D a hiding place

_____ 2. In the phrase "since my mother bore me," the word *bore* means —

    F the width of a tube

    G gave birth to

    H made me uninterested

    J gave lessons to

"The Talking Skull: A Nigerian Folktale" from *A Treasury of African Folklore* by Harold Courlander. Copyright © 1996 by Harold Courlander. Reproduced by permission of **Marlowe & Company**.

Collection 5 Summative Test   **111**

NAME	CLASS	DATE	SCORE

_____ 3. When you <u>accompany</u> a person you —
    A work with the person
    B go along with the person
    C give the person special powers
    D rule over the person

_____ 4. If you give a <u>summons</u>, you are asking someone to —
    F go away
    G give you a present
    H be your friend
    J appear before you

_____ 5. Doing something in <u>accordance</u> with something else is acting —
    A against your will
    B competitively
    C together
    D under pressure

COMPREHENSION (25 points; 5 points each)
On the line provided, write the letter of the *best* answer for each of the following items.

_____ 6. The hunter in the story found the skull —
    F after a thorough search
    G by accident
    H by using magic
    J at the command of the king

_____ 7. The king sends guards along with the hunter to —
    A protect him from lions
    B spy on him
    C kill him if the skull doesn't speak
    D make sure he comes back

_____ 8. What tells you that this tale is circular in structure?
    F Many African tales have a similar form.
    G The king wants to kill everyone.
    H The king, the skull, and the hunter are the same man.
    J The hunter ends up saying just what the skull said.

NAME	CLASS	DATE	SCORE

_____ 9. Which of the following statements *best* summarizes the story?

   A   A man finds an amazing thing, but talking about it leads to his doom.

   B   A man tries to do a favor for a king, but the king kills him instead.

   C   A skull that has been in the desert for a long time is found.

   D   A hunter does his duty and gets his just reward.

_____ 10. The dry skull probably doesn't speak when the guards are there because it —

   F   does not want to offend the king

   G   wants the hunter to be tricked too

   H   is unable to speak except to the hunter

   J   has finally died

READING SKILLS AND STRATEGIES: CONSTRUCTED RESPONSE *(40 points; 10 points each)*
Making Inferences

11. Some folk tales seek to do two things at once: entertain and instruct. Usually, the instruction in a folk tale takes the form of a simple lesson that has serious and far-reaching implications. "The Talking Skull" is a short piece built around a central, basic irony. See if you can infer from the story which type of irony this story presents. On a separate sheet of paper, write a paragraph that states whether the irony of this story is dramatic or situational and what led you to make this inference.

Understanding Text Structures

_____ 12. The hunter says the same thing at the end of the story as the skull said at the beginning. This text structure tells you the story may have a moral (or message). From the following possible messages in "The Talking Skull," choose the one that you think fits best. On a separate sheet of paper, write the letter of the answer you chose, and briefly defend your choice with supporting evidence from the folk tale.

   F   Haste makes waste.

   G   A penny saved is a penny earned.

   H   When in doubt, keep your mouth shut.

   J   Run, don't walk, to the nearest exit.

Understanding Cause and Effect

13. One way to view "The Talking Skull" is through the lens of cause and effect. The main character, the hunter, takes an action which leads to a very real effect. In a short paragraph on a separate sheet of paper, record what you think were the hunter's action and the result of that action. Support your reasoning with an example from the story.

Collection 5 Summative Test   113

Making Predictions

_____ 14. Sometimes it is fun to predict what might happen after a story is over, based on the patterns that have been set up. In this case the way the story is structured makes it possible to predict that something fairly specific will happen. From the list below, choose a prediction that you think is *most* likely, and support your choice with a brief statement. Write your answer on a separate sheet of paper.

    F The king will visit the skull himself.
    G The guards will lie to the king about what happened.
    H Another hunter will find the new talking skull.
    J The dead hunter will decide never to speak to anyone again.

LITERARY FOCUS: CONSTRUCTED RESPONSE *(15 points)*

15. The ironic structure of "The Talking Skull" presents a sort of pattern. By breaking the story into parts, this pattern can be made clear. On the diagram below, write a brief description of the action of "The Talking Skull" as the cycle works its way around to where it began. Divide the action of the plot into five separate events so that the cycle completes itself. The first line has been completed for you.

Cycle of Irony in "The Talking Skull"

a. A hunter finds a skull that talks to him.

b. _____

f. _____

c. _____

e. _____

d. _____

114 Holt Assessment: Literature, Reading, and Vocabulary

COLLECTION 6 DIAGNOSTIC TEST

LITERATURE
INFORMATIONAL TEXT
VOCABULARY

Symbolism and Allegory

On the line provided, write the letter of the *best* answer to each of the following items. *(100 points; 10 points each)*

_____ 1. What is a **public symbol**?

   A A symbol that relates to a particular country or region

   B A commonly accepted symbol

   C A symbol used to represent organizations or institutions

   D A symbol that stands for people

_____ 2. To interpret an ongoing storm in a story as a **symbol** of despair, a reader would need to —

   F make an association between elements of the story

   G examine the story's conflict

   H identify the author's purpose for writing

   J understand the characters' backgrounds

_____ 3. Which of the following statements about **symbols** is *false*?

   A A symbol may appear several times in a work.

   B Symbols are often visual.

   C Symbols can have more than one meaning.

   D All literary works contain symbols.

_____ 4. The characters, places, and events in **allegories** —

   F represent elements in a dream

   G stand for abstract ideas or moral qualities

   H have no figurative meaning

   J reflect the writer's life

_____ 5. In the **omniscient point of view,** the narrator —

   A has no role in the story but can tell us what all the characters are thinking and feeling

   B is a character in the story who tells about events from his or her viewpoint

   C is a minor character in the story who mostly observes the action

   D plays no part in the action but tells the story from the vantage point of one character

Collection 6 Diagnostic Test **115**

6. A story's **theme** —
   F is always directly stated in the story
   G summarizes the plot
   H is the same as the story's subject
   J offers some insight or idea about life

7. When you **paraphrase** a text, you —
   A discuss its strengths and weaknesses
   B state the main idea
   C restate it in your own words
   D connect it to other sources you have read

8. When you draw a **conclusion** based on several sources, you —
   F generate a question for further research
   G make a judgment or form an opinion based on evidence
   H compare and contrast the sources
   J evaluate the reliability of the information in the texts

9. To determine a word's meaning using **context clues,** you —
   A identify the root of the word
   B search for hints about the word's definition in the text
   C consider the associations the writer wishes to evoke by using a word
   D evaluate how the word suits the narrator or character who is using it

10. Which of the following relationships is *not* usually found in an **analogy**?
   F Synonyms
   G Characteristic of
   H Word families
   J Degree of intensity

| NAME | CLASS | DATE | SCORE |

SELECTION TEST LITERARY RESPONSE AND ANALYSIS

Through the Tunnel Doris Lessing

COMPREHENSION *(40 points; 4 points each)*
On the line provided, write the letter of the *best* answer to each of the following items.

_____ 1. Jerry's mother allows him to go to the beach by the wild bay because she —
   A would like some time to herself
   B does not realize how dangerous it is
   C wants him to make friends with the boys playing there
   D does not want to be overly protective

_____ 2. Jerry is especially fascinated by the local boys at the wild bay because they —
   F speak a language Jerry doesn't understand
   G are older and stronger than he is
   H dive from a rock and swim through an underwater tunnel
   J climb through a tunnel to reach a high rock from which they dive

_____ 3. When Jerry masks his shame at not having found the tunnel because he was clowning around, the other boys —
   A laugh at his antics
   B frown like his mother
   C speak English to him
   D smile and wave at him

_____ 4. Which statement *best* describes Jerry's attitude toward going through the tunnel?
   F He feels the tunnel is more than he can handle at his age.
   G He's frightened but determined to go through it.
   H The tunnel has little meaning but poses some interest to him.
   J He has no fears about getting through the tunnel.

_____ 5. As soon as the local boys leave the wild bay, Jerry doesn't go through the tunnel *mainly* because —
   A his mother made him promise not to overdo anything
   B Jerry doesn't know where the tunnel is located
   C Jerry can't hold his breath long enough
   D without goggles, Jerry can't see underwater

_____ 6. The event that forces Jerry to decide that he will make his attempt to go through the tunnel occurs —
   F after he watches the local boys go through the tunnel for a second time
   G when his ability to hold his breath surpasses two minutes
   H when he buys a pair of goggles enabling him to see clearly underwater
   J after his mother tells him that they will be leaving the beach in four days

Through the Tunnel   117

_____ 7. The *best* description of Jerry's approach to going through the tunnel is that he —
   A enters impulsively and swims around until he finds his way out
   B waits until one of the older boys dives first and then follows him to safety
   C decides to wait until the following summer when is older and stronger
   D carefully plans and practices for several days before trying

_____ 8. In addition to overcoming the dangers of the water, Jerry has to contend with —
   F his mother's reluctance
   G his own rigorous training
   H taunts from the other boys
   J weather problems

_____ 9. In the end, while eating lunch, Jerry tells his mother —
   A absolutely nothing about his adventure underwater
   B every detail of what happened as he swam through the tunnel
   C that he can hold his breath for three minutes underwater
   D that he wants to go swimming again that day

_____ 10. Which statement *best* expresses the theme of "Through the Tunnel"?
   F Friendship is life's great prize.
   G A mother's love conquers all.
   H Proving one's worth is never easy.
   J Never judge a book by its cover.

LITERARY FOCUS (20 points; 5 points each)
On the line provided, write the letter of the *best* answer to each of the following items.

_____ 11. A reader finds the symbolic meaning in a story by —
   A outlining the events in the story's plot
   B interpreting and making connections among all of the story's symbols
   C discovering the reasons a character acts the way he or she does
   D determining who the narrator is and how he or she is connected to the story's characters

_____ 12. Of the following details from "Through the Tunnel," the *most* important symbol in the story is the —
   F pair of goggles
   G umbrella
   H tunnel
   J villa

_____ 13. The wild bay is a symbol for —
   A Jerry's entrance into a new phase in his life
   B the ways in which Jerry's mother coddles him
   C life in a foreign country
   D vacations and other exciting adventures

_____ 14. Which of the following descriptions from the story helps to create a mood of danger?
   F "There she was, a speck of yellow under an umbrella that looked like a slice of orange peel."
   G "Soon the biggest of the boys poised himself, shot down into the water, and did not come up."
   H "It was as if he had eyes of a different kind—fish eyes that showed everything clear and delicate and wavering in the bright water."
   J "Rocks lay like discolored monsters under the surface."

VOCABULARY DEVELOPMENT *(20 points; 4 points each)*

Match the definition on the left with the Vocabulary word on the right. On the line provided, write the letter of the Vocabulary word.

_____ 15. small; tiny   a. contrition
_____ 16. appeal; request   b. supplication
_____ 17. disbelieving; skeptical   c. inquisitive
_____ 18. regret or sense of guilt at having done wrong d. minute
_____ 19. questioning; curious   e. incredulous

CONSTRUCTED RESPONSE *(20 points)*

20. On a separate sheet of paper, write a paragraph explaining what you think Jerry's accomplishments are and how you think they change him. Support your ideas with at least two instances of symbols or figurative language from the story.

Through the Tunnel

| NAME | CLASS | DATE | SCORE |

SELECTION TEST   INFORMATIONAL READING

Coming of Age, Latino Style: Special Rite Ushers Girls into Adulthood
Cindy Rodriguez

Vision Quest
from Encyclopaedia Britannica

Crossing a Threshold to Adulthood
Jessica Barnes

COMPREHENSION (50 points; 10 points each)
On the line provided, write the letter of the *best* answer to each of the following items.

_____ 1. What is the *main* idea of "Coming of Age, Latino Style"?
   A   Hispanic families in Lowell, Massachusetts, may give a birthday party or a $10,000 debutante ball for their teenage daughters.
   B   On their fifteenth birthday, Hispanic girls celebrate a *quinceañera*, which may be a religious or social event.
   C   Some families in the Hispanic community worry more about *quinceañeras* than they do about weddings.
   D   Iris and Martin have a daughter named Glenda who decides to celebrate her fifteenth birthday.

_____ 2. A vision quest is —
   F   a coming-of-age tradition in Indian cultures
   G   the sole work of a chief in an Indian tribe
   H   a wedding tradition for Indians of the Great Plains
   J   a traditional birthday celebration for Indians of the eastern woodlands

_____ 3. Which detail describes a specific custom practiced in a vision quest?
   A   Among certain tribes most boys, but never girls, became involved in vision quests.
   B   Some Indians in woodland areas or on the Great Plains become hunters.
   C   A very important person in the community is its shaman, a kind of religious leader.
   D   A religious specialist interprets a dream, a sighting of an animal, or a special stone that has been found.

_____ 4. In "Crossing a Threshold to Adulthood," the author *mostly* tells about —
   F   the Peace Corps for which she worked
   G   American coming-of-age customs
   H   marriage customs in Uzbekistan
   J   the quality of video productions in Uzbekistan

Holt Assessment: Literature, Reading, and Vocabulary

_____ **5.** The author of "Crossing a Threshold to Adulthood" feels that in America, unlike in Uzbekistan, —

    A there is no specific occasion that turns a child into an adult

    B people do not videotape important occasions and therefore do not preserve the past

    C young people marry at too young an age

    D all young adults should follow the same customs when they get married

VOCABULARY DEVELOPMENT *(50 points; 10 points each)*
Choose a Vocabulary word from the boldface list to complete each sentence below. On the line provided, write the appropriate word.

indigenous   solitary   vigil   formidable   inevitable

6. It is _____ that major differences in the customs of different countries exist.

7. To go out into nature and return with greater wisdom is a _____ feat.

8. Unusual thoughts may cross the mind of someone who stays awake all night on a _____.

9. Some of the _____ peoples of America share certain coming-of-age rites.

10. To be by yourself, completely _____, is more the mark of someone ready to be an adult than of someone wanting to stay a child.

Coming of Age . . . / Vision Quest / Crossing a Threshold . . .   **121**

| NAME | CLASS | DATE | SCORE |

SELECTION TEST　　　　　　　　　　　　　LITERARY RESPONSE AND ANALYSIS

The Masque of the Red Death Edgar Allan Poe
The Black Death from When Plague Strikes James Cross Giblin

COMPREHENSION *(40 points; 4 points each)*
On the line provided, write the letter of the *best* answer to each of the following items.

_____ 1. The events of this story are related to —
   A a popular ballroom dance
   B a spreading, infectious disease
   C a nickname for Prince Prospero
   D costumes for masquerade balls

_____ 2. What is unusual about where the masquerade takes place?
   F There is a ballroom as large as the entire imperial suite in Prince Prospero's palace.
   G Musicians play in a curved hall while guests dance in colored chambers.
   H It begins at sundown and does not end until an ebony clock strikes.
   J There are colored rooms that are not connected to each other or situated along a straight hall.

_____ 3. "Gaudy and fantastic appearances" are created at the masquerade ball by —
   A the prince who wears a frightening costume and dances in several rooms
   B a man in a red mask who enters the various rooms and does a bizarre dance
   C flames that shine through red glass windows in each of many rooms along a hallway
   D the guests who take turns putting on a red mask, which makes them act in strange ways

_____ 4. Few people dare to enter the black apartment because —
   F faces look frightening there, and an ebony clock makes a strange sound
   G without light, no one can see or dance without causing injury to others
   H it is the room where Prince Prospero wears the masque of the Red Death
   J in this room a strange voice can be heard whose origins no one can trace

_____ 5. Prince Prospero is a person who basically desires —
   A good company and entertainment
   B to face pain and suffering with courage
   C to be surrounded by people in simple clothes
   D others to share their feelings with him

122　　　　　　　　　　　　　　Holt Assessment: Literature, Reading, and Vocabulary

_____ **6.** Under the circumstances the appearance and behavior of guests at the ball come across as —
   F handsome
   G ordinary
   H elegant
   J grotesque

_____ **7.** When Prince Prospero confronts the strangely masked guest, the prince —
   A challenges the guest to a duel and then draws his sword in order to fight
   B demands that the masked guest leave since he or she was not invited
   C draws a dagger, then chases the masked guest by going from room to room
   D asks for the mask and costume so that he, the prince, can wear them

_____ **8.** The outcome of the story is that —
   F the pendulum clock strikes the hour of twelve, and the guest in the strange mask flees the palace of Prince Prospero
   G Prince Prospero kills the strangely masked guest in a duel, suddenly becomes ill from the Red Death, and dies
   H the guests die after grabbing the masked figure, whose costume turns out to be empty
   J the guests take revenge on the strangely masked guest, kill him or her in the black room, and then perform a bizarre dance

_____ **9.** According to "The Black Death," how did people in the fourteenth century get bubonic plague?
   A Infected fleas from infected rats bit humans and transmitted the disease.
   B A boat from Sicily with infected sailors traveled to other harbors in Europe, spreading the disease.
   C Rats entered the house of a sick person, contracted the disease, and then spread it to other animals.
   D Without modern refrigeration, leftover food became rotten and people who ate the food got sick.

_____ **10.** According to Boccaccio, the people of Florence took all of the following measures to avoid the plague *except* —
   F eat lightly, and receive no visitors and no news
   G enjoy life, and act as if news of the plague were a joke
   H arrest foreigners to keep them from spreading the disease in the city
   J flee to the countryside to escape the people who carried the disease

The Masque of the Red Death / The Black Death

NAME	CLASS	DATE	SCORE

LITERARY FOCUS *(20 points; 5 points each)*
On the line provided, write the letter of the *best* answer to each of the following items.

_____ 11. An **allegory** is a narrative story —
   A with an unexpected turning point and climax in its plot
   B told by a narrator who knows more about events than other characters know
   C that uses imaginary characters to tell about a historical event
   D in which characters and settings stand for abstract ideas or moral qualities

_____ 12. In "The Masque of the Red Death," the red mask probably stands for —
   F the bubonic plague that had been killing much of the population of fourteenth-century Europe
   G the desire that all people had to become a prince or princess
   H Prince Prospero's wish to be anything but ordinary
   J the people in fourteenth-century Europe who survived the bubonic plague

_____ 13. In "The Masque of the Red Death," Prince Prospero stands for —
   A a terrible, deadly disease that had been spreading through Europe
   B a future people who learned how to fight infectious diseases successfully
   C anyone who believed they could fool death by their cleverness
   D weak people who were easily infected by and died from bubonic plague

_____ 14. Which statement expresses the theme of this allegory?
   F Money can buy you happiness.
   G Laugh and the world laughs with you.
   H Live life to the fullest.
   J Death can master life.

VOCABULARY DEVELOPMENT *(20 points; 4 points each)*
On the lines provided, write the letter of the choice that is the *best* antonym for each Vocabulary word. Remember that an antonym is a word that means the *opposite* of another word.

_____ 15. sagacious
   A clever
   B humorous
   C foolish
   D somber

_____ **16.** profuse

        F plentiful

        G scarce

        H questionable

        J reluctant

_____ **17.** sedate

        A simplified

        B tranquil

        C boring

        D excited

_____ **18.** pervaded

        F contained

        G attacked

        H invented

        J spread

_____ **19.** propriety

        A respectability

        B indecency

        C modesty

        D possibility

CONSTRUCTED RESPONSE *(20 points)*

20. On a separate sheet of paper, describe how "The Masque of the Red Death" acts as an allegory for historical information you learn about in "The Black Death." Connect at least two details in "The Masque of the Red Death" to two facts in "The Black Death."

SELECTION TEST

LITERARY RESPONSE AND ANALYSIS

Stopping by Woods on a Snowy Evening Robert Frost
After Apple-Picking Robert Frost

COMPREHENSION *(60 points; 6 points each)*
On the line provided, write the letter of the *best* answer to each of the following items.

_____ 1. The reader can infer that the speaker in "Stopping by Woods on a Snowy Evening" —
   A is familiar with the area being described
   B is wealthy and owns much land
   C lives alone and has no one to go home to
   D has had a dispute with the man who owns the woods

_____ 2. What situation seems "queer," or unusual, to the speaker's horse?
   F An unpredictable spring snow has just occurred.
   G The speaker has become lost in unfamiliar woods.
   H There seems to be no reason why the speaker stopped.
   J The speaker forces the horse off of a familiar path.

_____ 3. Two sounds the speaker describes in "Stopping by Woods on a Snowy Evening" are —
   A his own voice and the voice of the owner of the woods
   B his own voice and his horse's neighing
   C harness bells on a horse and wind during a snowfall
   D wind howling in the bare branches and sleigh bells

_____ 4. Which of the following statements about Frost's poem is *not* true?
   F The speaker has a long distance left to travel.
   G The speaker is accompanied by a horse.
   H The woods are dark and very quiet.
   J The speaker is eager to leave the woods.

_____ 5. The speaker of "Stopping by Woods on a Snowy Evening" is a person who —
   A prefers nature to humankind
   B does not communicate well with horses
   C questions why he lives in a snowy place
   D takes time to think about his life

_____ 6. The situation described in "After Apple-Picking" is —
   F frustration the speaker feels about apples left unpicked
   G a dream the speaker has after picking apples all day
   H the danger the speaker realizes about the act of picking apples
   J worry about the coming snow that winter

NAME _____ CLASS _____ DATE _____ SCORE _____

_____ 7. For *most* of "After Apple-Picking," the speaker is located —
   A on a ladder picking apples in a dream
   B in a farmhouse cellar where he stores picked apples
   C by a water trough where he has fallen asleep
   D in a city where he now lives and writes

_____ 8. Which sentence explains the general state of apples in "After Apple-Picking"?
   F Every apple the speaker puts in the barrel is sweet and delicious.
   G Few apples live up to the standards the speaker expects.
   H Some apples are easy to pick, and some apples are best left ignored.
   J There are too many apples for the speaker to easily keep track of.

_____ 9. According to the speaker, apples that are used to make cider are —
   A the ones that fall to the ground
   B red and sweet
   C picked from the highest tree branches
   D found on the lowest tree branches

_____ 10. The speaker of "After Apple-Picking" can be described as someone who is —
   F angry with someone
   G bored with his job
   H weary from life
   J in love with a stranger

LITERARY FOCUS *(20 points; 5 points each)*
On the line provided, write the letter of the *best* answer to each of the following items.

_____ 11. A poet may turn objects into **symbols** that —
   A seem magical and not like ordinary objects from real life
   B create musical sounds through repeated word endings
   C stand for things other than themselves, suggesting a deeper meaning
   D have new meanings the poet explains in the narrative element of the poem

_____ 12. In "Stopping by Woods on a Snowy Evening," the phrase "miles to go before I sleep" symbolically means that the —
   F speaker has much to do in the next few days
   G nearest hotel is a long way off
   H speaker has much to do before stopping again
   J speaker has much to do before dying

Stopping by Woods . . . / After Apple-Picking

127

_____ **13.** The symbolic meaning of a poem may be understood by paying attention to all of the following elements *except* —

    A repetition

    B mysterious images

    C word associations

    D meter

_____ **14.** Which question does "After Apple-Picking" symbolically address?

    F How does a person deal with many hopes, wishes, and experiences?

    G Why are apples and other fruits so abundant?

    H What is the real importance of nature?

    J When does a person best fulfill life's hopes and dreams?

Constructed Response *(20 points)*

15. Robert Frost once said that a poem must start in delight and end in wisdom. Choose either "Stopping by Woods on a Snowy Evening" or "After Apple-Picking," and explain how the poem you selected starts in delight and ends in wisdom. Make at least two references to the poem to support your interpretation. Write your answer on a separate sheet of paper.

COLLECTION 6 SUMMATIVE TEST

Symbolism and Allegory

This test asks you to use the skills and strategies you have learned in this collection. Read the poem "Knives" by Jane Yolen, and then answer the questions that follow it.

Knives
by Jane Yolen

Love can be as sharp
as the point of a knife,
as piercing as a sliver of glass.
My sisters did not know this.
They thought love was an old slipper:
pull it on and it fits.
They did not know this secret of the world:
the wrong word can kill.
It cost them their lives.

Princes understand the world,
they know the nuance of the tongue,
they are bred up in it.
A shoe is not a shoe:
it implies miles, it suggests length,
it measures and makes solid.
It wears and is worn.
Where there is one shoe, there must be a match.
Otherwise the kingdom limps along.

Glass is not glass
in the language of love:
it implies sight, it suggests depth,
it mirrors and makes real,
it is sought and is seen.
What is made of glass reflects the gazer.
A queen must be made of glass.

I spoke to the prince in that secret tongue,
the diplomacy of courting,
he using shoes, I using glass,
and all my sisters saw was a slipper,
too long at the heel,
too short at the toe.
What else could they use but a knife?
What else could he see but the declaration of war?

Collection 6 Summative Test

129

| NAME | CLASS | DATE | SCORE |

> Princes understand the world,
> they know the nuance of the tongue,
> they are bred up in it.
> In war as in life they take no prisoners
> And they always marry the other shoe.

VOCABULARY SKILLS *(25 points; 5 points each)*
On the line provided, write the letter of the *best* answer to each of the following items.

_____ 1. The act of *piercing* may be compared to the act of —
   A directing
   B reversing
   C puncturing
   D obliterating

_____ 2. The meaning of the word *nuance* is —
   F something that is brand new
   G subtle distinction
   H strong emotion
   J incomplete thought or action

_____ 3. If someone is said to act with great *diplomacy*, that person —
   A practices the art of skillful negotiation
   B provokes hostility between two or more people
   C rapidly completes a thought
   D finds it difficult to communicate with others

_____ 4. To make a *declaration* is the same as to make a —
   F colorful pattern
   G change of mind
   H formal statement
   J meeting with many parties

"Knives" by Jane Yolen from *Snow White, Blood Red,* edited by Ellen Datlow and Terri Windling. Copyright © 1993 by Jane Yolen. Published by William Morrow & Company, 1993. All rights reserved. Reproduced by permission of **Curtis Brown, Ltd.**

NAME	CLASS	DATE	SCORE

_____ **5.** When something is *bred*, it is —

    A dough rising

    B raised, or reared

    C broken beyond repair

    D fragmented

COMPREHENSION *(30 points; 6 points each)*
On the line provided, write the letter of the *best* answer to each of the following items.

_____ **6.** "Knives" is based on the —

    F famous metaphor in which knives are slippers

    G popular fairy tale "Cinderella"

    H idea that glass is a kind of mirror of life

    J poet's autobiography

_____ **7.** In this poem a knife's point is compared to —

    A the high heels of women's dress shoes

    B cruel words that Cinderella speaks to her stepsisters

    C the eyes of a powerful prince when he wages war

    D love, as understood by the speaker

_____ **8.** For the prince in this poem, a shoe represents —

    F an attractive bride

    G a declaration of war

    H all that love implies

    J a sharp knife

_____ **9.** According to the speaker, glass suggests all of the following things *except* —

    A a language for love

    B the end of love

    C the depth of love

    D a reflection of a lover

_____ **10.** What is the outcome of the situation described in "Knives"?

    F The speaker and the prince unite in marriage.

    G A sister threatens the prince with a knife.

    H A prince declares war on women who wear glass slippers.

    J The speaker defends her sisters by refusing to marry the prince.

NAME _____ CLASS _____ DATE _____ SCORE _____

READING SKILLS AND STRATEGIES: CONSTRUCTED RESPONSE *(30 points; 15 points each)*
Understanding Symbols

11. Like the fairy tale "Cinderella," this poem tells about a speaker, the speaker's sisters, a prince, and the relationship they have to one another. The poem also uses the fairy tale's glass slipper.

    a. Use the following chart to examine what the poet says are the functions of glass and the shoe. For each symbol, write several details from the poem.

▶ Symbol	▶ Functions
glass	
shoe	

    b. On a separate sheet of paper, describe what the poem is trying to teach readers.

    c. Notice that the poet connects the shoe to the prince and the mirror to the speaker. Like the prince and his princess, the looking glass and the shoe have very different functions. What are they? What is their relationship to the prince and the speaker? Write your answer on a separate sheet of paper.

12. People as well as objects may function as symbols in poems. Choose the sisters, the prince, or the speaker of this poem, and explain what the person you chose represents on a symbolic level. Write your answer on a separate sheet of paper.

LITERARY FOCUS: CONSTRUCTED RESPONSE *(15 points)*

13. Trace the appearance of the word *knives, slipper,* or *glass* in this poem. Then, on a separate sheet of paper, explain the way the word you chose is used in a figure of speech. How does the **figurative language** that includes this word enhance the poem's meaning?

132 Holt Assessment: Literature, Reading, and Vocabulary

COLLECTION 7 DIAGNOSTIC TEST

Poetry

On the line provided, write the letter of the *best* answer to each of the following items.
(100 points; 10 points each)

_____ 1. Which of the following **images** would *most* likely evoke a feeling of peacefulness?

    A A snake slithering through the hot desert sand

    B Thunder rumbling quietly in the distance

    C A sailboat floating across a sparkling lake in a gentle breeze

    D Fireworks exploding against a velvety black sky

_____ 2. A **metaphor** that continues over several lines or throughout an entire poem is called a(n) —

    F extended metaphor

    G mixed metaphor

    H implied metaphor

    J direct metaphor

_____ 3. Which of the following statements contains an example of **personification**?

    A My brother was always a lone wolf.

    B The morning dew gleamed like a field of diamonds.

    C The bear's paws were as cold as ice.

    D The flowers bowed their heads in grief.

_____ 4. What is **lyric poetry**?

    F Poetry that has been passed down orally

    G Poetry that tells a story

    H Poetry that expresses a speaker's emotions or thoughts

    J Short, simple poetry that does not use figurative language

_____ 5. Which of the following elements is characteristic of an **English,** or **Shakespearean, sonnet**?

    A A two-part structure of eight lines and six lines

    B Three quatrains and a concluding couplet

    C A series of couplets

    D Sixteen lines

Collection 7 Diagnostic Test

| NAME | CLASS | DATE | SCORE |

_____ 6. **Free verse** is poetry that —
   F relies on rhyme to give it structure
   G does not use any sound devices
   H follows a strict metrical pattern
   J has no regular meter and rhyme scheme

_____ 7. Which of the following words is an example of an **iamb**?
   A excel
   B confident
   C homework
   D crater

_____ 8. Which of the following pairs of words is an example of **approximate rhyme**?
   F meet / feet
   G wings / sings
   H moon / mourn
   J bubble / trouble

_____ 9. A repeating word or phrase in a poem is called —
   A alliteration
   B a refrain
   C diction
   D an idiom

_____ 10. Which of the following sentences contains an example of **onomatopoeia**?
   F Frightened, the small boy ran away.
   G The oil crackled and hissed in the hot pan.
   H The leaky faucet needed to be repaired.
   J The cat wandered through the empty house.

| NAME | CLASS | DATE | SCORE |

SELECTION TEST LITERARY RESPONSE AND ANALYSIS

A Storm in the Mountains
Aleksandr Solzhenitsyn *translated by* Michael Glenny

COMPREHENSION *(50 points; 5 points each)*
On the line provided, write the letter of the *best* answer to each of the following items.

_____ 1. Why do Solzhenitsyn and his companions crawl out of the tents and run for shelter?
  A They hear a bear.
  B Rocks have begun to slide down the mountain.
  C A storm is coming.
  D They are afraid of the dark.

_____ 2. Solzhenitsyn writes that there were "no peaks, no valleys, no horizon" because he —
  F thinks it is the end of the world
  G wishes he were in a heated apartment
  H exaggerates to make events sound more exciting
  J can't see a thing in the pitch-black night

_____ 3. Belaya-Kaya and Djuguturlyuchat are —
  A Solzhenitsyn's camping buddies
  B mountains in Russia
  C rivers running down the mountain
  D types of pine trees

_____ 4. Lightning helps Solzhenitsyn see the mountains and trees, but when it is dark, he —
  F cannot believe they ever existed
  G remembers what they look like in his mind's eye
  H can't remember who he is
  J feels safe on terra firma

_____ 5. The thunder drowns out the sound of —
  A the roaring rivers
  B an avalanche
  C the frightful voices in his head
  D a sonic boom

_____ 6. The lightning reminds Solzhenitsyn of —
  F darts
  G spears
  H arrows
  J fishing poles

A Storm in the Mountains   135

| NAME | CLASS | DATE | SCORE |

_____ 7. A "droplet in the ocean has no fear of a hurricane," just as Solzhenitsyn is —
   A not afraid of a hurricane
   B afraid of the storm
   C not afraid of the storm
   D afraid of a hurricane

_____ 8. The events that the speaker describes make him feel —
   F insignificant
   G important
   H intelligent
   J indignant

_____ 9. The storm also makes the speaker feel grateful because he realizes that he is —
   A alive when it's over
   B a part of this world
   C clean and awake
   D as strong as a pine tree

_____ 10. Solzhenitsyn compares watching the storm, sky, and mountains that night to watching —
   F a battle between the ancient gods
   G ocean waves crashing on cliffs
   H a nature documentary
   J the creation of the world

LITERARY FOCUS (20 points; 5 points each)
On the line provided, write the letter of the *best* answer to each of the following items.

_____ 11. You can tell that "A Storm in the Mountains" is a prose poem because it —
   A answers the *5W-How?* questions
   B is hard to understand
   C is written in paragraph form but uses poetic elements
   D reads like a technical manual with metaphors

_____ 12. All of the following characteristics are elements of a prose poem *except* —
   F paragraph form
   G powerful images
   H a message
   J a moral

_____ 13. Allowing us to enter the writer's world and devise our own meaning is a characteristic of —

　　A persuasive writing
　　B poetry
　　C warranties
　　D advertising

_____ 14. Another clue that "A Storm in the Mountains" is a prose poem is that it has —

　　F long paragraphs
　　G circular logic
　　H a point not directly stated
　　J appeal to the lovelorn

Constructed Response *(30 points)*

15. On a separate sheet of paper, compare and contrast the form of a prose poem, using "A Storm in the Mountains" as an example, with the form of a newspaper article.

| NAME | CLASS | DATE | SCORE |

SELECTION TEST
LITERARY RESPONSE AND ANALYSIS

Same Song Pat Mora

COMPREHENSION *(50 points; 5 points each)*
On the line provided, write the letter of the *best* answer to each of the following items.

_____ 1. The speaker provides details that carefully describe —
   A how she feels about her son and daughter
   B where her son and daughter live
   C the routines her son and daughter follow
   D the mirrors in the house

_____ 2. The speaker's daughter is —
   F sixteen years old
   G twelve years old
   H six years old
   J twelve and a half years old

_____ 3. The speaker's daughter is concerned about her —
   A health
   B schoolwork
   C future
   D appearance

_____ 4. Why does the speaker's daughter frown when seeing her face in the mirror?
   F She doesn't like Aztec Blue eye shadow.
   G She looks like everyone else.
   H Her features are dark, not fair.
   J Her hair is not curly enough.

_____ 5. The phrase "mirror, mirror on the wall" is an allusion to the story of
   A Snow White
   B Goldilocks
   C Jack and Jill
   D Sleeping Beauty

_____ 6. The speaker's son is —
   F twelve years old
   G sixteen years old
   H sixteen and a half years old
   J six years old

| NAME | CLASS | DATE | SCORE |

_____ **7.** The speaker's son is concerned about —
   A looking better than his sister
   B building his physique
   C getting some shut-eye
   D clothes

_____ **8.** The speaker's son's routine takes place —
   F at six o'clock in the morning
   G in the afternoon
   H after school
   J after nine o'clock in the evening

_____ **9.** The narrator's daughter's routine takes place —
   A after her brother has gone to bed
   B at nine o'clock in the evening
   C at six o'clock in the morning
   D throughout the day

_____ **10.** The title "Same Song" probably refers to the fact that the speaker's daughter and son are critical of their —
   F schoolwork
   G parents
   H appearance
   J sharing a bathroom

LITERARY FOCUS *(20 points; 5 points each)*
On the line provided, write the letter of the *best* answer to each of the following items.

_____ **11.** The speaker describes all the details of her daughter's morning beauty routine to show how —
   A long a good beauty makeover can take
   B extensive and important the ritual is to her daughter
   C expensive it is to buy quality makeup
   D vain and self-centered her daughter is

_____ **12.** Naming the makeup colors —
   F demonstrates that the speaker's daughter doesn't know what colors go together
   G gives the reader a sense of what it is like to work at a cosmetic counter
   H confirms that these colors are not found in nature
   J suggests that the girl is blending Mexican and American cultures

Same Song

_____ 13. In spite of the effort the son makes, he frowns when he looks at himself in the mirror because he —

  A doesn't have beautiful hair

  B is tired from his intense routine

  C remembers a fairy tale

  D isn't satisfied with the reflection

_____ 14. The images in "Same Song" focus on rituals that boys and girls follow to —

  F prepare for adulthood

  G stay young

  H live up to an ideal standard of attractiveness

  J enter the competitive world of dating

Constructed Response *(30 points)*

15. On a separate sheet of paper, compare and contrast the son's and daughter's routines. What is the significance of the images associated with each?

| NAME | CLASS | DATE | SCORE |

SELECTION TEST   **LITERARY RESPONSE AND ANALYSIS**

Eating Together Li-Young Lee
Grape Sherbet Rita Dove

COMPREHENSION *(50 points; 5 points each)*
On the line provided, write the letter of the *best* answer to each of the following items.

_____ 1. What is the family having for lunch in "Eating Together"?
    A Rice and beans
    B Rice and onions
    C Trout and rice
    D Ham sandwiches

_____ 2. Which family member will not be eating lunch with the others?
    F Mother
    G Father
    H Sister
    J Brother

_____ 3. Why will the mother eat the meat from the trout's head?
    A She is continuing a tradition.
    B The children do not like the meat from the head.
    C It is the only part left.
    D She wants to leave the good parts for her children.

_____ 4. The simile "lay down / to sleep like a snow-covered road / winding through pines" refers to —
    F the beauty of nature
    G death
    H life
    J Mother

_____ 5. "Eating Together" suggests all of the following ideas *except* the —
    A continuity of life after death
    B importance of traditions
    C power of trout
    D peacefulness of death

_____ 6. In "Grape Sherbet" the image "swirled snow, gelled light" describes —
    F the diabetic grandmother
    G grape sherbet
    H the father
    J Memorial Day

Eating Together / Grape Sherbet

NAME	CLASS	DATE	SCORE

_____ 7. Dad "fights a smile" when he brings out the grape sherbet because he is —
  A trying not to laugh
  B playing a trick on his family
  C going to tell his secret
  D proud of his masterpiece

_____ 8. The phrase "a lost milk tooth" describes a —
  F porch
  G dessert
  H duck
  J tombstone

_____ 9. The speaker uses the metaphor "a torch / of pure refusal" to refer to the grandmother because she —
  A isn't able to eat the sherbet
  B won't go to the cemetery with the family
  C refuses to tell the secret of making the sherbet
  D can't accept the fact that she is diabetic

_____ 10. At the end of the poem, what does the speaker appreciate that Father "bothered" to do?
  F Doing special and memorable things for the children
  G Sharing his recipe for grape sherbet with her
  H Keeping secret his recipe for grape sherbet
  J Grilling on Memorial Day

LITERARY FOCUS (20 points; 5 points each)
On the line provided, write the letter of the *best* answer to each of the following items.

_____ 11. The speaker in "Eating Together" is —
  A the mother
  B an aunt
  C the father
  D the poet

_____ 12. In "Eating Together," what attitude toward death does the speaker convey?
  F Anger and resentment
  G Fear
  H Peaceful acceptance
  J Joy

NAME	CLASS	DATE	SCORE

_____ **13.** In "Grape Sherbet," what does the speaker at first think is "a joke"?

    A How lavender tastes

    B Death and burial

    C Dad's cap that looks like a duck

    D The secret recipe

_____ **14.** At the end of "Grape Sherbet," the speaker's attitude has changed because she has learned —

    F that her father was a master cook

    G the reality of death and how precious life is

    H to appreciate her grandmother

    J how to make grape sherbet

CONSTRUCTED RESPONSE *(30 points)*

15. On a separate sheet of paper, compare and contrast how the speaker feels on Memorial Day as an adult with the way she felt on that day when she was a child.

Eating Together / Grape Sherbet   **143**

| NAME | CLASS | DATE | SCORE |

SELECTION TEST LITERARY RESPONSE AND ANALYSIS

The Legend Garrett Hongo

COMPREHENSION *(50 points; 5 points each)*
On the line provided, write the letter of the *best* answer to each of the following items.

_____ 1. The first stanza of "The Legend" could be described as —
   A violent
   B humorous
   C peaceful
   D grim

_____ 2. In the second stanza the description of the man creates the impression of a(n) —
   F angry person who causes his own tragedy
   G heroic person
   H poor man who becomes a victim
   J kindly person who puts others before himself

_____ 3. In the second stanza the man has just —
   A robbed the package store
   B gotten into a fight with the boy
   C read about Descartes
   D finished washing his laundry

_____ 4. The boy in the poem —
   F helps the man put his laundry in the car
   G backs out of a store he has robbed
   H shovels snow in front of a package store
   J reads Descartes at the bus stop

_____ 5. The man is shot —
   A after interfering in a fight between two young men
   B because he is stealing laundry
   C simply because he is in the wrong place at the wrong time
   D for trying to stop the boy from fleeing

_____ 6. The onlookers do not comfort the man because they —
   F cannot understand him
   G are protecting the boy
   H fear for their own lives
   J are too shocked

NAME	CLASS	DATE	SCORE

_____ **7.** The speaker is ashamed because he —
   A doesn't understand Descartes
   B didn't help the man
   C hasn't done his laundry
   D puts reason ahead of feeling

_____ **8.** According to the speaker, Descartes doubted everything *except* —
   F the fact of his own existence
   G life after death
   H the existence of love
   J the need for taxes

_____ **9.** The speaker wishes that the dead man —
   A had never come out of the laundry
   B will be comforted in the afterlife
   C were alive and he was dead in his place
   D will wander the earth as a vengeful ghost

_____ **10.** At the end of the poem, the speaker reveals the name of the —
   F man who was killed
   G boy
   H poet's brother
   J person who was robbed

LITERARY FOCUS *(20 points; 5 points each)*
On the line provided, write the letter of the *best* answer to each of the following items.

_____ **11.** At first the speaker's tone toward the man who is shot is —
   A sarcastic
   B indifferent
   C sorrowful
   D outraged

The Legend

145

NAME _____ CLASS _____ DATE _____ SCORE _____

_____ 12. All of the following images create an impression of someone who is downtrodden *except* —

　　F "very skinny"
　　G "dressed as one of the poor"
　　H "a Rembrandt glow on his face"
　　J "plaid mackinaw, / dingy and too large"

_____ 13. In the end, how does the speaker come to feel about "the wounded man lying on the concrete"?

　　A The man is completely separate from him.
　　B Neither the man's life nor his death has any importance.
　　C The man was very similar to Descartes.
　　D The man's death should be mourned.

_____ 14. Garrett Hongo wants to make a "legend" of the man —

　　F so that people will consider the man a hero
　　G so that the man will be remembered
　　H so that people will write poetry about the man
　　J in order to conceal the man's identity

CONSTRUCTED RESPONSE (30 points)

15. On a separate sheet of paper, describe how the speaker feels about the event he witnessed. Cite details from the text to support your answer.

| NAME | CLASS | DATE | SCORE |

SELECTION TEST LITERARY RESPONSE AND ANALYSIS

Simile N. Scott Momaday

COMPREHENSION (20 points; 5 points each)
On the line provided, write the letter of the *best* answer to each of the following items.

_____ 1. To whom does the pronoun "we" refer in this poem?
   A The speaker and a deer
   B The speaker and a companion
   C The speaker and an enemy
   D Two deer

_____ 2. Before the poem begins, the speaker *probably* —
   F saw two deer
   G walked in single file
   H fell in love
   J had an argument

_____ 3. Which fact about the deer is significant?
   A They are in the woods.
   B There are only two of them.
   C They like to run.
   D They walk in single file.

_____ 4. The deer hold their heads high because they are —
   F looking for food
   G eating tree leaves
   H triumphant
   J alert to danger

LITERARY FOCUS (50 points; 10 points each)
On the line provided, write the letter of the *best* answer to each of the following items.

_____ 5. The appeal of this poem comes *primarily* from —
   A a visual image
   B details of taste, touch, and sound
   C philosophical ideals
   D a strong rhythmic pattern

Simile 147

_____ 6. The poet might have chosen deer for his simile because they are —
    F usually alone
    G quiet animals
    H often violent
    J rarely startled

_____ 7. The entire poem is a(n) —
    A sonnet
    B metaphor
    C narrative poem
    D extended simile

_____ 8. The lines "with ears forward / with eyes watchful" suggest that the two people —
    F like being together
    G are wary of each other and their surroundings
    H enjoy walking in the woods
    J have sharp ears that hear the least little sound

_____ 9. The phrase "in whose limbs there is latent flight" suggests that the two people —
    A are going on vacation
    B will run away from each other at the first sign of trouble
    C used to run together
    D have strong legs

CONSTRUCTED RESPONSE *(30 points)*

10. On a separate sheet of paper, describe how the speaker and his companion are like deer. Use details from the poem to support your answer.

SELECTION TEST — LITERARY RESPONSE AND ANALYSIS

I Am Offering This Poem Jimmy Santiago Baca
since feeling is first E. E. Cummings

COMPREHENSION (50 points; 5 points each)
On the line provided, write the letter of the *best* answer to each of the following items.

_____ 1. The speaker of Jimmy Santiago Baca's poem offers the poem as a gift because he —
   A does not have anything else to offer
   B values poetry over material things
   C knows the recipient loves poetry
   D wants the recipient to appreciate art

_____ 2. The speaker of "I Am Offering This Poem" asks the recipient to —
   F hide the poem in the forest
   G respond to his message quickly
   H keep and treasure the poem
   J read and then discard the poem

_____ 3. In Baca's poem the speaker hopes that his poem will —
   A be critically acclaimed
   B win the heart of someone dear
   C change the way people live their lives
   D offer comfort to the speaker's loved one as time goes by

_____ 4. In Baca's poem the repetition of the same line following each stanza —
   F creates a jarring rhythm
   G emphasizes the speaker's feelings
   H undercuts what has gone before
   J adds variety to the poem's structure

_____ 5. In the construction of "since feeling is first," E. E. Cummings —
   A uses the metaphor of "Spring" to express being unloved
   B describes love as being a parenthesis
   C relies on nonstandard punctuation, capitalization, and syntax
   D uses many similes

_____ 6. The premise of "since feeling is first" is that —
   F the brain's reasoning is stronger than emotion
   G emotion, not reason, fosters love
   H the power of the brain is stronger than the "eyelids' flutter"
   J death will eventually overcome love

I Am Offering This Poem / since feeling is first

149

_____ 7. According to the speaker of "since feeling is first," what is better than wisdom?
   A Flowers
   B The flutter of his lady's eyelids
   C Kisses
   D The brain's "best gesture"

_____ 8. Which of the following statements about Cummings's poem is *true*?
   F The speaker is delighted to be immersed in love.
   G The woman addressed by the speaker does not return his affection.
   H The speaker fears that death will ruin their love.
   J The poem follows a standard structure.

_____ 9. To Cummings the flutter of his love's eyelids tells him that —
   A she should see an eye doctor
   B they are meant to be together
   C she is flirting with him
   D he has forgotten to bring her flowers

_____ 10. Cummings urges his readers to —
   F look before you leap
   G consider alternatives
   H be fools in love
   J open their eyes to spring

LITERARY FOCUS *(20 points; 5 points each)*
On the line provided, write the letter of the *best* answer to each of the following items.

_____ 11. "I Am Offering This Poem" is considered a lyric poem *mainly* because it is a —
   A simple poem that tells a story
   B tragic poem that teaches a lesson
   C short poem that expresses strong emotion
   D rhyming poem that reveals passion

____ 12. The speaker of Baca's poem compares love to —
  F a wilderness that has never been explored
  G a treasure that will never be exhausted
  H a fire that burns out of control
  J food and clothing that provide warmth

____ 13. In "since feeling is first," the speaker uses the metaphor "life's not a paragraph" to suggest that —
  A life is not neat and orderly
  B the story of a person's life cannot be written down
  C people shouldn't pay any attention to the rules of grammar
  D life has no meaning

____ 14. The metaphor "death i think is no parenthesis" in the context of the poem means that —
  F the dead can't send love letters
  G death will not separate the lovers
  H life is better than death
  J death has no meaning

Constructed Response (30 points)

15. On a separate sheet of paper, explain what feeling the gift expresses in "I Am Offering This Poem." Support your answer with examples of figurative language from the poem that express the emotion.

| NAME | CLASS | DATE | SCORE |

SELECTION TEST LITERARY RESPONSE AND ANALYSIS

Heart! We will forget him! Emily Dickinson
Three Japanese Tankas Ono Komachi
translated by Jane Hirshfield *with* Mariko Aratani

COMPREHENSION *(50 points; 5 points each)*
On the line provided, write the letter of the *best* answer to each of the following items.

_____ 1. In "Heart! We will forget him!" the speaker tells —
   A her heart to forget the warmth of her loved one
   B her heart to remember the warmth of her loved one
   C her mind to forget her loved one's light
   D both her mind and her heart to pray

_____ 2. Which of the following statements about Emily Dickinson's poem is *true*?
   F The speaker's heart is unable to love anyone.
   G Her heart will never recover from this broken relationship.
   H She no longer loves a certain man.
   J The speaker no longer has a relationship with the man she loves.

_____ 3. In "Heart! We will forget him!" to whom or what does the pronoun *we* refer?
   A The speaker and her mind
   B The speaker and her heart
   C Warmth and light
   D The speaker's love and the speaker's heart

_____ 4. The speaker urges her heart to forget him —
   F in a fortnight
   G as soon as it is ready
   H tomorrow
   J tonight

_____ 5. In the three Japanese tankas the speaker does *not* send a tanka —
   A to a man who passed by the screens of her room
   B to a man who appears to have changed his mind
   C attached to a stalk of rice with an empty husk
   D attached to the stem of a red rose without thorns

152 Holt Assessment: Literature, Reading, and Vocabulary

6. The three tankas are about —
   F   marriage
   G   weather
   H   love
   J   power

7. In the first tanka the speaker feels that the "world of love" is —
   A   meant for astronomers
   B   mostly cloudy and dark
   C   a gap to fill in
   D   in the clouds

8. In the second tanka the speaker is actually —
   F   in a difficult love affair
   G   in an easygoing friendship
   H   alone on a ship
   J   wet and shivering

9. In the third tanka the speaker —
   A   wishes her life was full
   B   feels the wind on her face
   C   hopes to see her former love
   D   lives a breezy, carefree life

10. The speaker of all three tankas addresses —
   F   herself
   G   a person
   H   the world
   J   the elements

Heart! We will forget him! / Three Japanese Tankas

NAME _____ CLASS _____ DATE _____ SCORE _____

LITERARY FOCUS *(20 points; 5 points each)*
On the line provided, write the letter of the *best* answer to each of the following items.

_____ 11. Dickinson uses personification in "Heart! We will forget him!" when she —
  A speaks directly to her mind
  B addresses the man she loves
  C conducts a debate between her heart and her mind
  D speaks to her heart as if it were another person

_____ 12. "Heart! We will forget him!" has all of the following traits *except* that it —
  F is short
  G expresses strong feelings
  H does not tell a story
  J is rhymed

_____ 13. A tanka is a Japanese poem that contains —
  A fifteen unrhymed lines
  B five lines and thirty-one syllables
  C seven lines and a set meter
  D seven syllables in each of five lines

_____ 14. In tanka 3 the speaker compares her life to —
  F the wind
  G autumn
  H an empty stalk
  J a grain

CONSTRUCTED RESPONSE *(30 points)*

15. On a separate sheet of paper, explain the meaning of the three metaphors in the three tankas. Use details from the poems to support your answer.

154   Holt Assessment: Literature, Reading, and Vocabulary

| NAME | CLASS | DATE | SCORE |

SELECTION TEST   LITERARY RESPONSE AND ANALYSIS

Shall I Compare Thee to a Summer's Day?
William Shakespeare

COMPREHENSION *(50 points; 5 points each)*
On the line provided, write the letter of the *best* answer to each of the following items.

_____ 1. How does the loved one in Shakespeare's sonnet compare to a summer's day?
   A She is almost as beautiful as a summer's day.
   B She can never be as beautiful as a summer's day.
   C Her beauty will remain, but summer's beauty will fade.
   D Her beauty, like that of a summer's day, changes constantly.

_____ 2. The speaker claims that his sonnet —
   F can create an entirely new language
   G has the power to give his love immortality
   H is not as powerful as love itself
   J is a force as powerful as nature

_____ 3. According to Shakespeare's poem, summer is —
   A more golden than any woman can hope to be
   B too short, prone to intemperance, and sometimes too hot
   C always warm, pleasant, and fair
   D eternal

_____ 4. Which of the following statements is *not* true about the speaker of Shakespeare's sonnet?
   F He is in love.
   G He vows to immortalize his beloved.
   H He predicts that his beloved's beauty will never fade.
   J He fears that death will remove the glow of summer from his beloved.

_____ 5. The "eye of heaven" is the —
   A North Star
   B earth
   C moon
   D sun

_____ 6. The speaker considers summer —
   F more lovely and temperate than any person could be
   G constant and never changing
   H fickle and fleeting
   J too hot to bear

Shall I Compare Thee to a Summer's Day?   155

_____ 7. What are the "eternal lines"?
   A An infinite time line
   B Life's path toward death
   C Eternal truths
   D The lines of the poem

_____ 8. Shakespeare uses the word *fair* to mean —
   F reason
   G circus
   H exhibition
   J beauty

_____ 9. By "eternal summer" the speaker means —
   A youth and beauty
   B vacation
   C changeability and hot temper
   D death

_____ 10. This sonnet is about —
   F love and summer
   G summer and weather
   H love and poetry's power
   J love and death

LITERARY FOCUS (20 points; 5 points each)
On the line provided, write the letter of the *best* answer to each of the following items.

_____ 11. A **Shakespearean sonnet** does *not* —
   A tell a story
   B have fourteen lines
   C have a concluding couplet
   D have divisions of three quatrains

NAME _____ CLASS _____ DATE _____ SCORE _____

_____ 12. Which of the following quotations is an example of personification in this sonnet?
    F "Nor shall Death brag"
    G "eternal summer"
    H "Shall I compare thee to a summer's day?"
    J "Rough winds do shake"

_____ 13. The first two quatrains —
    A have irregular rhyme schemes
    B describe the beloved's eternal qualities
    C ask and answer a question
    D have six rhyming lines

_____ 14. In the final couplet, what does the speaker claim will give life to his beloved?
    F The summer
    G His poem
    H Her beauty
    J The eternal lines of time

CONSTRUCTED RESPONSE *(30 points)*

15. Consider the assertion in the final couplet. On a separate sheet of paper, write a paragraph telling whether you agree or disagree with it, and explain why.

Shall I Compare Thee to a Summer's Day?

SELECTION TEST

LITERARY RESPONSE AND ANALYSIS

Ode to My Socks Pablo Neruda *translated by* Robert Bly

COMPREHENSION *(50 points; 5 points each)*
On the line provided, write the letter of the *best* answer to each of the following items.

_____ 1. The socks come from —
    A schoolboys
    B Maru Mori
    C the jungle
    D firemen

_____ 2. Which words *best* describe the socks?
    F Made of goatskin
    G Soft but itchy
    H Knee-high
    J Hand-knitted wool

_____ 3. The speaker feels that the socks —
    A make his feet sweaty
    B are too tight
    C honor his feet
    D tempt him to run

_____ 4. The socks are so handsome that they make the speaker's feet seem —
    F clumsy and huge
    G unacceptable and unworthy
    H magnificent
    J like golden cages

_____ 5. The speaker resists the mad temptation to —
    A set the socks on fire
    B eat the socks
    C give the socks to learned men
    D put the socks in a cage

_____ 6. Finally the speaker —
    F pulls on the socks and then his shoes
    G gives the socks birdseed and pink melon
    H hides the socks in the pages of a sacred text
    J knits another pair of socks and a sweater

_____ 7. The speaker's attitude toward these socks is —
   A reverential
   B sarcastic
   C angry
   D disdainful

_____ 8. All of the following words describe the socks *except* —
   F magnificent
   G violent
   H woven
   J threadbare

_____ 9. The gift of socks makes the speaker —
   A hate cheap, homemade socks
   B love this beautiful present
   C feel guilty that he didn't get anything for Maru Mori
   D hope he can exchange them for mittens

_____ 10. The speaker says that the moral of his ode is that —
   F goodness and beauty are sometimes lost in the dryer
   G goodness is only half as good if you only have one sock
   H beauty is doubled in the case of two wool socks in winter
   J it is better to have two socks on your feet than one on your hand

LITERARY FOCUS *(20 points; 5 points each)*
On the line provided, write the letter of the *best* answer to each of the following items.

_____ 11. "Ode to My Socks" is not like traditional odes in that it is —
   A about a serious subject
   B not about a serious subject
   C intended to be recited or sung
   D written in a dignified style

Ode to My Socks

159

NAME _____ CLASS _____ DATE _____ SCORE _____

_____ **12.** Which of the following items is *not* a metaphor?

    F "my feet were / two fish"

    G "knitted / with threads of / twilight"

    H "two socks as soft / as rabbits"

    J "woven / fire / of those glowing / socks"

_____ **13.** Which of the following items is a simile?

    A "and each day give them / birdseed"

    B "my feet seemed to me / unacceptable / like two decrepit / firemen"

    C "two immense blackbirds, / two cannons: / my feet"

    D "I resisted / the mad impulse / to put them / into a golden / cage"

_____ **14.** The humorous nature of Pablo Neruda's poem makes it a(n) —

    F extended simile

    G extended metaphor

    H ode

    J parody

Constructed Response *(30 points)*

15. On a separate sheet of paper, identify an example of metaphor and one of simile in "Ode to My Socks," and explain their meanings. Use details from the poem to support your answer.

| NAME | CLASS | DATE | SCORE |

SELECTION TEST　　　　　　　　　　　　　　　　　　　**LITERARY RESPONSE AND ANALYSIS**

Sea Fever John Masefield

COMPREHENSION *(50 points; 5 points each)*
On the line provided, write the letter of the *best* answer to each of the following items.

_____ 1. The title of the poem "Sea Fever" refers to —
   A a particular disease
   B boiling water
   C a desire to sail
   D a stormy sea

_____ 2. The speaker "must go down to the seas again" because —
   F there is a tall ship waiting for him
   G the running tide is calling him
   H he must return to his gypsy family
   J he needs some quiet so that he can sleep

_____ 3. The speaker asks for all of the following things *except* —
   A "a merry yarn from a laughing fellow-rover"
   B "a windy day with the white clouds flying"
   C "a wild call and a clear call that may not be denied"
   D "a tall ship and a star to steer her by"

_____ 4. The speaker feels that going to sea again is —
   F his choice
   G at the whim of the boat owners
   H something he is compelled to do
   J unpleasant to consider

_____ 5. The speaker needs "a windy day" to —
   A fill the sails and keep the ship moving
   B keep the air temperature cool
   C make the sea gulls cry
   D keep the white clouds out of the sky

_____ 6. The "vagrant gypsy life," "the gull's way," and "the whale's way" are alike in that each —
   F lives life upon the sea
   G keeps moving from place to place
   H is land bound
   J is hunted by sailors

Sea Fever   **161**

| NAME | CLASS | DATE | SCORE |

_____ 7. The speaker compares the wind at sea to a whetted knife because the wind —
   A cuts through steel
   B can feel sharp
   C whets the taste for food
   D can be used to kill gulls

_____ 8. Which of the following statements about the speaker is *not* true?
   F He has spent time at sea in the past.
   G He loves the kind of life that sailors lead.
   H He fears leaving his home for the sea.
   J He can't resist the call of the sea.

_____ 9. A "merry yarn" is —
   A sheep's wool
   B a happy tale
   C a good knit cap
   D a sad story

_____ 10. "A quiet sleep and a sweet dream when the long trick's over" refers to —
   F his reward
   G napping
   H death
   J life

LITERARY FOCUS *(20 points; 5 points each)*
On the line provided, write the letter of the *best* answer to each of the following items.

_____ 11. Which of the following phrases repeats in each verse of "Sea Fever"?
   A "lonely sea and the sky" and "to the vagrant gypsy life"
   B "I must go down to the seas again" and "And all I ask"
   C "And all I ask" and "quiet sleep and a sweet dream"
   D "I must go down to the seas again" and "to the lonely sea and the sky"

_____ 12. Which statement about the rhyme scheme of "Sea Fever" is *true*?
   F Every other line rhymes.
   G The rhyme scheme is irregular.
   H Every pair of lines rhymes.
   J The first and fourth line in each stanza rhyme.

_____ **13.** Which of the following phrases contains an example of alliteration?
  A "a tall ship and a star to steer her by"
  B "a gray mist on the sea's face"
  C "from a laughing fellow-rover"
  D "I must go down to the seas again"

_____ **14.** The meter of this poem captures the —
  F motion of a ship on the high seas
  G loneliness of a sailor's life
  H wildness of a vagrant's life
  J unpredictable nature of the weather at sea

Constructed Response *(30 points)*

15. In "Sea Fever," how is a sense of the sea conveyed through repetition, rhyme, rhythm, and sound? On a separate sheet of paper, cite details from the poem to support your answer.

Sea Fever

NAME _____ CLASS _____ DATE _____ SCORE _____

SELECTION TEST LITERARY RESPONSE AND ANALYSIS

Bonny Barbara Allan Anonymous

COMPREHENSION *(50 points; 5 points each)*
On the line provided, write the letter of the *best* answer to each of the following items.

_____ 1. In order to save him from death, what does William ask of Barbara?
  A A rose
  B Her hand in marriage
  C A kiss
  D A drink

_____ 2. Barbara Allan refuses William's request because she —
  F felt slighted when he drank to the health of all the ladies in town
  G is afraid to touch him while he is ill and dying
  H is angry that he has refused to marry her the night before
  J is angry that he had been drinking

_____ 3. To explain his insult to Barbara Allan, William tells her that he —
  A still wants to marry her
  B won't go drinking again
  C pledged his love to her
  D will write her a ballad

_____ 4. After William dies, Barbara Allan —
  F is relieved to be rid of him
  G feels responsible for his death
  H plants a beautiful garden by his grave
  J is blamed by others for his death

_____ 5. All of the following quotations from the poem relate to Barbara Allan's being "hardhearted" *except* —
  A "every bell"
  B "every bird"
  C "his corpse"
  D "the ladies"

_____ 6. When she sees William's corpse, Barbara Allan —
  F realizes that she could not have saved him
  G swears she will join him in death
  H vows to join a convent
  J asks her father to plant flowers on William's grave

164 Holt Assessment: Literature, Reading, and Vocabulary

NAME	CLASS	DATE	SCORE

_____ **7.** What kills Barbara Allan?

  A A broken heart
  B Envy
  C Anger
  D Drinking

_____ **8.** What grew from Barbara Allan's and William's grave?

  F A love knot grew from her grave, and a rose grew from his.
  G A red rose grew from his grave, and a black rose grew from hers.
  H A green briar grew from her grave, and a red rose grew from his.
  J A rose grew from her grave, and a briar grew from his.

_____ **9.** William and Barbara Allan are united in death when —

  A "they could grow no higher"
  B "They buried them both"
  C "They grew and grew"
  D "The rose ran 'round the briar"

_____ **10.** What emotions triumph in "Bonny Barbara Allan"?

  F jealousy and hate
  G love and forgiveness
  H anger and despair
  J greed and selfishness

LITERARY FOCUS *(20 points; 5 points each)*
On the line provided, write the letter of the *best* answer to each of the following items.

_____ **11.** "Bonny Barbara Allan" is defined as a ballad *primarily* because it —

  A has an unknown author
  B tells of love and death
  C offers a moral lesson
  D tells a story and is like a song

_____ **12.** What is the refrain in "Bonny Barbara Allan"?

  F "They grew and grew so very high"
  G "And he sent for Barbara Allan"
  H "Oh, take him away! Oh, take him away!"
  J "Hardhearted Barbara Allan"

Bonny Barbara Allan

_____ 13. The repeated vowel sounds in the refrain create a —
   A happy feeling
   B melancholy feeling
   C frightening feeling
   D boring feeling

_____ 14. In "Bonny Barbara Allan" a formulaic phrase common to folk ballads is —
   F "Hardhearted Barbara Allan"
   G "she saw his corpse a-coming"
   H "in the merry month of May"
   J "William came from the Western states"

Constructed Response (30 points)

15. On a separate sheet of paper, describe the characteristics of a ballad that are found in "Bonny Barbara Allan." Use details from the poem to support your answer.

| NAME | CLASS | DATE | SCORE |

SELECTION TEST LITERARY RESPONSE AND ANALYSIS

The Flying Cat Naomi Shihab Nye

COMPREHENSION *(50 points; 5 points each)*
On the line provided, write the letter of the *best* answer to each of the following items.

_____ 1. The speaker had never imagined the —
  A danger involved in a plane trip to a distant city
  B difficulty of traveling by plane with a cat
  C hazards of swallowing at twenty thousand feet
  D hardship of keeping a cat in a traveling case

_____ 2. The speaker mentions all of the following worries *except* whether —
  F the baggage compartment is pressurized
  G a soldier's footlocker will fall on the cat
  H the cat will freeze
  J the cat will spit up hairballs and start shedding

_____ 3. The worried speaker —
  A finds answers on the Internet
  B decides not to travel
  C asks questions about the problem
  D puts the cat on a bus

_____ 4. The problem of the flying cat affects —
  F everything the speaker does
  G the speaker at dinner
  H the speaker's dreams
  J how the speaker does laundry

_____ 5. The speaker dreams that the cat —
  A has a fishhead
  B is nauseous
  C calls over the phone
  D has propellers

_____ 6. The speaker asks all of the following questions *except* —
  F "Will the cat go deaf?"
  G "Are there mice on the plane?"
  H "Is the baggage compartment soundproofed?"
  J "Will he faint when the plane lands?"

The Flying Cat

| NAME | CLASS | DATE | SCORE |

_____ 7. The speaker feels that the responses to her fears are —
    A insensitive and indifferent
    B rude and cruel
    C courteous and helpful
    D short-tempered and curt

_____ 8. At the end of the poem, the speaker realizes that her fears and pain —
    F are shared by the cat
    G are unfounded
    H have a private language
    J are general knowledge

_____ 9. The reason the flying cat is so special is that he —
    A knows little of planets and satellites
    B trusts the speaker
    C can fly
    D has seen black holes

_____ 10. The poem is not only about the cat but also about —
    F planets and constellations
    G trust and fear
    H the dangers of flying
    J travel

LITERARY FOCUS *(20 points; 5 points each)*
On the line provided, write the letter of the *best* answer to each of the following items.

_____ 11. "The Flying Cat" has all of the following characteristics *except* —
    A irregular meter
    B irregular rhyme
    C conversational rhythm
    D iambic tetrameter

_____ 12. What example of parallelism is found *most* often in "The Flying Cat"?
    F rhymes
    G questions
    H alliteration
    J exclamations

NAME _____ CLASS _____ DATE _____ SCORE _____

_____ **13.** Run-on lines do not —
   A make literal sense
   B end with a punctuation mark
   C start with a capital letter
   D complete a thought

_____ **14.** The distinct rhythm of "The Flying Cat" is created by —
   F rhyming couplets in iambic pentameter
   G long and short sentences and many run-on lines
   H the regular rhythm of assonance
   J a catchy refrain

Constructed Response *(30 points)*

15. On a separate sheet of paper, describe the characteristics of free verse in "The Flying Cat." Use details from the poem to support your answer.

The Flying Cat

| NAME | CLASS | DATE | SCORE |

SELECTION TEST   LITERARY RESPONSE AND ANALYSIS

Ex–Basketball Player John Updike
miss rosie Lucille Clifton

COMPREHENSION *(50 points; 5 points each)*
On the line provided, write the letter of the *best* answer to each of the following items.

_____ 1. Pearl Avenue is "cut off / Before it has a chance" just as —
   A Flick's basketball shots were blocked
   B the gas pumps have run out of gas
   C Flick's life is a dead end
   D the inner tube has no air

_____ 2. Except for one that is "more of a football type," the "idiot pumps" represent —
   F hockey players
   G chess-club members
   H gymnasts
   J ex–basketball players

_____ 3. The speaker of "Ex–Basketball Player" makes a comparison between wild birds and —
   A Flick's legs
   B Flick's hands
   C the cheering crowd
   D the air hose

_____ 4. Flick does all of the following things *except* —
   F "runs past the high-school lot"
   G "sells gas, / Checks oil, and changes flats"
   H "nurses lemon phosphates"
   J "dribbles an inner tube"

_____ 5. The speaker of John Updike's poem suggests that Flick is not more successful in life because he —
   A expected to play in the NBA and make lots of money
   B spent too much time learning to repair cars
   C never learned to manage his money
   D never developed any abilities beyond playing basketball

170   Holt Assessment: Literature, Reading, and Vocabulary

NAME _____ CLASS _____ DATE _____ SCORE _____

_____ 6. The speaker of Lucille Clifton's poem compares Miss Rosie to —
   F "next week's grocery"
   G an "old man's shoes"
   H a "wet brown bag"
   J "old potato peels"

_____ 7. How did Rosie used to look?
   A Old and tired
   B Mean and ugly
   C Bitter and angry
   D Young and beautiful

_____ 8. Miss Rosie is now *probably* someone who —
   F works in a grocery store
   G works in a restaurant peeling potatoes
   H lives on the street
   J works with the poor and downtrodden

_____ 9. When the speaker says that Miss Rosie is "waiting for [her] mind," the speaker means that Miss Rosie —
   A has lost part of her mental capacity
   B is very peaceful and quiet
   C hasn't long to live
   D has the wisdom of a psychologist

_____ 10. The line "I stand up" indicates that the speaker —
   F is disgusted by Miss Rosie
   G feels responsible for Miss Rosie's destruction
   H respects what Miss Rosie has been through
   J thinks that she is no better than Miss Rosie

LITERARY FOCUS *(20 points; 5 points each)*
On the line provided, write the letter of the *best* answer to each of the following items.

_____ 11. "Ex–Basketball Player" uses all of the following devices *except* —
   A iambic pentameter
   B end rhyme
   C internal rhyme
   D alliteration

Ex–Basketball Player / miss rosie   171

_____ 12. All of the following phrases are examples of alliteration in "Ex–Basketball Player" *except* —

    F "loose and low"

    G "Grease-gray and kind of coiled"

    H "checks oil, and changes flats."

    J "on the corner facing west"

_____ 13. Which of the following quotations is an idiom in "miss rosie"?

    A "when I watch you"

    B "too old potato peels"

    C "the best looking gal in georgia"

    D "i stand up;"

_____ 14. The conversational tone of "miss rosie" tells you that this poem is —

    F free verse

    G a ballad

    H an ode

    J a sonnet

CONSTRUCTED RESPONSE *(30 points)*

15. On a separate sheet of paper, compare and contrast the differences and similarities in the forms of "Ex–Basketball Player" and "miss rosie."

SELECTION TEST   LITERARY RESPONSE AND ANALYSIS

Remember Joy Harjo

COMPREHENSION *(50 points; 5 points each)*
On the line provided, write the letter of the *best* answer to each of the following items.

_____ 1. The speaker is *most* likely addressing a —
   A grandmother
   B father
   C mother
   D child

_____ 2. When is the "strongest point of time"?
   F Dawn
   G Sundown
   H Night
   J Afternoon

_____ 3. The speaker wants the listener to remember all of the following things *except* —
   A the moon
   B the sky
   C a bar in Iowa City
   D the sun's birth

_____ 4. The speaker compares the colors of the earth to —
   F eye color
   G hair color
   H skin color
   J fingernail polish

_____ 5. When the speaker urges the listener to remember that plants, trees, and animals all have their tribes, the speaker is emphasizing that they —
   A are all alive and should be valued
   B are members of the human family
   C follow the ways of Native Americans
   D live together in groups

_____ 6. The speaker believes that plant and animal life are —
   F historical documents
   G living poems
   H related to people
   J good to eat

Remember   173

NAME _____ CLASS _____ DATE _____ SCORE _____

_____ 7. What knows the "origin of the universe"?
  A The wind
  B Poems
  C Red earth
  D The sky

_____ 8. The speaker tells the listener that language and life are a —
  F song
  G joke
  H play
  J dance

_____ 9. The speaker wants us to know that we are —
  A unique in the natural world
  B happiest when we are singing
  C all part of the universe
  D a joke that the universe laughs at

_____ 10. This poem is about —
  F the star's stories
  G a birth
  H the natural world
  J the unity of life

LITERARY FOCUS *(20 points; 5 points each)*
On the line provided, write the letter of the *best* answer to each of the following items.

_____ 11. The word that acts as a refrain in Joy Harjo's poem is —
  A "Remember"
  B "you"
  C "the"
  D "earth"

_____ 12. The speaker personifies the moon as —
  F someone she met in a bar in Iowa City
  G her mother
  H a person singing Kiowa war–dance songs
  J a child

NAME _____ CLASS _____ DATE _____ SCORE _____

_____ **13.** "Remember" has all of the following characteristics of free verse *except* —
    A irregular meter
    B iambic pentameter
    C conversational rhythm
    D irregular rhyme

_____ **14.** The tone of "Remember" is —
    F ironic
    G humorous
    H reverential
    J suspicious

CONSTRUCTED RESPONSE *(30 points)*

15. On a separate sheet of paper, tell how the refrain conveys tone and meaning in "Remember." Cite details from the poem to support your answer.

Remember

SELECTION TEST

LITERARY RESPONSE AND ANALYSIS

We Real Cool Gwendolyn Brooks

COMPREHENSION *(50 points; 10 points each)*
On the line provided, write the letter of the *best* answer to each of the following items.

_____ 1. The "We" in "We Real Cool" is a(n) —
   A elderly couple watching their grandchildren
   B bunch of pool players
   C group of kids showing off on a basketball court
   D group of adults taunting some young kids

_____ 2. The first clue that the speakers are flirting with a dangerous way of life is that they —
   F have robbed a bank
   G have quit school
   H don't have jobs
   J are abusing alcohol

_____ 3. The "We" of the poem do all of the following things *except* —
   A "Thin gin"
   B "Sing sin"
   C "Lurk late"
   D "Ring wins"

_____ 4. "Strike straight" refers to hitting a pool ball with a cue, but in this context the phrase also connotes —
   F bowling a perfect game
   G telling the truth
   H fighting well
   J hitting a home run

_____ 5. Brooks hopes to persuade the pool players to —
   A learn trick shots
   B get a job
   C change their ways
   D join a choir

176 Holt Assessment: Literature, Reading, and Vocabulary

NAME _____ CLASS _____ DATE _____ SCORE _____

LITERARY FOCUS *(20 points; 5 points each)*
On the line provided, write the letter of the *best* answer to each of the following items.

_____ **6.** Which of the following lines contains internal rhyme?
   F   "Left school. We"
   G   "Lurk late. We"
   H   "Thin gin. We"
   J   "Strike straight. We"

_____ **7.** The word that acts as a refrain in Gwendolyn Brooks's poem is —
   A   "Pool"
   B   "cool"
   C   "real"
   D   "We"

_____ **8.** All of the following lines contain alliteration *except* —
   F   "Left school. We"
   G   "Lurk late. We"
   H   "Strike straight. We"
   J   "Jazz June. We"

_____ **9.** Brooks's tone toward her subject is —
   A   melancholy
   B   humorous
   C   ironic
   D   angry

CONSTRUCTED RESPONSE *(30 points)*

10. On a separate sheet of paper, describe how the use of sound effects in "We Real Cool" conveys tone and meaning. Use details from the poem to support your answer.

We Real Cool   **177**

SELECTION TEST

LITERARY RESPONSE AND ANALYSIS

Jazz Fantasia Carl Sandburg

COMPREHENSION *(50 points; 10 points each)*
On the line provided, write the letter of the *best* answer to each of the following items.

_____ 1. The speaker is addressing —
   A drummers
   B steamboat captains
   C jazzmen
   D motorcycle cops

_____ 2. What does the speaker want the people he is addressing to do?
   F Fight with one another
   G Make each other happy
   H Slip away from a motorcycle cop
   J Play music that will make people feel deep emotion

_____ 3. In "Jazz Fantasia" all of the following items are musical instruments *except* —
   A tin pans
   B sandpaper
   C tin cans
   D pianos

_____ 4. The speaker compares the sound of jazz to all of the following things *except* a(n) —
   F autumn wind
   G racing car
   H babbling brook
   J lonely person

_____ 5. The speaker thinks of jazz as —
   A something to fill with time
   B rough and soft
   C beautiful and haunting
   D difficult to understand

178 Holt Assessment: Literature, Reading, and Vocabulary

NAME	CLASS	DATE	SCORE

LITERARY FOCUS *(20 points; 5 points each)*
On the line provided, write the letter of the *best* answer to each of the following items.

_____ 6. Which of the following terms is *not* an example of **onomatopoeia**?
   F "ooze"
   G "bang-bang"
   H "hoo-hoo-hoo-oo"
   J "Mississippi"

_____ 7. The tone of "Jazz Fantasia" is —
   A playful
   B angry
   C sad
   D ironic

_____ 8. Which image does *not* appeal to the sense of hearing?
   F "batter on your banjoes"
   G "a red moon rides on the humps of the low river hills"
   H "cry like a racing car slipping away from a / motorcycle cop"
   J "let your trombones ooze, and go husha- / husha-hush"

_____ 9. The speaker asks the jazzmen to play their instruments in a way that can make people want to —
   A sing out
   B fight
   C dance
   D race cars

CONSTRUCTED RESPONSE *(30 points)*

10. On a separate sheet of paper, describe how diction, or word choice, conveys tone and meaning in "Jazz Fantasia." Use details from the poem to support your answer.

COLLECTION 7 SUMMATIVE TEST

Poetry

This test asks you to use the skills and strategies you have learned in this collection. Read "Child" by Sylvia Plath. Then, answer the questions that follow the poem.

Child
by Sylvia Plath

Your clear eye is the one absolutely beautiful thing.
I want to fill it with color and ducks,
The zoo of the new

Whose names you meditate—
April snowdrop, Indian pipe,
Little

Stalk without wrinkle,
Pool in which images
Should be grand and classical

Not this troublous
Wringing of hands, this dark
Ceiling without a star.

COMPREHENSION *(40 points; 8 points each)*
On the line provided, write the letter of the *best* answer to each of the following items.

_____ 1. To Sylvia Plath a child represents —
   A confusion
   B innocence
   C sadness
   D wisdom

_____ 2. The speaker wants to fill the "clear eye" with all of the following *except* —
   F "April snowdrop"
   G "ducks"
   H "hands"
   J "color"

"Child" from *Winter Trees* by Sylvia Plath. Copyright © 1963 and renewed © 1991 by Ted Hughes. Reproduced by permission of **HarperCollins Publishers, Inc.**

NAME _____ CLASS _____ DATE _____ SCORE _____

_____ **3.** What is "the zoo of the new"?

    A Grand and classical images

    B All the things the child will learn about

    C Baby animals that remind the speaker of the child

    D Snowdrops, pipes, pools, and stars

_____ **4.** The speaker wants the images the child absorbs to be —

    F troublous

    G grand and classical

    H dark like a ceiling

    J without stars

_____ **5.** The speaker wants to —

    A keep the child indoors to nap

    B take the child to the zoo

    C show the world outside to the child

    D give the child a star

READING SKILLS AND STRATEGIES: CONSTRUCTED RESPONSE *(20 points; 10 points each)*
Using Prior Knowledge

6. The last word in this poem is *star*. Think about this word. What do you associate it with? Can you think of any famous quotations that use it? What do you think Plath means by *star* in this poem? Support your ideas with details from the poem.

_____

_____

_____

_____

_____

Collection 7 Summative Test   **181**

Paraphrasing

7. In your own words, paraphrase what the speaker is saying to the child.

_____

_____

_____

_____

_____

LITERARY FOCUS *(40 points; 8 points each)*

_____ **8.** "Child" has all of the following characteristics *except* —
  F conversational tone
  G regular rhythm and rhyme
  H strong images
  J figurative language

_____ **9.** As "Child" begins, its tone is one of —
  A affection and admiration
  B cynicism and irony
  C sorrow and regret
  D mockery and bitterness

_____ **10.** The "wringing of hands" refers to the action of a(n) —
  F child who can't learn anything
  G teacher having difficulty in her job
  H overwhelmed and bewildered person
  J adult reaching out to comfort a crying child

_____ 11. The change in tone in Plath's poem shows a —
   A clever use of free verse
   B deliberate contrast between delight and despair
   C determination to throw off melancholy
   D moralistic message about how to raise children

12. The left-hand column of the chart below contains two metaphors from "Child." Write your interpretation of these metaphors in the right-hand column.

"Little stalk without wrinkle"	
"this dark Ceiling without a star"	

Collection 7 Summative Test

NAME _____ CLASS _____ DATE _____ SCORE _____

COLLECTION 8 DIAGNOSTIC TEST

Evaluating Style

LITERATURE
INFORMATIONAL TEXT
VOCABULARY

On the line provided, write the letter of the *best* answer to each of the following items.
(100 points; 10 points each)

_____ 1. Which of the following elements constitute a writer's **style**?

    A Plot and character

    B Point of view and sequence of events

    C Diction and sentence structure

    D Time and place of a story

_____ 2. A writer can create an elaborate, poetic **style** by —

    F using slang and contractions

    G relying on irony

    H presenting anecdotes

    J including figures of speech

_____ 3. The **tone** of a story represents —

    A its symbolic meaning

    B the author's attitude toward the characters or subject

    C the speech patterns of characters

    D an insight about human experience revealed by the writer

_____ 4. Which of the following elements contributes the *most* to the creation of **mood** in a story?

    F Imagery

    G Conflict

    H Genre

    J Dialogue

_____ 5. The purpose of **flashbacks** is to —

    A suggest what will happen to characters in the future

    B connect a story to its historical period

    C create a story that is not located in a particular time or place

    D reveal events that happened prior to the beginning of a story

NAME _____ CLASS _____ DATE _____ SCORE _____

_____ 6. **Motivation** reveals the —
   F author's purpose for writing
   G identity of the narrator
   H reasons for a character's actions
   J resolution of a story

_____ 7. Which of the following statements about **emotional appeals** is *false*?
   A They can be proven.
   B They are not evidence.
   C They appeal to a reader's emotions.
   D They include loaded words.

_____ 8. Which of the following strategies is *not* a common way to structure an **argument**?
   F Most important idea to least important idea
   G Spatial order
   H Least important idea to most important idea
   J Comparison and contrast

_____ 9. The **literal meaning** of a word refers to —
   A its abstract meaning
   B its dictionary definition
   C a meaning that is implied, not stated
   D the associations that the word evokes

_____ 10. Knowing a word's **root** will help you —
   F determine the word's part of speech
   G understand how to use the word in context
   H figure out the meaning of related words
   J identify synonyms of the word

Collection 8 Diagnostic Test

| NAME | CLASS | DATE | SCORE |

SELECTION TEST LITERARY RESPONSE AND ANALYSIS

Geraldo No Last Name Sandra Cisneros

COMPREHENSION *(60 points; 6 points each)*
On the line provided, write the letter of the *best* answer to each of the following items.

_____ 1. Marin met Geraldo —
   A at the hospital
   B at a dance
   C in school
   D at a restaurant

_____ 2. The relationship between Marin and Geraldo is one of —
   F best friends
   G relatives
   H acquaintances
   J girlfriend and boyfriend

_____ 3. This story does *not* include any dialogue between Marin and Geraldo because —
   A they spoke little as they danced
   B Marin speaks English and Geraldo speaks Spanish
   C they had not yet been introduced by their mutual friend
   D Marin was angry with Geraldo that night

_____ 4. Geraldo met his fate through —
   F the indifference of the narrator
   G a jealous quarrel at a dance
   H the blunders of the police department
   J a hit-and-run car accident

_____ 5. Geraldo was —
   A sending money home to his family
   B the owner of a successful nightclub
   C a distant relative of Marin's
   D Marin's steady boyfriend

_____ 6. The narrator imagines that Geraldo's family —
   F is wondering what happened to him
   G is glad to be rid of him
   H will eventually forget about him
   J is sending money to him when he needs it

186 Holt Assessment: Literature, Reading, and Vocabulary

_____ 7. After the accident, Marin —
   A accompanies Geraldo to the hospital
   B runs away until the police find her
   C returns to the dance
   D goes to jail

_____ 8. When the narrator says that Marin can do *salsas*, she means that Marin can —
   F cook Mexican food
   G dance popular dances
   H paint murals
   J perform gymnastics

_____ 9. The narrator says of Geraldo, "Just another wetback." The word *wetback*, an offensive term, refers to —
   A someone who sweats easily
   B a boy who wears shiny shirts to impress girls
   C the fact that Geraldo only pretended to know Marin
   D a Mexican laborer who illegally enters the United States

_____ 10. Which sentence states a theme of "Geraldo No Last Name"?
   F The first impressions you have of someone are true.
   G Never judge a book by its cover or a person by his or her clothes.
   H Even someone you have met only recently can have a strong impact on your life.
   J If you want to be happy, avoid making new friends at dances.

LITERARY FOCUS *(20 points; 5 points each)*
On the line provided, write the letter of the *best* answer to each of the following items.

_____ 11. A writer's **style** refers to the way writers —
   A entertain themselves when they are not writing
   B choose characteristics for main characters
   C develop a plot with rising and falling actions
   D use language to express feelings and ideas

_____ 12. If critics say that Sandra Cisneros's diction is colloquial, they mean that she —
   F uses words that her characters would actually speak
   G makes use of short sentences
   H includes difficult or foreign words
   J makes use of a variety of sentence lengths

Geraldo No Last Name

NAME _____ CLASS _____ DATE _____ SCORE _____

_____ **13.** A reviewer would *most* likely describe the sentences in "Geraldo No Last Name" as —
  A poetic and varied
  B elegant and lengthy
  C short and to the point
  D complicated and hard to follow

_____ **14.** The tone of "Geraldo No Last Name" is *mostly* —
  F polite and amiable
  G brusque and offhand
  H humorous
  J suspenseful

CONSTRUCTED RESPONSE *(20 points)*

15. Why does Marin keep thinking about Geraldo? How does she feel about him? On a separate sheet of paper, write a paragraph that explains your interpretation. Support your ideas with at least two references to details in the selection.

| NAME | CLASS | DATE | SCORE |

SELECTION TEST   LITERARY RESPONSE AND ANALYSIS

Night Calls Lisa Fugard
Waiting for *E. gularis* Linda Pastan

COMPREHENSION *(40 points; 4 points each)*
On the line provided, write the letter of the *best* answer to each of the following items.

_____ 1. The narrator of "Night Calls" is —
   A the daughter of a caretaker for the Modder River Wildlife Sanctuary
   B someone other than a main character in the story
   C the boarding school roommate of a girl who comes from Modder River
   D the father of the girl who can imitate the sounds of animals in the wild

_____ 2. The first scene in the story takes place in the —
   F future, when the red-crested night heron is discovered
   G present, at the daughter's boarding school
   H past, at the mother's funeral in Johannesburg
   J past, as the daughter returns home to visit her father

_____ 3. Marlene has a special gift for —
   A making her father laugh
   B writing personal journal entries
   C imitating calls of animals and birds
   D tracking and capturing animals in the wild

_____ 4. During the story, the relationship of the father and daughter is traced through —
   F the decision made by an aunt in Johannesburg to send Marlene to a boarding school
   G the father's decision to keep Marlene with him at the Modder River Wildlife Sanctuary after the mother's death
   H what happens to King and Blitz, the dogs at Modder River Wildlife Sanctuary, after Marlene goes to boarding school
   J the story of an endangered red-crested night heron, which arrived at the sanctuary the year that the mother died in a car accident

_____ 5. How does the arrival of the red-crested night heron affect the lives of Marlene and her father?
   A Its presence creates distance between Marlene and her father.
   B Because of the heron, the father continues on as warden at the sanctuary.
   C The arrival of the heron instantly cheers up the grieving father.
   D The arrival of the heron forces the father to dig a pond on land where water is scarce.

Night Calls / Waiting for *E. gularis*   **189**

_____ 6. What happens to the red-crested night heron in the story?
   F Marlene opens the cage accidentally and then recaptures the bird.
   G The father frees it from its cage, but the bird dies in the wild.
   H A jackal breaks into the bird's cage and kills the bird.
   J The dogs knock the cage over, injuring the bird.

_____ 7. Marlene learns about the father's relationship to the red-crested night heron —
   A from reading entries in his journal
   B by secretly following him
   C by talking with him at breakfast
   D from reading a letter from her aunt

_____ 8. During the story the father's character goes from —
   F happy-go-lucky to sad
   G distant to expressive
   H friendly to mysterious
   J tranquil to indifferent

_____ 9. The response of the father and daughter to the red-crested night heron shows how they deal with —
   A living in isolation in the South African countryside and learning to enjoy it
   B mourning the death of a family member and moving on with their lives
   C learning ways to help preserve endangered species of African wildlife
   D developing better communication techniques between humans

_____ 10. Why does the speaker go to a pond in "Waiting for *E. gularis*"?
   F She hopes to find *E. gularis*, an African heron that has been sighted there.
   G She enjoys swimming at *E. gularis*, a famous pond on Nantucket Island.
   H An African rock band named *E. gularis* is going to perform at a local pond.
   J She dreams that she is in Africa, when she actually is on a pond in Nantucket.

LITERARY FOCUS (20 points; 5 points each)
On the line provided, write the letter of the *best* answer to each of the following items.

_____ 11. The **mood** of a piece of literature is —
   A the sentence structure a writer chooses
   B the point of view from which the story is told by a narrator
   C the feeling or atmosphere created by the writer's language
   D either the formal or informal diction used by the writer

_____ 12. Read the last stanza of the poem "Waiting for *E. gularis*" below:

> binoculars
> raised
> like pistols

The mood evoked by the poem, especially in this last stanza, is —

F tense
G subdued
H absurd
J disinterested

_____ 13. Which of the following sentences from "Night Calls" includes a figure of speech?

A "It was hot, and the only other car at the small station pulled away."
B "Once in the truck, I was filled with anxiety about how close to him I could sit."
C "I felt like a thief and moved a little closer to the window."
D "I mimicked their rattling cry again, and they stopped."

_____ 14. Read the last sentence of "Night Calls."

> He took three more small steps toward my side of the river and his hands fluttered like giant, tawny moths in the moonlight.

This sentence allows you to sense the father's character and the mood of the story by —

F describing both the daughter and the father in one sentence
G focusing on two sides of a river at one time
H comparing hands and a moth in a figure of speech
J presenting the symbol of hands, which stand for the idea of time

VOCABULARY DEVELOPMENT (20 points; 4 points each)

Choose a Vocabulary word to complete each sentence below. On the line provided, write the word.

avid   abutting   opulent   indigenous   patina

15. The setting sun on the water created a shiny orange _____.

16. Marlene's aunt was a(n) _____ supporter of boarding schools.

17. _____ the sanctuary lay dusty wilderness and nothing else.

Night Calls / Waiting for *E. gularis*   191

NAME _____ CLASS _____ DATE _____ SCORE _____

18. Head feathers of the heron were a deep, _____ shade of ruby red.

19. The sanctuary allowed visitors to view _____ animals of the region in their natural habitat.

CONSTRUCTED RESPONSE *(20 points)*

20. On a separate sheet of paper, describe the mood that Lisa Fugard evokes in her story "Night Calls." Explain how she uses language to create this mood, and include at least two examples from the story that support your idea.

NAME _____ CLASS _____ DATE _____ SCORE _____

SELECTION TEST   INFORMATIONAL READING

Call of the Wild—Save Us!
Norman Myers

COMPREHENSION (50 points; 10 points each)
On the line provided, write the letter of the *best* answer to each of the following items.

_____ 1. The *main* point the author hopes to get across is that readers should —
   A write to government representatives
   B take action to save plants and animals
   C use plants to cure serious human diseases
   D spend money on the future of their children

_____ 2. Which of the following sentences is *not* a reason given to support the author's opinion?
   F Plants and animals are more important than anything else.
   G Important medicines come from wild plants.
   H Plants and animals, like humans, deserve the right to survive.
   J Future generations deserve to live on a diverse planet.

_____ 3. Which of the following sentences from the article is an example of an opinion rather than a fact?
   A "We chop down their forests, dig up their grasslands, drain their marshes, pollute their rivers and lakes, pave over their other habitats, and generally jump on whatever corners of the earth they have chosen to make their last stand."
   B "The U.N. is putting together a global treaty to safeguard wildlife."
   C "There will ultimately be no healthy place for wildlife except on a planet that is healthy all 'round."
   D "A rich-nation couple spends $175,000 to bring up a child from cradle through college."

_____ 4. Which quotation from the section under the heading "What Will It Cost" appeals to emotion?
   F "that alone would generate health benefits worth several billions annually"
   G "For the cost of a beer or a hamburger, we could do it."
   H "bereft of much of what makes the world diverse and interesting, spectacular and special"
   J "There are 1.2 billion of us."

_____ 5. The tone of this article may be described by all of the following adjectives *except* —
   A concerned
   B sincere
   C serious
   D hysterical

Call of the Wild—Save Us!   **193**

VOCABULARY DEVELOPMENT *(50 points; 10 points each)*

Match the definition on the left with the Vocabulary word on the right. On the line provided, write the letter of the Vocabulary word.

_____ 6. end
_____ 7. places where animals live
_____ 8. actual
_____ 9. decline
_____ 10. not having what is needed

a. habitats
b. degradation
c. bereft
d. terminal
e. veritable

NAME _____ CLASS _____ DATE _____ SCORE _____

SELECTION TEST   LITERARY RESPONSE AND ANALYSIS

A Very Old Man with Enormous Wings
Gabriel García Márquez *translated by* Gregory Rabassa
Sonnet for Heaven Below   Jack Agüeros

COMPREHENSION *(40 points; 4 points each)*
On the line provided, write the letter of the *best* answer to each of the following items.

_____ 1. The neighbor's first explanation of the angel's arrival is that the angel came to —
   A help the child
   B keep the crabs away
   C help the village
   D take the child away

_____ 2. When he visits the angel, Father Gonzaga —
   F falls to the ground in awe
   G is suspicious because the angel doesn't speak Latin
   H announces that the angel is a gift from God
   J runs away in fear

_____ 3. When the people in the community are considering what to do with the angel, they do *not* suggest that the —
   A angel be sent to a circus
   B government make the angel a five-star general
   C people of Macondo make the angel the mayor
   D angel be put out to stud

_____ 4. Elisenda considers the angel to be a(n) —
   F miracle
   G annoyance
   H diversion
   J embarrassment

_____ 5. What turns the attention of the people of Macondo away from the angel?
   A The angel catches chicken pox and becomes sick just like any human.
   B A woman turned into a spider entertains the people of Macondo.
   C A leper heals, and sunflowers sprout from the scars.
   D Elisenda and Pelayo build a mansion for the angel to live in quietly.

A Very Old Man with Enormous Wings / Sonnet for Heaven Below   **195**

_____ 6. Because of the angel, —
   F Elisenda and Pelayo observe three miracles
   G the child of Elisenda and Pelayo is cured
   H the crabs are scared away
   J Elisenda and Pelayo become rich

_____ 7. Which of the following details in the story is a turning point that leads to the story's outcome?
   A The angel begins to sprout new feathers.
   B Elisenda exclaims that she lives in a "hell full of angels."
   C The child and the angel catch chicken pox and die.
   D The angel speaks tongue twisters in a foreign language.

_____ 8. By using the magical element of the angel in an ordinary world, Gabriel García Márquez —
   F attempts to show the problems with religious beliefs
   G forces readers to view outsiders in a new way
   H shows how angels truly live their everyday lives
   J tries to convey his own political beliefs to the reader

_____ 9. In telling the story, the author does *not* present the perspective of —
   A Elisenda
   B Father Gonzaga
   C the angel
   D Pelayo

_____ 10. The angels described in "Sonnet for Heaven Below" are really —
   F visitors from Macondo who have just arrived in New York
   G people from Calcutta, India, who lived long ago
   H homeless people who live in New York City
   J barges on the Gowanus that have been magically turned into angels

LITERARY FOCUS (20 points; 5 points each)

_____ 11. Which of the following statements is the *best* example of magic realism?
   A It rains for three days, bringing crabs into the house.
   B The angel does not speak.
   C The angel's wings are filled with parasites.
   D Father Gonzaga had been a woodcutter.

_____ 12. What magical element was involved in the healing of the leper?

    F Speaking in tongues

    G Seeing a vision of the Virgin Mary

    H Being completely healed but not knowing how

    J His sores sprouting sunflowers

_____ 13. When Pelayo and Elisenda built their mansion, they added "iron bars on the windows." The *best* explanation of this image is that —

    A Pelayo and Elisenda are able to build a mansion

    B the couple is showing off

    C the window bars are there to keep angels away

    D a mansion attracts robbers

_____ 14. The neighbor woman thought that angels were "fugitive survivors of a celestial conspiracy." The *best* interpretation of this image is that —

    F the woman thinks about angels

    G angels have to flee from the heavens

    H angels are survivors

    J the woman thinks about conspiracies

VOCABULARY DEVELOPMENT *(20 points; 4 points each)*
On the line provided, write the letter of the choice that is the *best* synonym for the Vocabulary word.

_____ 15. reverence

    A repetition

    B respect

    C fortitude

    D balance

_____ 16. prudence

    F inclination

    G mourning

    H caution

    J threat

_____ 17. lament

    A to calculate

    B to move slowly

    C to adhere

    D to feel great sorrow

NAME _____ CLASS _____ DATE _____ SCORE _____

_____ **18.** magnanimous
      F generous
      G stingy
      H attractive
      J suspicious

_____ **19.** impeded
      A destroyed
      B angered
      C delivered
      D blocked

CONSTRUCTED RESPONSE *(20 points)*

20. Why might people in the community react differently to the angel than they do to the spider woman? On a separate sheet of paper, write a paragraph explaining your opinion. Support your ideas with at least two details from the selection.

COLLECTION 8 SUMMATIVE TEST
Evaluating Style

This test asks you to use the skills and strategies you have learned in this collection. Read this story, "The Bracelet" by Colette, and then answer the questions that follow it.

The Bracelet
by Colette
translated by Matthew Ward

"... Twenty-seven, twenty-eight, twenty-nine ... There really are twenty-nine ..."

Madame Augelier mechanically counted and recounted the little *pavé*[1] diamonds. Twenty-nine square brilliants, set in a bracelet, which slithered between her fingers like a cold and supple snake. Very white, not too big, admirably matched to each other—the pretty bijou[2] of a connoisseur. She fastened it on her wrist, and shook it, throwing off blue sparks under the electric candles; a hundred tiny rainbows, blazing with color, danced on the white tablecloth. But Madame Augelier was looking more closely instead at the other bracelet, the three finely engraved creases encircling her wrist above the glittering snake.

"Poor François ... what will he give me next year, if we're both still here?"

François Augelier, industrialist, was traveling in Algeria at the time, but, present or absent, his gift marked both the year's end and their wedding anniversary. Twenty-eight jade bowls, last year; twenty-seven old enamel plaques mounted on a belt, the year before ...

"And the twenty-six little Royal Dresden[3] plates ... And the twenty-four meters of antique Alençon lace[4] ..." With a slight effort of memory Madame Augelier could have gone back as far as four modest silver place settings, as far as three pairs of silk stockings ...

"We weren't rich back then. Poor François, he's always spoiled me so ..." To herself, secretly, she called him "poor François," because she believed herself guilty of not loving him enough, underestimating the strength of affectionate habits and abiding fidelity.

Madame Augelier raised her hand, tucked her little finger under, extended her wrist to erase the bracelet of wrinkles, and repeated intently, "It's so pretty ... the diamonds are so white ... I'm so pleased ..." Then she let her hand fall back down and admitted to herself that she was already tired of her new bracelet.

"But I'm not ungrateful," she said naively with a sigh. Her weary eyes wandered from the flowered tablecloth to the gleaming window. The smell of some Calville apples in a silver bowl made her feel slightly sick and she left the dining room.

In her boudoir[5] she opened the steel case which held her jewels, and adorned her left hand in honor of the new bracelet. Her ring had on it a black onyx band and a blue-tinted brilliant; onto her delicate, pale, and somewhat wrinkled little finger, Madame Augelier slipped a circle of dark sapphires. Her prematurely white hair,

---

1. **pavé:** setting of jewelry in which the gems are placed close together so that no metal shows.
2. **bijou:** jewel.
3. **Royal Dresden:** fine, decorated porcelain or chinaware made near Dresden, a city in south-central Germany.
4. **Alençon lace:** needlepoint lace with a solid design on a net background.
5. **boudoir:** woman's bedroom, dressing room, or private sitting room.

which she did not dye, appeared even whiter as she adjusted amid slightly frizzy curls a narrow fillet sprinkled with a dusting of diamonds, which she immediately untied and took off again.

"I don't know what's wrong with me. I'm not feeling all that well. Being fifty is a bore, basically . . ."

She felt restless, both terribly hungry and sick to her stomach, like a convalescent whose appetite the fresh air has yet to restore.

"Really, now, is a diamond actually as pretty as all that?"

Madame Augelier craved a visual pleasure which would involve the sense of taste as well; the unexpected sight of a lemon, the unbearable squeaking of the knife cutting it in half, makes the mouth water with desire . . .

"But I don't want a lemon. Yet this nameless pleasure which escapes me does exist, I know it does, I remember it! Yes, the blue glass bracelet . . ."

A shudder made Madame Augelier's slack cheeks tighten. A vision, the duration of which she could not measure, granted her, for a second time, a moment lived forty years earlier, that incomparable moment as she looked, enraptured, at the color of the day, the iridescent, distorted image of objects seen through a blue glass bangle, moved around in a circle, which she had just been given. That piece of perhaps Oriental glass, broken a few hours later, had held in it a new universe, shapes not the inventions of dreams, slow, serpentine animals moving in pairs, lamps, rays of light congealed in an atmosphere of indescribable blue . . .

The vision ended and Madame Augelier fell back, bruised, into the present, into reality.

But the next day she began searching, from antique shops to flea markets, from flea markets to crystal shops, for a glass bracelet, a certain color of blue. She put the passion of a collector, the precaution, the dissimulation[6] of a lunatic into her search. She ventured into what she called "impossible districts," left her car at the corner of strange streets, and in the end, for a few centimes, she found a circle of blue glass which she recognized in the darkness, stammered as she paid for it, and carried it away.

In the discreet light of her favorite lamp she set the bracelet on the dark field of an old piece of velvet, leaned forward, and waited for the shock . . . But all she saw was a round piece of bluish glass, the trinket of a child or a savage, hastily made and blistered with bubbles; an object whose color and material her memory and reason recognized; but the powerful and sensual genius who creates and nourishes the marvels of childhood, who gradually weakens, then dies mysteriously within us, did not even stir.

Resigned, Madame Augelier thus came to know how old she really was and measured the infinite plain over which there wandered, beyond her reach, a being detached from her forever, a stranger, turned away from her, rebellious and free even from the bidding of memory: a little ten-year-old girl wearing on her wrist a bracelet of blue glass.

6. **dissimulation:** hiding of one's feelings or motives by pretense.

"The Bracelet" from *The Collected Stories of Colette*, edited by Robert Phelps, translated by Matthew Ward. Translation copyright © 1957, 1966, 1983 by **Farrar, Straus and Giroux, LLC.** Reproduced by permission of the publisher.

NAME _____ CLASS _____ DATE _____ SCORE _____

VOCABULARY SKILLS *(25 points; 5 points each)*
On the line provided, write the letter of the *best* answer to each of the following items.

_____ 1. If you believe in *fidelity*, you —
   A speak humbly
   B act arrogantly
   C are religious
   D act with loyalty

_____ 2. If you have acted *naively*, you have acted —
   F without worldly wisdom
   G generously
   H on the suggestion of others
   J secretly

_____ 3. A *fillet* that women might wear in their hair would be —
   A gems strung on gold or silver
   B a small ceramic figure
   C decorative seashells from France
   D a hair band

_____ 4. If you are a *convalescent*, the *most* likely activity you would engage in would be —
   F travel
   G rest
   H walk
   J dance

_____ 5. A person *enraptured* by a book would —
   A quickly forget the main events in the plot
   B be familiar with the settings before reading beyond the beginning
   C never stop thinking about it
   D write a critical review pointing out its many flaws

Collection 8 Summative Test   **201**

| NAME | CLASS | DATE | SCORE |

COMPREHENSION *(30 points; 6 points each)*
On the line provided, write the letter of the *best* answer to each of the following items.

_____ 6. Mrs. Augelier comes to own the diamond bracelet —
  F after she buys it in an antique store
  G because her husband gives it to her for their anniversary
  H when she turns fifty years old
  J as a farewell gift from her husband who has moved to Algeria

_____ 7. Mrs. Augelier's response to the diamond bracelet goes from —
  A delight to boredom
  B ignorance to knowledge
  C indifference to interest
  D anger to pleasure

_____ 8. Why does Mrs. Augelier search for a blue glass bracelet?
  F Blue glass is as popular as *pavé* diamonds.
  G Diamonds are her least favorite of all jewels.
  H She hopes it will thrill her as it did when she was a child.
  J She no longer needs valuable jewelry to prove her worth.

_____ 9. The result of Mrs. Augelier's search for a blue glass bracelet is that she —
  A cannot find one as old as she is
  B discovers the same one she wore as a ten-year-old girl
  C finds one, but it doesn't affect her as she hoped it would
  D receives in the mail from Algeria the one she had been looking for

_____ 10. What is a theme in this story?
  F Age is just a number.
  G The joys of youth are fleeting.
  H Diamonds are a girl's best friend.
  J A bird in the hand is worth two in the bush.

NAME _____ CLASS _____ DATE _____ SCORE _____

READING SKILLS AND STRATEGIES: CONSTRUCTED RESPONSE *(30 points; 15 points each)*

Evaluating Style

11. On a separate sheet of paper, describe the writing style of "The Bracelet"—is it straightforward, humorous, or thought provoking? Choose one of these terms or a term of your own to describe Colette's writing style. Then, point out two examples or details related to the diction (word choice) or sentence structure in the story to support your choice.

Evaluating Figurative Language

12. Figures of speech—unusual comparisons that are not literally true—enhance a writer's style. On a separate sheet of paper, identify a figure of speech that Colette uses in "The Bracelet," and explain how her use of figurative language affects the style of her writing and the story's meaning.

LITERARY FOCUS: CONSTRUCTED RESPONSE *(15 points)*

13. **Tone** is the writer's attitude toward life, the characters in a story, or both. A writer's **tone** will often influence the emotional atmosphere, or **mood**, in the story. Choose one or two words that describe the tone and the mood of "The Bracelet." Write your choices in the appropriate portions of the circles in the Venn diagram. Then, find two words or phrases from the story that display the tone and the mood to you. Write them in the appropriate portion of the diagram. If a word or phrase relates to both the tone and the mood, place it in the overlapping, middle section of the diagram.

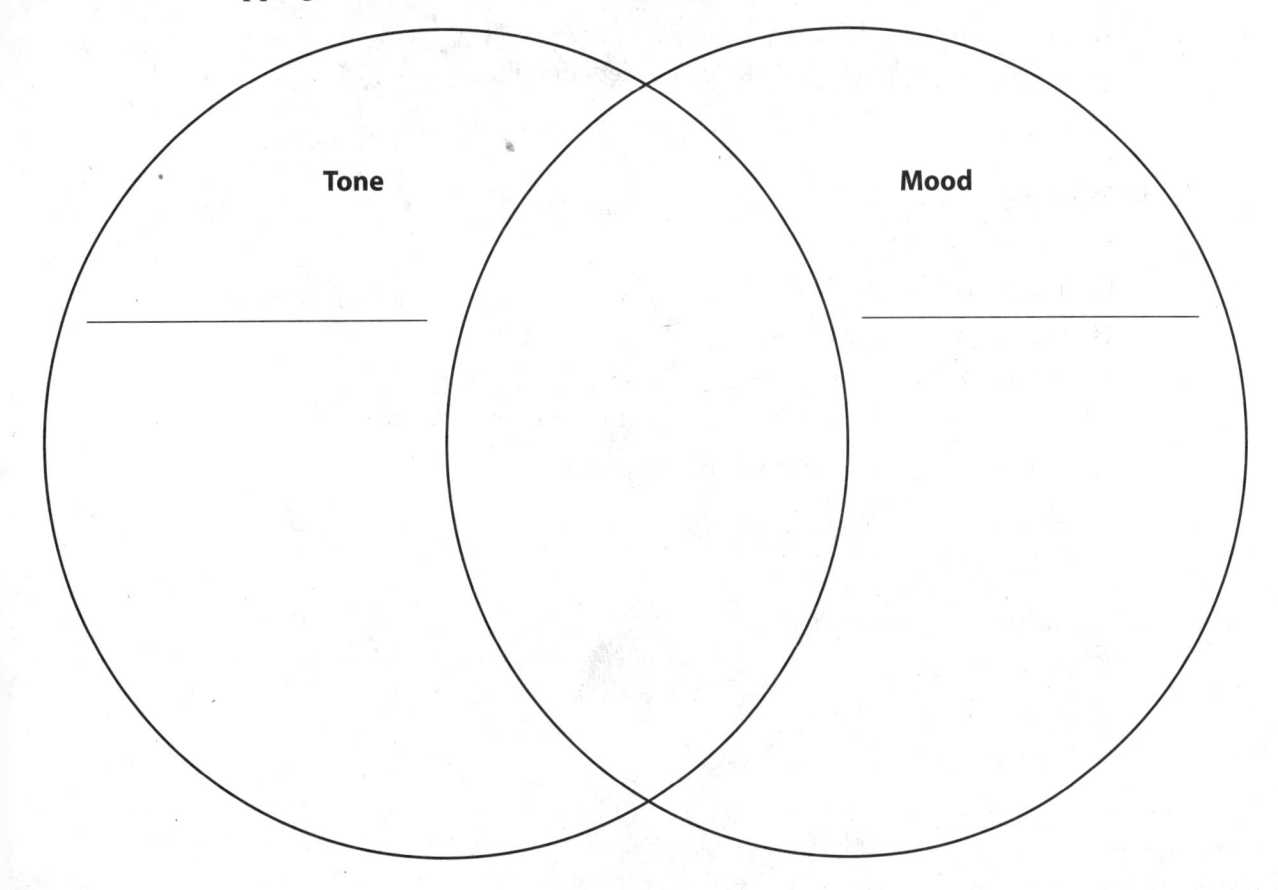

Tone | Mood

Collection 8 Summative Test

203

COLLECTION 9 DIAGNOSTIC TEST

LITERATURE
INFORMATIONAL TEXT
VOCABULARY

Biographical and Historical Approach

On the line provided, write the letter of the *best* answer to each of the following items.
(100 points; 10 points each)

_____ 1. Which would be the *best* approach to take in analyzing a war story by a writer who had been a soldier?

  A Assume that the story is completely based on facts.

  B Use the writer's background to understand the characters and attitudes expressed in the story.

  C Look for arguments in the story that support the writer's feelings about war.

  D Recognize that a literary work does not reflect an author's experiences, and view the story purely as a work of fiction.

_____ 2. When you use a **historical approach** to analyze a story, you —

  F think about the story in relation to the time period in which it is set

  G consider what critics have said about the story

  H view it in relationship to other works written by the author

  J examine the series of events that lead up to the story's conflict and resolution

_____ 3. Which of the following statements about **myths** is *false*?

  A Myths are linked to a particular society or culture.

  B Religious beliefs are a strong influence in myths.

  C Myths reflect a society's values.

  D Myths accurately record historical events.

_____ 4. What is an **archetypal character**?

  F A minor character in a story or myth

  G A character type that recurs over and over again in literature

  H A hero who goes on a quest and triumphs over many obstacles

  J A character that reflects values of the past

_____ 5. Writers use a character's actions for all of the following purposes *except* to —

  A establish their writing style

  B help convey a story's theme

  C further the plot

  D reveal character traits

NAME	CLASS	DATE	SCORE

_____ 6. A **primary source** is —
   F   written in clear, simple language
   G   the earliest source written about a particular event
   H   the most authoritative source written about a subject
   J   written by someone who participated in the events described

_____ 7. In a nonfiction work a writer's **main idea** is —
   A   the specific information that supports an argument
   B   his or her most important point, opinion, or message
   C   the subject, or topic, being discussed in a text
   D   his or her purpose for writing

_____ 8. Which of the following statements expresses a **fact**?
   F   We are approaching a crossroads in our national life.
   G   We must stop polluting our state's magnificent river.
   H   The unemployment rate is higher this month than it has been in the past two years.
   J   A vote for Leora Smith is a vote for better health benefits for all people.

_____ 9. Which of the following statements about **synonyms** is *false*?
   A   They may have different connotations.
   B   They may be used in different contexts.
   C   They have opposite meanings.
   D   They have the same part of speech.

_____ 10. English words are **derived** from all of the following sources *except* —
   F   the names of the authors of Roman myths
   G   the names of characters in Greek mythology
   H   the names of Norse gods and goddesses
   J   the Anglo-Saxon language

Collection 9 Diagnostic Test

NAME	CLASS	DATE	SCORE

SELECTION TEST LITERARY RESPONSE AND ANALYSIS

Where Have You Gone, Charming Billy? Tim O'Brien
The Friendship Only Lasted a Few Seconds
Lily Lee Adams

COMPREHENSION (40 points; 4 points each)

On the line provided, write the letter of the *best* answer to each of the following items.

_____ 1. The title "Where Have You Gone, Charming Billy?" refers to a(n) —
   A missing soldier that Paul Berlin finds during a march
   B experienced soldier who helps Paul adjust to the war
   C song the soldiers sang as they looked for their dead comrades
   D antiwar song popular during the Vietnam War

_____ 2. Paul's character is *best* described as —
   F young, impressionable, and afraid
   G young, passionate, and fearless
   H weary, jaded, and hopeless
   J straightforward, obedient, and industrious

_____ 3. What is unique about Paul's situation among his fellow soldiers?
   A This march is his first war experience.
   B He is the only one who did not know Billy personally.
   C He sacrifices his own life to save theirs.
   D His father had not wanted him to be a soldier.

_____ 4. To avoid being afraid, Paul —
   F meditates
   G writes
   H reads
   J counts

_____ 5. Paul tells himself that he will stop being afraid when he sees —
   A the next village
   B the sea
   C his parents
   D Billy

206 Holt Assessment: Literature, Reading, and Vocabulary

_____ 6. Paul would like his father to see him as —
   F self-sufficient
   G unafraid
   H smart
   J honorable

_____ 7. Paul imagines Billy's family receiving —
   A a telegram
   B an award
   C money
   D Billy's diary

_____ 8. What *most* disturbs Paul about Billy Boy's death?
   F They had been childhood friends.
   G Now Paul would have to take Billy's place.
   H Paul realizes how terrified he was.
   J Billy's body had fallen into the paddy.

_____ 9. Which of the following statements *best* describes the story's theme?
   A Fear is a powerful enemy.
   B Fear causes errors in judgment.
   C War is morally wrong.
   D War is justified in some cases.

_____ 10. What do the title and the repeated words refer to in "The Friendship Only Lasted a Few Seconds"?
   F The speaker made good friends in hospitals during the Vietnam War.
   G Soldiers left hospitals before having a chance to thank their nurses.
   H The speaker let dying soldiers think she was anyone they wanted her to be.
   J During her time in Vietnam, the speaker found that getting to know people was difficult.

LITERARY FOCUS *(20 points; 5 points each)*
On the line provided, write the letter of the *best* answer to each of the following items.

_____ 11. One historical element that would *not* appear in this story if it had been set during World War I is the reference to —
   A bloodshed
   B aluminum cans
   C helmets
   D land mines

_____ 12. If you are familiar with the historical context of this story, you know that —
   F prowar sentiment in the United States was at an all-time high
   G the soldiers would be sent home shortly
   H the soldiers used guerrilla-style tactics
   J most of the soldiers were glad to fight the war

_____ 13. Both the author and Paul Berlin —
   A knew a boy nicknamed Charming Billy
   B went camping with their fathers as young boys
   C served in the military during the Vietnam War
   D had a best friend named Buffalo

_____ 14. An element of the author's biography that is *least* related to the story is the —
   F vivid description of the climate and landscape in Vietnam
   G fear that soldiers feel during wartime
   H geography of the Vietnamese coastline
   J smell of mildew in a Vietnamese village

NAME _____ CLASS _____ DATE _____ SCORE _____

VOCABULARY DEVELOPMENT *(20 points; 4 points each)*
On the line before each sentence, write the Vocabulary word that has a meaning *similar* to the italicized word or phrase in the sentence.

stealth   diffuse   skirted   agile   inertia

_____ 15. The soldiers *passed around rather than through* the village.

_____ 16. Once he had lain down, Paul felt *the tendency to remain at rest.*

_____ 17. No one heard the soldier in the grass because of his *sly behavior and movement.*

_____ 18. Soldiers practiced on obstacle courses to make themselves *able to move easily and quickly.*

_____ 19. The soldiers sometimes believed they were less safe if their concentration was *unfocused.*

CONSTRUCTED RESPONSE *(20 points)*

20. Every war is unique, but many war experiences are universal. On a separate sheet of paper, identify a universal war experience that appears in "Where Have You Gone, Charming Billy?" Then, identify details from the story that show how the Vietnam War was unique to its historical period.

Where Have You Gone . . . / The Friendship Only Lasted . . .

SELECTION TEST   **INFORMATIONAL READING**

The War Escalates *from* The American Nation Paul Boyer
Dear Folks Kenneth W. Bagby
from Declaration of Independence from the War in Vietnam Martin Luther King, Jr.

COMPREHENSION *(50 points; 10 points each)*
On the line provided, write the letter of the *best* answer to each of the following items.

_____ 1. All of the following elements of "The War Escalates" represent primary sources *except* the —

  A excerpt from President Johnson's speech on August 4, 1964
  B quotation from Senator Morse of Oregon about the Tonkin Gulf Resolution
  C call-up of draftees by the Selective Service in April, 1965
  D interview with Edie Meeks from *Newsweek* magazine on March 8, 1999

_____ 2. What is the *main* idea in "The War Escalates"?

  F The Tonkin Gulf Resolution, passed by Congress in 1965, may have been based on faulty information.
  G Only a few government officials correctly predicted the outcome of U.S. military involvement in Vietnam.
  H Thousands of women, like Edie Meeks, held noncombat positions in the military and served alongside male soldiers in Vietnam.
  J Because of an incident on the Gulf of Tonkin, Congress granted war powers to President Johnson.

_____ 3. The author's purpose in writing "Dear Folks" was to —

  A persuade the average American citizen to support the war
  B express his feelings about the war to his parents
  C describe the life of a U.S. soldier in Vietnam for parents everywhere
  D write a letter to the parents of a Vietnamese soldier killed in the war

_____ 4. In writing his speech, Martin Luther King, Jr., hoped to —

  F persuade Americans to stop the war in Vietnam
  G increase awareness of the war on poverty
  H convince England to get their troops out of Vietnam
  J celebrate Vietnam's independence from France

_____ 5. In his speech, Martin Luther King, Jr., says, "We must move past indecision to action." The action he recommends is a(n) —

    A total military victory in Vietnam

    B end to the war and a commitment to fight social injustice

    C continuation of the war on land but not in the air

    D escalation of the war to include other parts of Asia

VOCABULARY DEVELOPMENT *(50 points; 10 points each)*
Write the letter of the choice that is the *best* synonym for the Vocabulary word.

_____ 6. facile

    F true

    G difficult

    H whimsical

    J easy

_____ 7. aghast

    A determined

    B stunned

    C equipped

    D relieved

_____ 8. manipulation

    F withdrawal

    G management

    H completion

    J removal

_____ 9. rehabilitation

    A victory

    B connection

    C remedy

    D consequence

_____ 10. compassion

    F volume

    G ability

    H condition

    J sympathy

The War Escalates . . . Declaration of Independence . . .

NAME	CLASS	DATE	SCORE

SELECTION TEST LITERARY RESPONSE AND ANALYSIS

The Sword in the Stone *from* Le Morte d'Arthur
Sir Thomas Malory *retold by* Keith Baines
"The Magic Happened" John Steinbeck

COMPREHENSION *(40 points; 4 points each)*
On the line provided, write the letter of the *best* answer to each of the following items.

_____ 1. The nobles gather in London in order to find out who will be the next —
  A to be knighted
  B king of Britain
  C advisor to the king
  D archbishop at St. Paul's

_____ 2. Before the story begins, the person who knows the identity of the future king of Britain is —
  F Arthur
  G Sir Kay
  H Merlin
  J the archbishop

_____ 3. Why does Arthur *first* pull the sword from the stone?
  A He wants everyone to know that he is the person who should be king.
  B He wants Sir Ector to favor him over Sir Kay.
  C It's a challenge, and Arthur likes challenges.
  D He intends to give it to Sir Kay, whose sword is missing.

_____ 4. Besides pulling the sword from the stone, what else makes Arthur the rightful heir to the crown?
  F He is the oldest son of Sir Ector.
  G He is the son of King Uther.
  H The Archbishop of Canterbury has appointed him king.
  J Arthur has received magical powers from Merlin.

_____ 5. When Sir Kay brings Sir Ector the magical sword, —
  A Sir Kay says that he, himself, should be king
  B he tells Sir Ector that Arthur pulled it from the stone
  C Arthur denies knowing anything about the sword
  D Sir Ector demands that Sir Kay replace the sword

212 Holt Assessment: Literature, Reading, and Vocabulary

_____ **6.** Sir Ector asks that Sir Kay be —
  F made a prince
  G made royal seneschal
  H punished for lying
  J appointed as Arthur's heir

_____ **7.** The political atmosphere at the New Year's Day tournament can *best* be described as —
  A unsettled
  B resigned
  C cooperative
  D treacherous

_____ **8.** Why are the nobles hesitant to accept Arthur as their king, even though he has pulled the sword from the stone?
  F Arthur's strength makes them jealous.
  G They say that Arthur is too young and not of noble birth.
  H They don't trust the Archbishop of Canterbury.
  J They prefer to have Sir Kay as their king.

_____ **9.** What finally persuades the nobles to recognize Arthur as their king?
  A Arthur pulls the sword from the stone at the New Year's Day tournament.
  B Merlin casts a spell on the nobles.
  C The archbishop urges the nobles to accept Arthur.
  D The commoners demand that Arthur be declared king.

_____ **10.** At the end of this selection, Arthur's attitude toward the nobles is one of —
  F jealousy
  G indifference
  H forgiveness
  J vengeance

LITERARY FOCUS *(20 points; 5 points each)*
On the line provided, write the letter of the *best* answer to each of the following items.

_____ **11.** All of the following statements about **legends** are true *except* that—
  A they are written by hand and passed along in secret
  B they often have magical elements
  C they tell about the adventures of a hero
  D their events are often based on historical fact

The Sword in the Stone / "The Magic Happened"   213

_____ 12. The legend of Arthur probably evolved from —
   F stories about a sixth-century warlord
   G a knight that Sir Thomas Malory knew
   H a painting of a warrior pulling a sword from a stone
   J the imagination of a fourth-century writer

_____ 13. When Sir Thomas Malory wrote about Arthur, —
   A a new British king was being chosen
   B no one had ever heard of a Celtic hero named Arthur
   C commoners and nobles got along well
   D the time of knights and chivalry had long been over

_____ 14. John Steinbeck uses the legend of King Arthur to express the idea that —
   F most kings are evil
   G only the wealthy can be trusted with power
   H writers generally like to write about the privileged
   J the magic of literature lives in the struggle between good and evil

VOCABULARY DEVELOPMENT (20 points; 4 points each)

Match the definition on the left with the Vocabulary word on the right. On the line provided, write the letter of the Vocabulary word.

_____ 15. crowning ceremony for royalty   a. realm
_____ 16. lowly, not of the upper class   b. inscription
_____ 17. kingdom   c. ignoble
_____ 18. something engraved or written   d. tumultuous
_____ 19. wild and noisy   e. coronation

CONSTRUCTED RESPONSE (20 points)

20. The characteristics of honor, loyalty, and generosity were considered the most important traits of heroes in the days of King Arthur. Is Arthur really a hero in the legend? On a separate sheet of paper, explain how Arthur does or does not display these characteristics.

SELECTION TEST

LITERARY RESPONSE AND ANALYSIS

The Tale of Sir Launcelot du Lake
from Le Morte d'Arthur   Sir Thomas Malory   *retold by* Keith Baines
The Romance: Where Good Always Triumphs
David Adams Leeming

COMPREHENSION *(40 points; 4 points each)*
On the line provided, write the letter of the *best* answer to each of the following items.

_____ 1. All of the following words describe Sir Launcelot *except* —

    A loyal

    B cautious

    C strong

    D clever

_____ 2. Sir Launcelot leaves Camelot because he —

    F is bored

    G has been rejected by Queen Gwynevere

    H has quarreled with King Arthur

    J wants to take a long nap in the forest

_____ 3. Based on details about the four queens' behavior, the reader can infer that the queens are —

    A forgiving and do not intend to kill Sir Launcelot

    B in love with the four knights who carry the canopy

    C playing a practical joke and plan to free Sir Launcelot

    D spoiled and used to getting what they want

_____ 4. Sir Launcelot tells Morgan le Fay that he would like to prove that —

    F he has a magic sword that helps him win every fight

    G King Arthur was wrong to have banished him from Camelot

    H Queen Gwynevere is better than any of the other queens

    J he is the greatest knight in the kingdom

_____ 5. Sir Launcelot does not behave like a knight when he —

    A accepts the offer of the daughter of King Bagdemagus

    B falls asleep under an apple tree at noon

    C rides through the forest and searches for the abbey

    D rejects Morgan le Fay's proposal

The Tale of Sir Launcelot du Lake / The Romance . . .

_____ 6. The reason Sir Launcelot fights with Sir Belleus is that —
   F Sir Launcelot believes Sir Belleus is a knight for Morgan le Fay
   G Sir Belleus mistakes Sir Launcelot for his lover
   H both knights are in love with the same woman
   J this is the promise he made to the daughter of King Bagdemagus

_____ 7. When Sir Launcelot encounters the three Round Table knights at the tournament, he —
   A enlists their aid
   B sends them to King Arthur for help
   C is defeated by them
   D defeats them

_____ 8. During the battle, Sir Launcelot concentrates on —
   F breaking the tips of his enemies' swords
   G knocking off his enemies' helmets
   H separating his enemies from their horses
   J making holes in his enemies' armor

_____ 9. In general the characters in "The Tale of Sir Launcelot du Lake" can be described as either —
   A educated or ignorant
   B good or evil
   C strong or weak
   D common or noble

_____ 10. The last statement that Sir Launcelot makes to the daughter of King Bagdemagus shows that Sir Launcelot —
   F honors his promises
   G has fallen in love with her
   H gives his allegiance to her father rather than to King Arthur
   J is planning to seek revenge against Morgan le Fay

LITERARY FOCUS (20 points; 5 points each)
On the line provided, write the letter of the *best* answer to each of the following items.

_____ 11. The term **romance**, when it was first used to describe stories like those of Sir Thomas Malory, referred to —
   A   romantic love
   B   the heroic quest
   C   loyalty to one's king
   D   the languages first used to tell these stories

_____ 12. **Chivalry** refers to —
   F   stories that are based on magic and fantasy
   G   the name of King Arthur's kingdom
   H   stories told about King Arthur
   J   medieval knights' code of behavior

_____ 13. According to the essay, all cultures have stories about —
   A   women who pose evil threats to male heroes
   B   heroes who solve problems using magic
   C   heroic quests
   D   the knights of the Round Table

_____ 14. David Adams Leeming tells us that in historical legends as well as modern-day science fiction —
   F   magical powers allow the hero to overcome evil
   G   the hero's quest is not always between good and evil forces
   H   women take risks and undertake quests of their own
   J   incredible luck and strength aid the heroes in their quests

The Tale of Sir Launcelot du Lake / The Romance . . .   **217**

| NAME | CLASS | DATE | SCORE |

VOCABULARY DEVELOPMENT (20 points; 4 points each)
Choose a Vocabulary word to complete each sentence. On the line provided, write the word.

diverted   fidelity   oblige   champion   wrath

15. Sir Launcelot's _____ to Queen Gwynevere influenced his decisions.

16. Morgan le Fay was a _____ of her selfish needs.

17. Whenever Sir Launcelot became tired, he was _____ from his course of action.

18. Sir Belleus did not feel _____ for Sir Launcelot when Launcelot's story was revealed.

19. To receive her help, Sir Launcelot had to first _____ the daughter of King Bagdemagus with a promise.

CONSTRUCTED RESPONSE (20 points)

20. On a separate sheet of paper, discuss how Sir Launcelot's actions embody the ideals of chivalry. Use at least two details from the story to support your idea.

SELECTION TEST — LITERARY RESPONSE AND ANALYSIS

Theseus retold by Edith Hamilton
"All We Need Is That Piece of String"
Bill Moyers *with* Joseph Campbell

COMPREHENSION *(60 points; 6 points each)*
On the line provided, write the letter of the *best* answer to each of the following items.

_____ 1. Theseus grows up —
   A in Athens, where his father is the king
   B with his mother in southern Greece
   C within the Labyrinth of Crete
   D on a ship with a black sail

_____ 2. Theseus proves that he is ready to go to his father when he —
   F kills the Minotaur and marries Ariadne
   G lifts the stone and takes possession of the sword
   H rids Greece of the thieves
   J casts a spell on Medea

_____ 3. The young Theseus —
   A follows the path his father took
   B chooses the easiest path to success
   C takes up challenges in order to test his strength
   D follows the advice of his elders

_____ 4. Why is Theseus given a poisoned drink?
   F Medea wants Aegeus in her power without outside interference.
   G Aegeus is threatened by his son's ideas about government.
   H His mother would rather see her son dead than sacrificed to King Minos.
   J Theseus refuses to accept Medea as his father's new wife.

_____ 5. All of the following events occur after Theseus is given a poisoned drink *except* —
   A Medea leaves Athens
   B Aegeus discovers that Theseus is his son
   C Theseus proves himself by going to Crete
   D Theseus defeats Procrustes

NAME _____ CLASS _____ DATE _____ SCORE _____

_____ 6. Every nine years fourteen young Athenians go to Crete to —
   F pay back King Minos for the loss of Androgenes
   G test their intelligence by going through the Minotaur's Labyrinth
   H persuade Minos to become a friend of Athens rather than an enemy
   J see Ariadne, whose only other friend is the Minotaur

_____ 7. Theseus is able to escape the Labyrinth because —
   A he learns its secret pathway
   B Ariadne gives him a ball of string
   C the bull has fallen asleep
   D the Minotaur shows him the way out

_____ 8. All of the following events happen as Theseus returns to Athens *except* —
   F the Minotaur tracks him down with the help of Medea.
   G Ariadne is left behind on the island of Naxos
   H Aegeus jumps off a cliff and into the sea
   J Theseus's ship has black sails when it enters the harbor

_____ 9. As the king of Athens, Theseus decides that —
   A the people of Athens should choose their own government officials
   B Athens should go to war against Minos
   C the sea off the coast of Greece should be called the Aegean Sea
   D Athenians should side with Thebes in the war

_____ 10. The decisions and actions of Theseus could be considered —
   F weak and thoughtless
   G indecisive and dictatorial
   H daring and democratic
   J selfish and arrogant

LITERARY FOCUS *(20 points; 5 points each)*
On the line provided, write the letter of the *best* answer to each of the following items.

_____ 11. **Myths** contain all of the following elements *except* —
   A a hero's quest
   B a mystery about life that is solved
   C characters who are gods, humans, or both
   D a hero with no negative qualities

220   Holt Assessment: Literature, Reading, and Vocabulary

_____ **12.** According to Joseph Campbell in "All We Need Is That Piece of String," the trials of a hero are designed to show that —

    F he is up to the task

    G humans are related to gods

    H might makes right

    J popular stories were written down

_____ **13.** In "All We Need Is That Piece of String," Joseph Campbell implies that Theseus succeeded as a hero because —

    A all he wished for was the love of a woman

    B his bravery surpassed his fears

    C he had several ways to solve each problem

    D he had the simplest solution to the problem

_____ **14.** According to Joseph Campbell, myths are generally about —

    F overcoming the world's evils

    G gods and goddesses

    H the adventure of being alive

    J human victory over supernatural forces

CONSTRUCTED RESPONSE *(20 points)*

15. On a separate sheet of paper, describe the dominant character traits that led Theseus to create the first people's democracy in ancient Athens. Use at least two details from the selection to support your ideas.

Theseus / "All We Need Is That Piece of String"

| NAME | CLASS | DATE | SCORE |

SELECTION TEST LITERARY RESPONSE AND ANALYSIS

Sigurd, the Dragon Slayer *retold by* Olivia E. Coolidge

COMPREHENSION *(60 points; 6 points each)*
On the line provided, write the letter of the *best* answer to each of the following items.

_____ 1. Throughout this story, Regin's goal is to —
   A forge the best sword in the kingdom
   B turn his brother into a dwarf
   C possess Andvari's gold
   D kill Sigurd and share the gold with his brother

_____ 2. At the beginning of the story, Sigurd shows all of the following qualities *except* —
   F physical strength
   G luck
   H love of family
   J wisdom

_____ 3. Sigurd's choice of a horse is *mostly* influenced by —
   A his mother's love
   B Regin's teachings
   C Odin's advice
   D Fafnir's threat

_____ 4. We know that Queen Hiordis favors Sigurd because —
   F she has saved Sigmund's sword for him
   G he is the strongest of all her children
   H Odin has advised her to pay special attention to him
   J Sigurd has promised never to leave her alone

_____ 5. All but one of the swords Regin makes smash to pieces because —
   A they are all made with fires from earth
   B they all contain silver from an evil world of giants
   C Regin is not a true blacksmith
   D Sigurd is more powerful than men or gods

_____ 6. Regin tells Sigurd to slay the dragon and then to —
   F roast the dragon's heart for Regin to eat
   G claim the crown to Alf's kingdom
   H slay any dwarf that challenges him
   J save a portion of gold for Odin

222   Holt Assessment: Literature, Reading, and Vocabulary

_____ 7. Just before agreeing to Regin's plan, Sigurd states that he —
   A will be ruled by no one but himself
   B plans to gain total control of Odin's kingdom
   C has been invited to live in Asgard
   D secretly has possession of a magic sword

_____ 8. Sigurd attacks Fafnir —
   F as the dragon dreams of his childhood in a dark cave
   G when Regin wakes him and signals for him to draw his sword
   H after the gray horse crosses the river where the dragon drinks
   J as the dragon walks to the river in the morning

_____ 9. Eating the dragon's heart enables —
   A Regin to gain the wisdom of dwarves
   B wild animals to speak the words of humans
   C Sigurd to become wise to Regin's plans
   D the Andvari's gold to melt

_____ 10. Sigurd learns from his experience with Regin that —
   F greed corrupts
   G dwarves are generous
   H strength is better than beauty
   J the gods are really humans

LITERARY FOCUS *(20 points; 5 points each)*
On the line provided, write the letter of the *best* answer to each of the following items.

_____ 11. In **myths,** dragons usually —
   A gain wisdom
   B hoard treasure
   C sleep deeply
   D rule over the gods

_____ 12. In Norse mythology, **sagas** are —
   F gods who live in Asgard
   G stories that take place in Iceland
   H tales about heroes
   J dragons and other monsters

Sigurd, the Dragon Slayer

223

_____ 13. **Norse myths** are different from Greek myths in that they —
   A present gods as kindhearted
   B explain the human condition
   C recount the adventures of heroes
   D predict the end of the world

_____ 14. Norse myths generally include all of the following elements *except* —
   F rowdy humor
   G happy endings
   H heroes who perform acts of courage
   J challenges that must be overcome

CONSTRUCTED RESPONSE *(20 points)*

15. Identify a lesson or theme that you learned by reading "Sigurd, the Dragon Slayer." On a separate sheet of paper, discuss what this theme teaches you about Norse culture and the history of the Vikings. Use at least two details from the myth to support your ideas.

COLLECTION 9 SUMMATIVE TEST

Biographical and Historical Approach

This test asks you to use the skills and strategies you have learned in this collection. Read the folk tale "Green Willow," retold by Paul Jordan-Smith, and then answer the questions that follow it.

Green Willow
retold by Paul Jordan-Smith

In the era of Bummei, there lived a young samurai, Tomotada, in the service of the daimyo of Noto. He was a native of Echizen, but had been accepted at a young age into the palace of the Lord of Noto, where he proved himself a good soldier and a good scholar as well, and enjoyed the favor of his prince. Handsome and amiable, he was admired also by his fellow samurai.

One day the Lord of Noto called for Tomotada and sent him on a special quest to the Lord of Kyoto. Being ordered to pass through Echizen, Tomotada asked and was granted permission to visit his widowed mother. And so he set out on his mission.

Winter had already come; the countryside was covered with snow, and though his horse was among the most powerful in the Lord of Noto's stable, the young man was forced to proceed slowly. On the second day of his journey, he found himself in mountain districts where settlements were few and far between. His anxiety was increased by the onslaught of a heavy snowstorm, and his horse was showing signs of extreme fatigue. In the very moment of his despair, however, Tomotada caught sight of a cottage among the willows on a nearby hill. Reaching the dwelling, he knocked loudly on the storm doors, which had been closed against the wind. Presently the doors opened, and an old woman appeared, who cried out with compassion at the sight of the noble Tomotada. "Ah, how pitiful! Traveling in such weather, and alone! Come in, young sir, come in!"

"What a relief to find a welcome in these lonely passes," thought Tomotada, as he led his horse to a shed behind the cottage. After seeing that his horse was well sheltered and fed, Tomotada entered the cottage, where he beheld the old woman and her husband, and a young girl as well, warming themselves by a fire of bamboo splints. The old couple respectfully requested that he be seated, and proceeded to warm some rice wine and prepare food for the warrior. The young girl, in the meantime, disappeared behind a screen, but not before Tomotada had observed with astonishment that she was extremely beautiful, though dressed in the meanest attire. He wondered how such a beautiful creature could be living in such a lonely and humble place. His thoughts, however, were interrupted by the old man, who had begun to speak.

"Honored sir," he began. "The next village is far from here and the road is unfit for travel. Unless your quest is of such importance that it cannot be delayed, I would advise you not to force yourself and your horse beyond your powers of endurance. Our hovel is perhaps unworthy of your presence, and we have no comforts to offer; nevertheless, please honor us by staying under this miserable roof."

Tomotada was touched by the old man's words—and secretly, he was glad of the chance afforded him to see more of the young girl. Before long, a simple meal was

225

Collection 9 Summative Test

set before him, and the girl herself came from behind the screen to serve the wine. She had changed her dress, and though her clothes were still of homespun, her long loose hair was neatly combed and smoothed. As she bent to fill his cup, Tomotada was amazed to see that she was even more beautiful than he had first thought: she was the most beautiful creature he had ever seen. She moved with a grace that captivated him, and he could not take his eyes from her. The old man spoke apologetically, saying, "Please forgive the clumsy service of our daughter, Green Willow. She has been raised alone in these mountains and is only a poor, ignorant girl." But Tomotada protested that he considered himself lucky indeed to be served by so lovely a maiden. He saw that his admiring gaze made her blush, and he left his wine and food untasted before him. Suddenly struck by inspiration, he addressed her in a poem.

> As I rode through the winter
> I found a flower and thought,
> "Here I shall spend the day."
> But why does the blush of dawn appear
> When the dark of night is still around us?

Without a moment's hesitation, the girl replied:

> If my sleeve hides the faint color of dawn,
> Perhaps when morning has truly come
> My lord will remain.

Then Tomotada knew that the girl had accepted his admiration, and he was all the more taken by the art of her verse and the feelings it expressed. "Seize the luck that has brought you here!" he thought to himself, and he resolved to ask the old couple to give him the hand of their daughter in marriage. Alas for the Lord of Noto's quest!

The old couple were astonished by the request of Tomotada, and they bowed themselves low in gratitude. After some moments of hesitation, the father spoke: "Honored master, you are a person of too high a degree for us to consider refusing the honor your request brings. Indeed our gratitude is immeasurable. But this daughter of ours is merely a country girl, of no breeding and manners, certainly not fit to become the wife of a noble samurai such as yourself. But since you find the girl to your liking, and have condescended to overlook her peasant origins, please accept her as a gift, a humble handmaiden. Deign, O Lord, to regard her henceforth as yours, and act toward her as you will."

Now a samurai was not allowed to marry without the consent of his lord, and Tomotada could not expect permission until his quest was finished. When morning came, Tomotada resumed his journey, but his heart grew more apprehensive with every footfall of his horse. Green Willow rode behind her lord, saying not a word, and gradually the progress of the young man slowed to a halt. He could not tear his thoughts from the girl, and did not know whether he should bring her to Kyoto. He was afraid, moreover, that the Lord of Noto would not give him permission to marry a peasant girl, and afraid also that his daimyo might be likewise captivated by her beauty and take her for himself. And so he resolved to hide with her in the mountains, to settle there and become himself a simple farmer. Alas for the Lord of Noto's quest!

For five happy years, Tomotada and Green Willow dwelt together in the mountains, and not a day passed that did not bring them both joy and delight in each other and their life together. Forgotten was the time before Green Willow had come into his life. But one day, while talking with her husband about some household matter, Green Willow uttered a loud cry of pain, and became very white and still. "What is it, my wife?" cried Tomotada as he took her in his arms. "Forgive me, my lord, for crying out so rudely, but the pain was so sudden . . . My dear husband, hold me to you and listen—do not let me go! Our union has been filled with great joy, and I have known with you a happiness that cannot bear description. But now it is at an end: I must beg of you to accept it."

"Ah!" cried Tomotada, "It cannot be so. What wild fancies are these? You are only a little unwell, my darling. Lie down and rest, and the pain shall pass."

"No, my dearest, it cannot be. I am dying—I do not imagine it. It is needless to hide from you the truth any longer, my husband. I am not a human being. The soul of a tree is my soul, the heart of a tree my heart, the sap of a willow is my life. And someone, at this most cruel of moments, has cut down my tree—even now its branches have fallen to the ground. And this is why I must die! I have not even the strength left to weep, nor the time . . ."

With another cry of pain, Green Willow turned her head and tried to hide her face behind her sleeve. In the same moment, her form seemed to fold in upon itself, and before Tomotada's astonished and grief-stricken eyes, her robes crumpled in the air and fell empty to the ground.

Many years after this, an itinerant[1] monk came through the mountain passes on his way to Echizen. He stopped for water beside a stream, on the banks of which stood the stumps of three willow trees—two old and one young. Nearby, a rude stone memorial had been set up, which showed evidence of regular care unusual in such a remote place. He inquired about it from an old priest who lived in the neighborhood and was told the story of Green Willow.

"And what of Tomotada?" asked the mendicant,[2] when the priest had finished his tale. But the old man had fallen into a reverie and gazed at the shrine, oblivious of his guest.

"Alas for the Lord of Noto's quest!" the old man sighed to himself and fell silent. The air grew chill as evening drew on. At length, the old priest shook himself from his dreams.

"Forgive me!" he told his guest. "As age creeps upon me, I sometimes find myself lost in the memories of a young samurai."

1. **itinerant:** traveling from place to place.
2. **mendicant:** monk or priest who lives mostly on charitable contributions.

"Green Willow," retold by Paul Jordan-Smith from *Parabola, The Magazine of Myth and Tradition*, vol. VIII, no. 1, Winter 1983. Copyright © 1983 by **Paul Jordan-Smith.** Reproduced by permission of the author.

Collection 9 Summative Test

227

NAME _____ CLASS _____ DATE _____ SCORE _____

VOCABULARY SKILLS *(30 points; 6 points each)*
On the line provided, write the letter of the *best* answer to each of the following items.

_____ 1. If you are *amiable*, you are —
   A mean
   B likable
   C smart
   D confused

_____ 2. Someone who shows *fatigue* is —
   F exhausted
   G desperate
   H friendly
   J hungry

_____ 3. The *meanest* clothing is the —
   A most expensive
   B most contemporary
   C loveliest
   D shabbiest

_____ 4. When someone is *afforded* an opportunity, that person is —
   F overwhelmed by opportunity
   G paying for the opportunity
   H given an opportunity
   J denied an opportunity

_____ 5. Someone who is *captivated* is —
   A imprisoned
   B charmed
   C harmed
   D frightened

NAME _____ CLASS _____ DATE _____ SCORE _____

COMPREHENSION *(30 points; 6 points each)*
On the line provided, write the letter of the *best* answer to each of the following items.

_____ 6. Tomotada stops at the cottage among the willows to —
   F find a bride
   G begin his quest
   H rest himself and his horse
   J beg for money

_____ 7. The old couple shows Tomotada —
   A fear
   B respect
   C love
   D pity

_____ 8. Tomotada recites a poem for the girl in order to —
   F intimidate her
   G confuse her
   H show her how educated he is
   J show his admiration for her

_____ 9. Tomotada decides against returning with the girl to Kyoto for all of the following reasons *except* fear that his lord will —
   A argue that she cannot adapt to the city
   B disapprove of her peasant status
   C want her for himself
   D deny him permission to marry her

_____ 10. At the end of the story, Tomotada —
   F returns to Kyoto
   G becomes a willow tree
   H becomes a priest
   J acts like a samurai

Collection 9 Summative Test

229

NAME _____ CLASS _____ DATE _____ SCORE _____

READING SKILLS AND STRATEGIES: CONSTRUCTED RESPONSE *(20 points; 10 points each)*

Analyzing Heroes and History

11. Think about this tale in the context of the culture and the time in which it is set. With this background in mind, in what way is Tomotada a Japanese hero? Which of his actions is not heroic? Use at least two examples from "Green Willow" to support your ideas. Write your answer on a separate sheet of paper.

Analyzing the Relationship of History and Its Tales and Myths

12. Like myths, tales are stories that are closely linked to a particular society. They reflect the values of the culture that gives rise to them. What is one aspect of Japanese culture that you learn about from reading "Green Willow"? Use two details from the story to support your claim. Write your answer on a separate sheet of paper.

LITERARY FOCUS: CONSTRUCTED RESPONSE *(20 points; 10 points each)*

13. Women often posed dangers or acted deceitfully in medieval English tales, like "The Tale of Sir Launcelot du Lake." In the Japanese tale "Green Willow," Tomotada is spellbound by the young girl when he stops at her parents' cottage. In this tale the young girl represents —

    A   the beauty and delicacy of nature
    B   the ephemeral, or short-lived, things of this world
    C   an ideal object of perfection
    D   another ideal, such as . . .

    On a separate sheet of paper, write the letter of the answer you choose, and briefly defend your choice. Use at least one example from the folk tale to support your ideas.

14. Complete the chart by listing two **characteristics** of **romance literature**. Then, explain how each characteristic is reflected in "Green Willow." Use one specific example to illustrate each characteristic.

Characteristics of Romance Literature	How Characteristic Is Shown

230 Holt Assessment: Literature, Reading, and Vocabulary

COLLECTION 10 DIAGNOSTIC TEST

LITERATURE
INFORMATIONAL TEXT
VOCABULARY

Drama

On the line provided, write the letter of the *best* answer to each of the following items.
(100 points; 10 points each)

_____ 1. The conflict in a **comedy** usually relates to a(n) —

    A accident

    B joke

    C romance

    D birth or death

_____ 2. In a tragedy a **tragic flaw** refers to the main character's —

    F background

    G motive

    H personal weakness

    J downfall

_____ 3. The **turning point** in a play is the event that —

    A ties up the loose ends in the plot and ends the play

    B determines the rest of the action and leads to a happy or an unhappy ending

    C informs the audience of something that the characters onstage do not yet know

    D defines the main conflict that the characters hope to resolve

_____ 4. All of the following elements are part of **scene designs** in plays *except* —

    F costumes

    G lighting

    H props

    J stage directions

_____ 5. In a **soliloquy** a character —

    A engages other characters in conversation

    B makes comments that are heard by only one other character onstage

    C speaks alone onstage, expressing private thoughts

    D makes remarks that are unrelated to the main subject of the dialogue

Collection 10 Diagnostic Test   **231**

_____ 6. A **foil** is a character who —
   F behaves in an exaggerated manner
   G provides a contrast to another character
   H is based on a stereotype
   J plays a subordinate role in a dramatic work

_____ 7. When evaluating the **credibility** of an argument, you should consider all of the following factors *except* —
   A the type of evidence presented
   B the amount of evidence provided
   C the author's qualifications
   D your personal feelings about the author

_____ 8. What **tone** would be *most* appropriate for a review of a play?
   F Critical
   G Uncertain
   H Mocking
   J Scolding

_____ 9. In a **word analogy,** if the words in the first pair are antonyms, then the words in the second pair should —
   A be antonyms of each other
   B be synonyms of each other
   C explain the relationship in the first pair
   D define the words in the first pair

_____ 10. The **connotations** of a word are always —
   F positive
   G negative
   H subjective
   J objective

NAME	CLASS	DATE	SCORE

SELECTION TEST
LITERARY RESPONSE AND ANALYSIS

The Brute: A Joke in One Act
Anton Chekhov *translated by* Eric Bentley

COMPREHENSION *(40 points; 4 points each)*
On the line provided, write the letter of the *best* answer to each of the following items.

_____ 1. Mrs. Popov will not leave her home because she is —
  A unwilling to pay her husband's debts
  B mourning her husband's death
  C too shy to meet new men
  D following the advice of Luka

_____ 2. Luka acts toward Mrs. Popov with —
  F fear
  G anger
  H concern
  J disgust

_____ 3. For what reason does Smirnov visit the Popov home?
  A Luka wants him to court Mrs. Popov.
  B He is owed money by Mr. Popov.
  C Toby requires a new supply of oats.
  D He hopes to make friends with Mrs. Popov.

_____ 4. All of the following qualities describe Mr. Smirnov *except* —
  F excitable
  G stubborn
  H jealous
  J aggressive

_____ 5. All of the following qualities describe Mrs. Popov *except* —
  A stubborn
  B relaxed
  C loyal
  D daring

_____ 6. The dialogue between Smirnov and Mrs. Popov is *best* described as —
  F friendly
  G reserved
  H quarrelsome
  J serious

The Brute: A Joke in One Act

| NAME | CLASS | DATE | SCORE |

_____ 7. Which sentence states the basic conflict between Mr. Smirnov and Mrs. Popov throughout *most* of the play?
- A He demands immediate payment of a debt, but she refuses.
- B She refuses to acknowledge any debts she or her husband owe in relation to Toby.
- C He wants her to acknowledge that women are awful, but she disagrees with him.
- D She wants Luka to throw out Mr. Smirnov, but Luka sides with him.

_____ 8. A change in the relationship between Smirnov and Mrs. Popov occurs when —
- F Mrs. Popov accepts a duel with Smirnov
- G Smirnov protests about women who have jilted him
- H Mrs. Popov admits that her husband has cheated on her
- J Luka advises Mrs. Popov that Toby needs to be fed

_____ 9. Smirnov's feelings about Mrs. Popov go from —
- A fear to anger
- B frustration to love
- C indifference to curiosity
- D friendship to confusion

_____ 10. At the end of the play, why does Mrs. Popov tell Luka that "Toby is not to have any oats today"?
- F Unable to pay her debt, she can no longer afford to feed Popov's favorite horse.
- G She has decided never to leave her home until the time of her funeral.
- H She no longer mourns Popov and has fallen in love with Smirnov.
- J Luka has succeeded in convincing her to ignore Smirnov's demands.

LITERARY FOCUS (20 points; 5 points each)
On the line provided, write the letter of the *best* answer to each of the following items.

_____ 11. The **central situation** in most comedies is —
- A a death or a birth
- B the meeting of two people
- C an accident
- D a love relationship

_____ 12. Which event would *most* likely occur in a **farce**?
- F A man disguises himself as a woman.
- G A man asks a woman for a date.
- H Two people have an argument and cannot resolve it.
- J Two people fall in love.

_____ **13.** The title of this play is sometimes translated as *The Bear*. How would this title *enhance* the comedy in the play?

   A By acting like an angry bear, Smirnov makes Mrs. Popov seem funnier than she really is.

   B The title, like the characters and actions in the play, is a ridiculous exaggeration.

   C When Mrs. Popov suddenly acts as violently as a bear and wields a gun, she surprises the audience and makes them laugh.

   D When Luka makes fun of Smirnov and Mrs. Popov, he is revealed as a bumbling bearlike person who is not so much threatening as funny.

_____ **14.** The tone of *The Brute* is —

   F rational

   G reasonable

   H mocking

   J somber

VOCABULARY DEVELOPMENT *(20 points; 4 points each)*
On the line provided, write the letter of the choice that is the *best* antonym for the Vocabulary word.

_____ **15.** incoherent

   A rambling
   B unrelated
   C clear
   D wrong

_____ **16.** impudence

   F respect
   G volume
   H humor
   J refusal

_____ **17.** indisposed

   A withdrawn
   B fulfilled
   C calm
   D healthy

_____ **18.** emancipation

   F freedom
   G captivity
   H despair
   J maturity

The Brute: A Joke in One Act

_____ **19.** malicious
  - **A** clever
  - **B** invisible
  - **C** considerate
  - **D** remade

CONSTRUCTED RESPONSE *(20 points)*

20. Choose either Smirnov or Mrs. Popov. On a separate sheet of paper, explain how the character you chose helps to make *The Brute* a farce. Include at least two details from the play to support your idea.

SELECTION TEST   LITERARY RESPONSE AND ANALYSIS

The Tragedy of Julius Caesar, Act I William Shakespeare

COMPREHENSION *(60 points; 6 points each)*
On the line provided, write the letter of the *best* answer to each of the following items.

_____ 1. Judging from the events in Act I, the political mood and behavior of the Romans are *best* described as —
   A unswervingly patriotic and firm
   B discontented and angry
   C cowardly and timid
   D fickle and changeable

_____ 2. When we first see Brutus, he appears to be —
   F envious of Caesar
   G at war with himself
   H scornful of all politicians
   J timid and elderly

_____ 3. Which line from Act I foreshadows what will happen to Caesar?
   A "yet, if you be out, sir, I can mend you"
   B "You blocks, you stones, you worse than senseless things!"
   C "Beware the ides of March."
   D "for the eye sees not itself / But by reflection, by some other things"

_____ 4. "Truly, sir ... I am but, as you would say, a cobbler" is an example of
   F suspense
   G a pun
   H a simile
   J foreshadowing

_____ 5. Cassius states,

   Men at some time are masters of their fates:
   The fault, dear Brutus, is not in our stars,
   But in ourselves, that we are underlings.

From this you can infer that Cassius —
   A believes that fate determines the outcome of one's life
   B implies that Caesar does not deserve to be their master
   C thinks that it is up to them to change what they do not like
   D wants Brutus to know that they are destined for greatness

The Tragedy of Julius Caesar, Act I   237

_____ 6. The crowd shouts three times for —
   F the soothsayer to speak
   G Caesar to accept a crown
   H Calphurnia to bear a son
   J Cicero to become a Roman senator

_____ 7. Who are the *most* loyal supporters of Caesar in Act I?
   A Cassius and Brutus
   B Casca and Cicero
   C The tribunes
   D The common people

_____ 8. At the end of Scene 2, Cassius plans —
   F a ceremony in which Caesar will be removed from power
   G a speech that he will deliver to the common people of Rome
   H to take over the leadership of Rome without the support of Brutus
   J to persuade Brutus to join the conspiracy against Caesar

_____ 9. In Scene 3, Shakespeare uses a violent storm and other unusual natural events to suggest —
   A the onset of chaos in Rome
   B the conflict between Cassius and Brutus
   C Caesar's inner turmoil
   D the coming intervention of the gods

_____ 10. In Scene 3, Cicero says to Casca, "this disturbèd sky / Is not to walk in." Other than the actual weather, Cicero refers to the fact that he —
   F is afraid of other kinds of natural phenomena
   G wants no part in the conspiracy against Caesar
   H prefers to walk alone through the streets of Rome
   J agrees with Casca about the meaning of storms

NAME _____ CLASS _____ DATE _____ SCORE _____

LITERARY FOCUS *(20 points; 5 points each)*
On the line provided, write the letter of the *best* answer to each of the following items.

_____ 11. Act 1, the **exposition**, includes all of the following elements *except* —
   A the establishment of the setting
   B introductions to the main characters and their conflicts
   C a series of complications during characters' attempts to resolve conflicts
   D necessary background information to follow the characters and their conflicts

_____ 12. The **protagonist** is the character who —
   F predicts events
   G drives the action
   H says the most lines
   J experiences a conflict

_____ 13. Cassius's character can *best* be described as —
   A noble
   B idealistic
   C cunning
   D honest

_____ 14. The central conflict introduced in Act I is between —
   F Brutus and Cassius
   G Brutus and Caesar
   H Caesar and the soothsayer
   J Caesar and his opponents

CONSTRUCTED RESPONSE *(20 points)*

15. Dialogue not only reveals the play's action and the characters' motives but often shows various arguments or positions or an opinion or event. In Scene 3, lines 34–35, Cicero says of the storm, "But men may construe things after their fashion, / Clean from the purpose of the things themselves." How does this idea vary from Cassius's attitude toward the storm? How else could the storm be interpreted? Write your answer on a separate sheet of paper, using at least two examples from the play to support your ideas.

The Tragedy of Julius Caesar, Act I

SELECTION TEST

LITERARY RESPONSE AND ANALYSIS

The Tragedy of Julius Caesar, Act II William Shakespeare

COMPREHENSION *(60 points; 6 points each)*
On the line provided, write the letter of the *best* answer to each of the following items.

_____ **1.** Brutus's soliloquy reveals his true feelings about —
   A Caesar
   B Antony
   C his servant
   D his wife

_____ **2.** As Act II progresses, Portia becomes more —
   F concerned about her health
   G sympathetic to the augurer's reports
   H anxious over Brutus's plans
   J convinced that Caesar should accept the crown

_____ **3.** Cassius, as a foil, influences Brutus in all of the following actions *except* the —
   A decision to keep Cicero out of the conspiracy
   B realization that others hold Brutus in high regard
   C agreement that all of the conspirators are trustworthy
   D decision that Antony should also be murdered

_____ **4.** Caesar's initial decision to stay at home rather than to go to the Senate is a response to —
   F the omens he interprets
   G the words of Decius
   H his desire not to appear ambitious
   J the concerns of Calphurnia

_____ **5.** Caesar's conflict about whether or not to go to the Senate is resolved by —
   A Calphurnia's changing her mind and telling Caesar to go with Antony
   B the augurers' telling him that it is safe to go to the Senate
   C Decius's giving him a positive interpretation of Calphurnia's dream
   D Antony's arriving to take Caesar to the Senate

240 Holt Assessment: Literature, Reading, and Vocabulary

_____ 6. As Caesar decides whether or not to go to the Senate, he says,

> Mark Antony shall say I am not well,
> And for thy humor, I will stay at home.

When Caesar refers to *humor*, he means —

F laughter

G opinion

H intelligence

J mood

_____ 7. Caesar disregards the omens for all of the following reasons *except* —

A he does not trust the augurers

B he does not want to appear cowardly

C he feels fate is inescapable

D he feels invincible

_____ 8. Brutus compares Caesar to a newly hatched serpent to show that Caesar is —

F Rome's greatest leader

G corrupt and destructive

H capable of becoming a tyrant

J ineffective but honorable

_____ 9. When he arrives to take Caesar to the Senate, Decius can be characterized as —

A honest and patient

B petty and angry

C manipulative and persuasive

D friendly but sarcastic

_____ 10. An attempt to warn Caesar of the conspiracy occurs in the form of a —

F confession from Brutus

G letter from Artemidorus

H message Portia sends with Lucius

J conversation with Cicero

The Tragedy of Julius Caesar, Act II

NAME _____ CLASS _____ DATE _____ SCORE _____

LITERARY FOCUS *(20 points; 5 points each)*
On the line provided, write the letter of the *best* answer to each of the following items.

_____ 11. When Brutus delivers a soliloquy in Scene 1, he does all of the following things *except* —
  A stand alone onstage
  B address Portia
  C speak his inner thoughts
  D talk to the audience

_____ 12. Act II includes the **rising action** of the play, which is —
  F the changing of sets to another time or place
  G a series of complications in the plot
  H the introduction of a main character
  J clues to the play's theme or message

_____ 13. Shakespeare builds suspense by having Calphurnia do all of the following things *except* —
  A urge Caesar not to go to the Senate
  B recount the disturbing omens
  C suggest that Caesar pretend to be ill
  D give a speech telling of her dream of Caesar's assassination

_____ 14. When Portia delivers a soliloquy at the end of Act II, —
  F she stands alone and reveals her feelings about Brutus
  G Lucius is onstage, but not all of her speech is directed to him
  H Lucius receives clear instructions about how to help Brutus
  J she admits that Calphurnia's dream interpretation is correct

CONSTRUCTED RESPONSE *(20 points)*

15. In Scene 1, lines 63–69, Brutus says,

>   Between the acting of a dreadful thing
>   And the first motion, all the interim is
>   Like a phantasma, or a hideous dream.
>   The genius and the mortal instruments
>   Are then in council, and the state of a man,
>   Like to a little kingdom, suffers then
>   The nature of an insurrection.

How do these lines reflect both Brutus's inner conflict and the overall conflict that builds in Act II? Write your answer on a separate sheet of paper, using at least two examples from the play to support your ideas.

Holt Assessment: Literature, Reading, and Vocabulary

| NAME | CLASS | DATE | SCORE |

SELECTION TEST LITERARY RESPONSE AND ANALYSIS

The Tragedy of Julius Caesar, Act III William Shakespeare

COMPREHENSION *(60 points; 6 points each)*
On the line provided, write the letter of the *best* answer to each of the following items.

_____ 1. The conspirator who *first* prevents Artemidorus from warning Caesar is —
   A Brutus
   B Decius
   C Cicero
   D Cassius

_____ 2. Caesar's dying words express —
   F regret for not having followed Calphurnia's advice
   G sorrow over murdering Pompey before returning to Rome
   H love for the Roman people he hoped to serve as king
   J surprise that Brutus is one of the assassins

_____ 3. Immediately after Caesar's death, Antony sends a servant to Brutus to —
   A report that he is ill
   B ask whether he can safely speak to Rome
   C collect Caesar's body
   D declare his love for Brutus and to ask for an explanation

_____ 4. Which of the following sentences is *not* a reason Brutus allows Antony to speak at Caesar's funeral?
   F Brutus intends to speak first.
   G Antony has been told what he can and cannot say.
   H Brutus fears Antony.
   J Brutus thinks proper rites for Caesar will please the people.

_____ 5. Among the conspirators the one who warns Brutus that Antony will scheme against them is —
   A Decius
   B Cassius
   C Casca
   D Metellus

_____ 6. In Act III, Antony speaks of all the following feelings *except* his —
   F love of Rome
   G respect for Brutus and the conspirators
   H desire to bury Caesar
   J distrust of the Roman people

The Tragedy of Julius Caesar, Act III   **243**

NAME	CLASS	DATE	SCORE

_____ 7. The reaction of plebeians to the speeches by Brutus and Antony may *best* be described as —

    A content
    B fickle
    C disinterested
    D annoyed

_____ 8. What is the difference between the two funeral orations?

    F Brutus offends the Roman mob; Antony wins its approval.
    G Brutus concentrates on Caesar; Antony concentrates on Rome's greatness.
    H Brutus argues that Caesar was ambitious; Antony argues that he wasn't.
    J Brutus is rational; Antony is fiery and emotional.

_____ 9. Antony says to the assembled mob,

> Good friends, sweet friends, let me not stir you up
> To such a sudden flood of mutiny.

By saying this, Antony —

    A actually moves the mob toward thoughts of mutiny against the conspirators
    B calms down the plebeians and creates a peaceful atmosphere in Rome
    C supports the conspirators by justifying their action against Caesar
    D expresses his hope that Rome will be destroyed by a terrible storm

_____ 10. The plebeians mistake Cinna for —

    F a conspirator and attack him unfairly
    G Brutus and applaud him for his bravery
    H Caesar's servant and beg for more money
    J Antony and elect him king of Rome

LITERARY FOCUS (20 points; 5 points each)
On the line provided, write the letter of the *best* answer to each of the following items.

_____ 11. The turning point of the play occurs when —

    A Caesar is assassinated
    B Brutus allows Antony to speak
    C Brutus makes his own speech
    D Antony speaks at Caesar's funeral

_____ **12.** After the conspirators kill Caesar, they bathe their hands and swords in Caesar's blood. These actions foreshadow the end of the play, when —

    F the blood of the conspirators will be spilled
    G hunters will kill brave harts
    H Antony will die
    J the conspirators will recite the poems of Cinna

_____ **13.** When Cassius speaks in an aside to Brutus about whether Antony should speak at Caesar's funeral, —

    A all of the characters listen and respond
    B his words are heard only by Cassius and the audience
    C he stands alone on stage, probably in front of the curtain
    D his words are heard by the audience, but he is seen by no one

_____ **14.** Antony's funeral speech is *not* considered a soliloquy because —

    F he praises Caesar as well as Brutus
    G the ideas are off the main subject of the play
    H both characters and audience hear the speech
    J it expresses personal thoughts only the audience learns

Constructed Response *(20 points)*

15. In Scene 2, Antony turns a shocked, confused crowd of mourners into an angry mob of rioters. On a separate sheet of paper, write a paragraph that describes how this transformation occurs. Cite at least three specific ways by which Antony achieves this effect.

The Tragedy of Julius Caesar, Act III

The Tragedy of Julius Caesar, Act IV — William Shakespeare

SELECTION TEST — LITERARY RESPONSE AND ANALYSIS

COMPREHENSION *(60 points; 6 points each)*
On the line provided, write the letter of the *best* answer to each of the following items.

_____ 1. The planned military conflict in Act IV is between —
   A Antony, Brutus, and Lepidus on one side and Octavius on the other
   B Brutus and Cassius on one side and Antony and Octavius on the other
   C Brutus and Cassius
   D Antony and Octavius

_____ 2. In his attitude toward Lepidus, Antony is characterized as —
   F honest
   G foolish
   H arrogant
   J indecisive

_____ 3. Brutus is motivated *mainly* by thoughts of —
   A honor
   B friendship
   C power
   D Rome

_____ 4. An issue that stands between Cassius and Brutus is —
   F Cassius's taking of bribes
   G Brutus's guilt about Caesar's death
   H the decision to fight at Philippi
   J Cassius's mistrust of Messala

_____ 5. In his treatment of Cassius, Brutus is characterized as —
   A arrogant and condescending
   B cynical and punishing
   C carefree and funloving
   D righteous but forgiving

_____ 6. The poet who appears in Brutus's tent in Scene 3 —
   F brings news of Portia to Brutus
   G warns Brutus of Cassius's fading loyalty
   H keeps Brutus and Cassius at peace with each other
   J predicts the outcome of Antony's military campaign

246   Holt Assessment: Literature, Reading, and Vocabulary

_____ 7. Cassius and Brutus argue over where they should do battle with the triumvirate's troops. How is this conflict resolved?

    A Cassius and Brutus agree to wait at Sardis for Antony's troops.

    B As a gesture of friendship, Brutus decides to follow Cassius's plan.

    C Not wanting further disagreement, Cassius embraces Brutus's plan.

    D After initially opposing the plan to go to Philippi, Brutus agrees.

_____ 8. "To get a better view of Caesar's chariot as it travels down the road, Cassius first tries a mirror and then a telescope." In the preceding sentence, the anachronism is —

    F mirror

    G telescope

    H chariot

    J road

_____ 9. "Brutus was the last to raise his dagger and plunge it into Caesar's cloak, narrowly missing the watch in his pocket." In the preceding sentence, the anachronism is the —

    A dagger

    B steel

    C cloak

    D watch

_____ 10. What happens to Portia?

    F An emissary of Antony's poisons her.

    G She is silenced when she tries to warn Brutus about Cassius.

    H She tells Brutus that she will see him at Philippi.

    J She takes her life.

LITERARY FOCUS *(20 points; 5 points each)*
On the line provided, write the letter of the *best* answer to each of the following items.

_____ 11. In the **falling action** of Act IV, main characters —

    A provide background for the resolution

    B fall deeper into disaster

    C experience a turning point

    D become involved in the plot's climax

The Tragedy of Julius Caesar, Act IV

12. Before the battle of Philippi, Brutus tells Cassius,

> There is a tide in the affairs of men
> Which, taken at the flood, leads on to fortune;
> Omitted, all the voyage of their life
> Is bound in shallows and in miseries.

Brutus means that —

F success depends on seizing opportunity
G fate is inescapable
H fortune is fickle
J hasty action brings certain defeat

13. The appearance of Caesar's ghost is an example of —

A understatement
B characterization
C hyperbole
D foreshadowing

14. Caesar's ghost —

F warns Cassius to act honorably
G tells Brutus that they will meet at Philippi
H predicts that Antony will die at Philippi
J accepts an apology from Brutus

CONSTRUCTED RESPONSE *(20 points)*

15. What function do you think the ghost of Julius Caesar serves at the end of Act IV? On a separate sheet of paper, write a paragraph describing your interpretation of the ghost scene. Use at least two examples from the play to support your ideas.

SELECTION TEST LITERARY RESPONSE AND ANALYSIS

The Tragedy of Julius Caesar, Act V William Shakespeare
The Fear and the Flames Jimmy Breslin

COMPREHENSION *(60 points; 6 points each)*
On the line provided, write the letter of the *best* answer to each of the following items.

_____ 1. All of the action in Act V takes place during the span of —
   A a single day
   B two days
   C a week
   D a month

_____ 2. Shakespeare's use of minor characters to report on the battle's progress helps to create —
   F unbiased reports
   G comedy
   H horror
   J suspense

_____ 3. In Scene 1, lines 46–47, Cassius says to Octavius,

   This tongue had not offended so today,
   If Cassius might have ruled.

   Cassius means that they would not be having their present conversation if —
   A Brutus had agreed with Cassius to murder Antony
   B Cassius and Brutus had not mended their friendship
   C Caesar had not been assassinated
   D Brutus had fought without first engaging in conversation

_____ 4. What incorrect conclusion does Pindarus come to about what is happening on the battlefield?
   F Titinius is killed.
   G The battle is lost.
   H Titinius is captured.
   J Brutus has surrendered.

_____ 5. The consequence of Pindarus's misreading of the battlefield is —
   A the death of Portia
   B the death of Cassius
   C the surrender of Brutus's army
   D Antony's surrender to Brutus

The Tragedy of Julius Caesar, Act V / The Fear . . .   249

_____ 6. What really happens on the battlefield?

    F Brutus's army overpowers Octavius's army.

    G The army of Lepidus retreats to Philippi.

    H Antony takes Brutus as a prisoner.

    J Brutus's army chases off Antony's army.

_____ 7. What is ironic, or surprising, about Brutus's suicide?

    A Unaware that Antony was about to surrender, Brutus misread the battlefield.

    B He did not know that Cassius had already committed suicide nearby.

    C At the beginning of Act IV, he claimed that suicide was cowardly and vile.

    D He did not know that he had been pardoned for Caesar's assassination.

_____ 8. The arguments, battles, and deaths in the final act serve to —

    F suggest that Rome will again be free and happy

    G indicate that power always destroys itself

    H make clear the tragic irony in Brutus's motives

    J destroy the reputations of Brutus and Cassius

_____ 9. In "The Fear and the Flames," chaos comes to Washington, D.C., because of —

    A the assassination of Martin Luther King, Jr.

    B hospitals that refuse emergency patients

    C looters who have no regard for society

    D the National Guard was protecting the city

_____ 10. What do "The Fear and the Flames" and "The Tragedy of Julius Caesar" have in common?

    F Rome and Washington are great cities to visit but not to live in.

    G The assassination of great leaders often incites a population to riot.

    H Romans and Americans live under the rule of democratic governments.

    J Rioters will cause trouble in any city if given the opportunity.

LITERARY FOCUS (20 points; 5 points each)
On the line provided, write the letter of the *best* answer to each of the following items.

_____ 11. The character who *most* closely fits Aristotle's definition of a tragic hero is —
   A Cassius, because he is a good man who is easily influenced by his underlings
   B Caesar, because he is assassinated
   C Antony, because he praises Caesar and later speaks well of Brutus
   D Brutus, because he is noble but flawed and causes his own downfall

_____ 12. The climax of the play occurs when —
   F Octavius, Antony, Cassius, and Brutus speak before battle
   G Pindarus misreads the battlefield
   H Cassius dies
   J Brutus dies

_____ 13. The last act of a play includes all of the following elements *except* —
   A moments of tension and suspense
   B an event that serves as the climax
   C background information
   D a resolution

_____ 14. In the resolution of the play, —
   F Antony accepts the crown for Rome
   G Brutus is given a respectful burial
   H Octavius, Antony, and Lepidus form a triumvirate
   J Octavius and Antony argue over Brutus

CONSTRUCTED RESPONSE (20 points)

15. In Act I, Brutus tells Cassius that though he would not have Caesar for a king, he still loves him. Throughout the play, characters express what seem to be contradictory feelings or act in apparent contradiction to their professed beliefs. On a separate sheet of paper, write a paragraph in which you explore at least two examples of contradictory feelings or actions in Act V.

The Tragedy of Julius Caesar, Act V / The Fear . . .   251

NAME	CLASS	DATE	SCORE

SELECTION TEST INFORMATIONAL READING

Julius Caesar in an Absorbing Production
John Mason Brown

COMPREHENSION *(50 points; 10 points each)*
On the line provided, write the letter of the *best* answer to each of the following items.

_____ 1. John Mason Brown's purpose for writing "*Julius Caesar* in an Absorbing Production" is to —
  A compare the conspirators in *Julius Caesar* to fascists
  B convince theatergoers of William Shakespeare's talents
  C comment on Orson Welles's interpretation of the role of Marcus Brutus
  D persuade readers to see *Julius Caesar* at the Mercury Theater

_____ 2. Brown discusses all of the following points in "*Julius Caesar* in an Absorbing Production" *except* —
  F the effect of modern costumes
  G changing sets within each act of the play
  H the actors' interpretations of their roles
  J changes to Shakespeare's original text

_____ 3. What basic opinion does Brown express in "*Julius Caesar* in an Absorbing Production"?
  A *Julius Caesar* is William Shakespeare's greatest tragedy.
  B Orson Welles's *Julius Caesar* is superior to Tallulah Bankhead's *Antony and Cleopatra*.
  C The Mercury Theater production of *Julius Caesar* is not only original but successful.
  D Orson Welles gives a commanding, honest performance as Brutus.

_____ 4. Brown supports his opinion with all of the following pieces of evidence *except* —
  F Welles's production addresses modern-day concerns
  G Welles takes liberties by changing the original script
  H the mob creates the sound of thunder with their feet
  J the audience is asked to participate in the mob scenes

_____ 5. "*Julius Caesar* in an Absorbing Production" expresses a tone of —
  A doubt
  B admiration
  C humor
  D mystery

VOCABULARY DEVELOPMENT *(50 points; 10 points each)*
On the line provided, write the letter of the *best* answer to each of the following items.

_____ 6. Something that is <u>gaunt</u> is —
   F far away
   G energized
   H reliable
   J grim

_____ 7. The Latin root *–vital–*, meaning "life," appears in the word <u>vitality</u>, which means —
   A energy
   B contempt
   C reason
   D sport

_____ 8. The behavior of a person who is <u>surly</u> would *most* likely be —
   F sociable
   G rude
   H intelligent
   J old-fashioned

_____ 9. If you act in an <u>unorthodox</u> way, you act —
   A selfishly
   B unusually
   C spontaneously
   D in imitation

_____ 10. If you are an actor who feels <u>perplexed</u>, which of the following situations would you *most* likely be in?
   F You're unsure of how to deliver a monologue.
   G You have just been praised for your reading of dialogue.
   H Another actor speaks his or her lines to you.
   J You take many bows as the audience applauds wildly.

Julius Caesar in an Absorbing Production

COLLECTION 10 SUMMATIVE TEST

Drama

This test asks you to use the skills and strategies you have learned in this collection. Read this excerpt from Shakespeare's tragedy *Macbeth*. After Macbeth has won a great battle, King Duncan visits his castle to reward him by naming him Thane (Chief) of Cawdor. Macbeth, however, is not content with this new title. He wishes to be king. Lady Macbeth is even more ambitious than her husband. She wants him to murder King Duncan and claim the crown. As the excerpt opens, Macbeth and Lady Macbeth are discussing King Duncan.

FROM Macbeth
by William Shakespeare

[*Enter* LADY MACBETH]

Macbeth. How now! What news?
Lady Macbeth. He has almost supp'd: why have you left the chamber?
Macbeth. Hath he ask'd for me?
Lady Macbeth. Know you not he has?
Macbeth. We will proceed no further in this business:
He hath honour'd me of late; and I have bought
Golden opinions from all sorts of people,
Which would be worn now in their newest gloss,
Not cast aside so soon.
Lady Macbeth. Was the hope drunk
Wherein you dress'd yourself? hath it slept since,
And wakes it now, to look so green and pale
At what it did so freely? From this time
Such I account thy love. Art thou afeard
To be the same in thine own act and valor
As thou art in desire? Wouldst thou have that
Which thou esteem'st the ornament of life,
And live a coward in thine own esteem,
Letting 'I dare not' wait upon 'I would,'
Like the poor cat i' the adage?
Macbeth. Prithee, peace.
I dare do all that may become a man;
Who dares do more is none.
Lady Macbeth. What beast was't, then,
That made you break this enterprise to me?
When you durst do it then you were a man;
And, to be more than what you were, you would
Be so much more the man. Nor time nor place
Did then adhere, and yet you would make both:
They have made themselves, and that their fitness now
Does unmake you. I have given suck, and know
How tender 'tis to love the babe that milks me:

	I would, while it was smiling in my face,
	Have pluck'd my nipple from his boneless gums,
	And dash'd the brains out, had I so sworn as you
	Have done to this.

Macbeth. If we should fail,—

Lady Macbeth. We fail!
But screw your courage to the sticking-place,
And we'll not fail. When Duncan is asleep,
Whereto the rather shall his day's hard journey
Soundly invite him, his two chamberlains
Will I with wine and wassail so convince
That memory, the warder of the brain,
Shall be a fume, and the receipt of reason
A limbeck only; when in swinish sleep
Their drenched natures lie, as in a death,
What cannot you and I perform upon
The unguarded Duncan? what not put upon
His spongy officers, who shall bear the guilt
Of our great quell?

Macbeth. Bring forth men-children only;
For thy undaunted mettle should compose
Nothing but males. Will it not be receiv'd,
When we have mark'd with blood those sleepy two
Of his own chamber, and us'd their very daggers,
That they have done't?

Lady Macbeth. Who dares receive it other,
As we shall make our griefs and clamour roar
Upon his death?

Macbeth. I am settled, and bend up
Each corporal agent to this terrible feat.
Away, and mock the time with fairest show:
False face must hide what the false heart doth know.

[*Exeunt.*]

Collection 10 Summative Test

255

NAME _____ CLASS _____ DATE _____ SCORE _____

VOCABULARY SKILLS *(20 points; 4 points each)*
On the line provided, write the letter of the *best* answer to each of the following items.

_____ 1. Someone who has valor acts with —
   A   pride
   B   fear
   C   suspicion
   D   courage

_____ 2. Prithee is a way of saying —
   F   you
   G   please
   H   listen
   J   stop

_____ 3. An enterprise is a kind of —
   A   plan
   B   promise
   C   news report
   D   reminder

_____ 4. If you are a warder, you —
   F   marry
   G   guard
   H   whisper
   J   chase

_____ 5. Someone who is undaunted acts —
   A   tired
   B   resolute
   C   wholesome
   D   perplexed

256   Holt Assessment: Literature, Reading, and Vocabulary

COMPREHENSION *(25 points; 5 points each)*
On the line provided, write the letter of the *best* answer to each of the following items.

_____ 6. The major conflict in the passage is between —
   F Macbeth and Duncan
   G youth and age
   H Lady Macbeth's love and her fear
   J Macbeth's ambition and his conscience

_____ 7. The reader knows the conflict is resolved when —
   A Macbeth says, "If we should fail"
   B Macbeth says, "I am settled"
   C Macbeth says, "Bring forth men-children only"
   D Lady Macbeth says, "Screw your courage to the sticking-place"

_____ 8. In this excerpt, Macbeth is mobilized to act by his —
   F deep hatred of Duncan
   G patriotism
   H wife's ambitious taunting
   J fear of detection

_____ 9. Lady Macbeth uses the horrifying image of killing a child to show that she —
   A does not love her children
   B is not afraid
   C loves her husband
   D keeps her promises

_____ 10. Macbeth believes that Duncan's death will be blamed on —
   F him
   G the guards
   H his wife
   J Duncan himself

Collection 10 Summative Test

NAME	CLASS	DATE	SCORE

READING SKILLS AND STRATEGIES: CONSTRUCTED RESPONSE *(10 points)*
Paraphrasing

11. In Lady Macbeth's second speech to Macbeth, which begins with the line "What beast was't, then," she tries to convince her husband to commit murder. On a separate sheet of paper, use your own words to paraphrase this speech.

LITERARY FOCUS: CONSTRUCTED RESPONSE *(45 points; 15 points each)*

12. Review the conversation that takes place between Macbeth and Lady Macbeth in the second half of the excerpt, starting with Macbeth's line "If we should fail,—." What does this **dialogue** reveal about the relationship between Macbeth and Lady Macbeth? Pay special attention to the places in the dialogue where the speaker changes. On a separate sheet of paper, write your answer in a paragraph.

13. Choose two of the qualities below that you think *best* describe the **character** of Lady Macbeth. On a separate sheet of paper, write the letters of the qualities you choose, and then briefly defend your choices. Use at least one example from the excerpt to support your idea for each choice.

    A courage
    B determination
    C honor
    D ambition

14. Macbeth, like Brutus in *The Tragedy of Julius Caesar,* is considered a **tragic hero.** On a separate sheet of paper, compare and contrast these characters, specifically exploring their motives for murder and misgivings over their actions. (Macbeth is ultimately killed for slaying Duncan.) Use at least two examples from the play and the excerpt you have read to support your answer.

COLLECTION 11 DIAGNOSTIC TEST

INFORMATIONAL TEXT

Consumer and Workplace Documents

On the line provided, write the letter of the *best* answer to each of the following items. (100 points; 10 points each)

_____ 1. Which of the following items is a **consumer document**?
   A Government regulations
   B Newspaper article
   C Instruction manual
   D Business letter

_____ 2. People usually read various **workplace documents** for all of the following reasons *except* —
   F to familiarize themselves with their employer's policies
   G to find out about the authors' lives
   H to learn about their job responsibilities
   J to help them do their job more efficiently

_____ 3. If you bought a computer and it stopped working two weeks later, which of the following documents would be the *most* useful to you?
   A A warranty
   B A memorandum
   C A schedule of events
   D Product information

_____ 4. **Technical directions** are instructions —
   F that contain many details
   G written for experts in a particular field
   H for using electronic and mechanical products
   J that are not essential for using a product

_____ 5. A set of **directions** will *not* be useful if —
   A it contains many graphics
   B it uses spacing between each major section
   C it is written in specific language
   D the steps are out of order

Collection 11 Diagnostic Test

259

NAME _____ CLASS _____ DATE _____ SCORE _____

_____ 6. What type of **sequence** does a recipe follow?
   F   Step-by-step
   G   Spatial
   H   Alphabetical
   J   Most important to least important

_____ 7. A **point-by-point** sequence in a functional document is often indicated by —
   A   transitional words for comparing and contrasting
   B   numbered sections
   C   the author's narration
   D   a list of generalizations

_____ 8. Which of the following items is *not* an element of a functional document's **format**?
   F   Boldface type
   G   Drawings
   H   Color
   J   Main idea

_____ 9. The purpose of a **header** in a functional document is usually to —
   A   provide explanation
   B   present background information
   C   state the purpose or subject of the text
   D   make the document more attractive

_____ 10. Why should you include a *Works Cited* list at the end of a report?
   F   To rate the quality of the sources you used
   G   To let your reader know which sources you used
   H   To list all of the sources available on a particular subject
   J   To refer the reader to sources on related topics

| NAME | CLASS | DATE | SCORE |

SELECTION TEST INFORMATIONAL READING

Evaluating the Logic of Functional Documents

COMPREHENSION (50 points; 10 points each)
On the line provided, write the letter of the *best* answer to each of the following items.

_____ 1. *Audio Assertions* explains that if your computer has a free expansion slot, you must be sure of all of the following information *except* that —
   A the card you choose fits the free slot
   B the card you choose runs at the required speed
   C the card you choose will not use too much power
   D the card you choose and your computer are made by the same manufacturer

_____ 2. *Audio Assertions* makes the general statement that in order to make your system more powerful, it is *best* to —
   F spend the limit on a sound card and economize on speakers
   G spend the limit on speakers and economize on a sound card
   H spend as much as you can on a sound card and speakers
   J economize on a sound card and speakers and buy a top-of-the-line computer

_____ 3. The reviews of the speakers seem to indicate that the reviewer —
   A is open to systems in different price ranges
   B prefers only the most expensive speakers
   C prefers systems with less bass output
   D is not listening carefully

_____ 4. According to "Buying Guides and Reviews," which of the following statements is *true*?
   F SonicBombardier and SonicBoltblaster are the newest cards.
   G SonicBonanza was reviewed most recently.
   H TD3S200 was reviewed longest ago.
   J TD3S200 is the card that has been around the longest.

_____ 5. If your computer has fixed, pre-installed sound capabilities, to improve your sound, you must —
   A buy a new computer
   B buy better speakers
   C buy a sound-card package only
   D spend more on speakers and a sound card

Evaluating the Logic of Functional Documents   **261**

NAME _____ CLASS _____ DATE _____ SCORE _____

READING INFORMATIONAL TEXT *(50 points; 10 points each)*
On the line provided, write the letter of the *best* answer to each of the following items.

_____ 6. Like other functional documents a **product** review must have all of the following characteristics *except* —

    F clear organization
    G nontechnical language
    H easily understandable information
    J a logical sequence of information and/or procedures

_____ 7. All of the following structures are types of logical sequences in a functional document *except* —

    A lowest to highest
    B highest to lowest
    C easiest to hardest
    D step-by-step

_____ 8. In addition to product reviews, other types of **functional documents** include all of the following items *except* —

    F warranties
    G instructions
    H contracts
    J essays

_____ 9. If an item is out of sequence in a list of instructions for using a product, the product is likely to —

    A break
    B outsell the competition
    C win awards
    D be returned

_____ 10. A **step-by-step** sequence would *most* likely be used in —

    F articles
    G recipes
    H product reviews
    J legal documents

SELECTION TEST INFORMATIONAL READING

Following Technical Directions

COMPREHENSION *(50 points; 10 points each)*
On the line provided, write the letter of the *best* answer to each of the following items.

_____ 1. To locate the appropriate slot for the sound card on your computer's motherboard, —
   A try the new card in all of the slots
   B choose the slot without a metal cover
   C look for the slot that resembles the new card
   D consult the user's manual for instructions

_____ 2. The sound card is connected by cable to the —
   F speaker jacks
   G CD-drive
   H slot cover
   J external ground

_____ 3. If you follow the instructions in "Installing a Computer Sound Card," you save a small step in the installation if —
   A your new card has an integrated slot cover
   B the slot is currently in use by the old card
   C the connector strip's metal conductors are visible
   D the computer is battery operated

_____ 4. How is the software for the sound card installed?
   F It is pre-installed on the sound card.
   G It is inserted into a slot next to the sound card.
   H It is on a CD that is inserted into the disk drive.
   J It is pre-installed in the computer.

_____ 5. It is *not* clear from the instructions —
   A whether the new sound card comes with an audio cable
   B how the sound card should fit into the motherboard
   C when you can plug in the power cord
   D whether or not slots should be covered

Following Technical Directions **263**

NAME	CLASS	DATE	SCORE

READING INFORMATIONAL TEXT *(50 points; 25 points each)*
On the line provided, write the letter of the *best* answer to each of the following items.

_____ **6.** **Technical directions** would be necessary for all of the following activities *except* —

    F using computers

    G designing jewelry

    H recording videos

    J dissecting frogs

_____ **7.** When using technical directions, it is important to —

    A follow each step in the sequence presented

    B check them over to see if all the steps are necessary

    C have someone assist you in the task at hand

    D do a preliminary run-through, omitting the last step

NAME	CLASS	DATE	SCORE

SELECTION TEST **INFORMATIONAL READING**

Analyzing Functional Workplace Documents

COMPREHENSION *(50 points; 10 points each)*
On the line provided, write the letter of the *best* answer to each of the following items.

_____ 1. A musical **lead sheet** may contain all of the following information *except* —
   A lyrics
   B guitar chords
   C microphone placement
   D lead vocal melody line

_____ 2. The collaboration agreement between Sara Songster and Mike Melodic includes everything *except* —
   F the publishers' share of all royalties
   G legal costs
   H the authors' share of all royalties
   J copyright arrangements

_____ 3. The structure and format of the collaboration agreement uses all of the following elements *except* —
   A spacing between each major section
   B Roman numerals to mark each major section
   C a main header
   D a copy of the words and music

_____ 4. The composition is registered with —
   F ASCAP
   G ACLU
   H FBI
   J AARP

_____ 5. Judging from the collaboration agreement between Sara Songster and Mike Melodic, what were they *most* concerned about?
   A The quality of their recordings
   B Protecting their composition legally
   C Making lots of money
   D Preventing disputes over artistry

Analyzing Functional Workplace Documents   **265**

NAME	CLASS	DATE	SCORE

READING INFORMATIONAL TEXT *(50 points; 10 points each)*
On the line provided, write the letter of the *best* answer to each of the following items.

_____ **6.** To emphasize important points and to present their information clearly, most workplace documents rely on —
    F font style, headers, and definitions
    G font style, headers, and graphics
    H line spacing, font style, and graphics
    J headers, definitions, and graphics

_____ **7.** A **collaboration agreement** is a kind of —
    A contract
    B IOU
    C warranty
    D lead sheet

_____ **8.** In **legal documents** each main idea is often —
    F printed in different color type
    G printed in boldface type
    H given its own section
    J centered as a title

_____ **9.** What kind of sequence is **point-by-point** sequence?
    A Spatial
    B Chronological
    C Logical
    D Alphabetical

_____ **10.** The **format** of a document performs all of the following functions *except* to —
    F dictate the sequence of ideas
    G highlight important information
    H call attention to key words
    J call attention to ideas

NAME _____ CLASS _____ DATE _____ SCORE _____

SELECTION TEST **INFORMATIONAL READING**

Citing Internet Sources

COMPREHENSION *(50 points; 10 points each)*
On the line provided, write the letter of the *best* answer to each of the following items.

_____ 1. Why do the bibliographic entries from the university-library site and the reference database lack names of authors?

   A These types of entries never require authors' names.
   B The authors' names were not given on the site.
   C This information is given elsewhere in the bibliography.
   D The reader is expected to visit the sites and find out the names.

_____ 2. In the entry for *The Columbia Electronic Encyclopedia*, 15 July 2001 is the date on which the —

   F site first appeared on the Web
   G site was last updated
   H source was accessed
   J article was written

_____ 3. In a bibliographic citation of an online source, the information in angled brackets is the —

   A author's name
   B name of the Web site
   C title of the work
   D electronic address (URL)

_____ 4. In the entry for *Audio Assertions*, 8 Aug. 2001 may be the date on which the —

   F source was accessed
   G article was written
   H article was posted on the Web
   J bibliography was compiled

_____ 5. The entry for the e-mail communication lacks all of the usual features of bibliographic citations for Web sites *except* —

   A a URL
   B a subject
   C the name of a publication
   D a geographic location

Citing Internet Sources **267**

| NAME | CLASS | DATE | SCORE |

READING INFORMATIONAL TEXT *(50 points; 10 points each)*
On the line provided, write the letter of the *best* answer to each of the following items.

_____ **6.** **Bibliographical citations** for Internet sources —
   F are more streamlined than those for print sources
   G have made other types of citations obsolete
   H are made nearly useless by constant updates
   J require more documentation than print sources

_____ **7.** Note cards for Internet sources require all of the following information *except* —
   A the type of source and the URL
   B the author, if listed
   C the date on which the note card was written
   D the date on which the site was last updated, if noted

_____ **8.** In bibliographical citations for Internet sources, editors' names —
   F are rarely given
   G only follow the title of the work
   H are abbreviated
   J can appear in more than one place

_____ **9.** The latest update of an Internet source can often be found —
   A near the top of the site's home page
   B after the title
   C at the bottom of the site's home page
   D after the volume or issue number

_____ **10.** When preparing a bibliography of Internet sources, you should —
   F use only the Modern Language Association style
   G change styles throughout to minimize the length of each entry
   H find a style that requires the least information
   J select one style and stick to it

NAME _____ CLASS _____ DATE _____ SCORE _____

SELECTION TEST INFORMATIONAL READING

Reading Consumer Documents

COMPREHENSION *(50 points; 10 points each)*
On the line provided, write the letter of the *best* answer to each of the following items.

_____ 1. The service contract from Aulsound Warranty Service Corporation for the digital multitrack recorder DMR88 provides coverage for —
   A ninety days
   B one year
   C two years
   D five years

_____ 2. The cost of renewing the service contract for the recorder, at the discretion of the administrator, is —
   F based on how much the unit has been used
   G a predetermined fraction of the original cost minus annual depreciation
   H twenty-five dollars
   J based on the age of the product and other factors

_____ 3. The procedures in the recorder's troubleshooting guide are based on an assumption of —
   A the usual flaws in electronic products
   B consumer error and oversight
   C consumer damage
   D known problems with the model

_____ 4. Based on the FCC information provided with this recorder, you might assume that this model has a history of —
   F breakdowns during extended or heavy usage
   G burning out cables
   H interference with other electronic devices
   J overloading electronic circuits

_____ 5. Under the terms and conditions of the service contract, the manufacturer of the recorder assumes responsibility for —
   A damage during maintenance as recommended in the product owner's guide
   B failures occurring during normal use
   C damage due to acts of God
   D repairs necessary because of improper installation

Reading Consumer Documents

READING INFORMATIONAL TEXT *(50 points; 10 points each)*
On the line provided, write the letter of the *best* answer to each of the following items.

_____ 6. The elements of consumer documents can include all of the following items *except* —
   F technical directions
   G warranties
   H owner testimonials
   J instruction manuals

_____ 7. A **transfer of ownership** —
   A always negates an original warranty agreement
   B usually requires a transfer fee within a time limit
   C always requires a renegotiation of the original agreement
   D usually is handled privately without manufacturer knowledge

_____ 8. The **features** of a warranty agreement —
   F always add cost
   G are really the only things to consider
   H often include labor as well as parts
   J turn out to mean little when you read them carefully

_____ 9. **Instruction manuals** —
   A contain essential information for making equipment work properly
   B protect the manufacturer against product return
   C protect the manufacturer against suits by owners
   D must be available in at least five languages

_____ 10. Instruction manuals usually do *not* include —
   F how to use the product
   G directions for installation
   H troubleshooting guides
   J illustrations

COLLECTION 11 SUMMATIVE TEST

Consumer and Workplace Documents

This test asks you to use the skills and strategies you have learned in this collection. Read this functional document from the Fire Safety Council. Then, answer the questions that follow it.

WHAT TO DO WHEN YOU ARE THREATENED BY WILDFIRE

First, if you see a fire approaching your home, report it immediately by dialing 911. Remember to stay on the phone to answer additional questions the emergency dispatcher may ask.

Next, dress properly to prevent burns and lifelong scars. Wear long pants, cotton or wool long-sleeve shirts or jackets. Gloves and a damp cloth provide added protection. Do not wear short sleeve shirts or clothing made of synthetic fabrics.

If there is time before the fire arrives, take the following actions:

EMERGENCY WILDFIRE SURVIVAL CHECKLIST

Preparing to Evacuate

- Park your car in the garage, point it toward the door, windows closed and keys in the ignition.
- Close the garage door, but leave it unlocked; disconnect the automatic garage-door opener in case of power failure.
- Place valuable documents, family mementos, and pets inside the car in the garage for quick departure if necessary.
- If you do evacuate, use your preplanned route, away from the approaching fire front.
- Keep a flashlight and portable radio with you at all times.
- If you are trapped by fire while evacuating via car, park in an area that is clear of vegetation, close all vehicle windows and vents, cover yourself with a blanket or jacket, and lie on the floor.
- If you are trapped by fire while evacuating on foot, select an area that is clear of vegetation and along a road, or lie in the ditch. Cover any exposed skin with a jacket or blanket. Avoid canyons, as they can concentrate and channel fire.

Outside Your Home

- Move combustible yard furniture away from the house, or store it in the garage; if it catches on fire while outside, the added heat could ignite your house.
- Cover windows, attic openings, eave vents, and subfloor vents with fire-resistant material such as half-inch or thicker plywood. Doing so will eliminate the possibility of sparks blowing into hidden areas in the house. Close window shutters if they are fire resistant.
- Attach garden hoses to spigots, and place them so that they can reach any area of your house.
- Fill trash cans and buckets with water, and place them where firefighters can find them.
- If you have an emergency generator or a portable gasoline-powered pump that will supply water from a swimming pool, pond, well, or tank, clearly mark its location, and make sure it is ready to operate.
- Place a ladder against the house on the side opposite the approaching fire to help firefighters rapidly gain access to the roof.
- Place a lawn sprinkler on flammable roofs, but don't turn it on unless the fire is an immediate threat. You do not want to reduce the firefighters' supply of water.

Inside Your Home

- Close all windows and doors to prevent sparks from blowing inside.
- Close all doors inside the house to hinder the spread of fire from room to room.
- Turn on a light in each room of your house, on the porch and in the yard, to make the house more visible in heavy smoke or darkness.
- Fill sinks, bathtubs, and buckets with water. These can be important extra water <u>reservoirs</u>.
- Shut off valves for liquefied petroleum gas (LPG) or natural gas.
- Move furniture away from windows and sliding glass doors: The heat of fire radiating through windows can ignite it.
- Remove your curtains and drapes. If you have metal blinds or special fire-resistant window coverings, close them to block heat radiation.

If You Stay in Your Home When a Fire Approaches

- Stay inside your house, away from outer walls.
- Close all doors, but leave them unlocked.
- Keep your entire family together, and remain calm.
- Remember: If it gets hot in the house, it is many times hotter and more dangerous outside.

After the Fire Passes

- Check the roof immediately, extinguishing all sparks and <u>embers</u>. If you must climb onto the roof, use caution, especially if it is wet.
- Check the attic for hidden burning embers.
- Check your yard for burning woodpiles, trees, fence posts, or other materials.
- Keep the doors and windows closed.
- Continue rechecking your home and yard for burning embers for at least twelve hours.

> "What To Do When You Are Threatened By Wildfire" from "Fire Safe—Inside and Out" from *Fire Safe Council* Web Site. Accessed February 4, 2002 at http://www.firesafecouncil.org/firesafebig6.html. Reproduced by permission of **California Department of Forestry and Fire Protection,** http://www.fire.ca.gov.

VOCABULARY SKILLS *(25 points; 5 points each)*
The Vocabulary words below are underlined in the selection. Write the letter
of the choice that is the *best* synonym for the Vocabulary word.

_____ 1. dispatcher
   A   correspondent
   B   sender
   C   fireman
   D   operator

_____ 2. synthetic
   F   fake
   G   luxurious
   H   fireproof
   J   cheap

_____ 3. mementos
   A   coins
   B   members
   C   souvenirs
   D   wills

_____ 4. reservoirs
   F   purifiers
   G   receptacles
   H   receivers
   J   farewells

_____ 5. embers
   A   eaves
   B   rodents
   C   insulation
   D   cinders

Collection 11 Summative Test

NAME _____ CLASS _____ DATE _____ SCORE _____

COMPREHENSION (25 points; 5 points each)
On the line provided, write the letter of the *best* answer for each of the following items.

_____ **6.** If you remain inside your home during a wildfire, the most dangerous places to be are —
   F the kitchen and the bathroom
   G the basement and the laundry room
   H near chimneys or flues
   J near windows or glass doors

_____ **7.** If you are trapped in a wildfire while evacuating via your car, —
   A drive into the nearest large body of water
   B park where there's no vegetation
   C put on fireproof clothes
   D keep the car windows open

_____ **8.** Lawn sprinklers should not be left on before evacuations because —
   F they don't distribute enough water to extinguish fire
   G grass doesn't burn
   H they'll just burn up with everything else
   J they may deplete the firefighters' water supply

_____ **9.** In a case of an evacuation, pets should be —
   A carried inside your clothes
   B released to fend for themselves
   C put in the car in advance
   D placed in sinks, bathtubs, or buckets

_____ **10.** If you are evacuating your home, it is important to —
   F take your fire-insurance policy with you
   G grab as many belongings as you can carry
   H try to spray the outside with water first
   J make things easier for the firefighters

NAME	CLASS	DATE	SCORE

READING FUNCTIONAL DOCUMENTS
Understanding the Format of Functional Documents *(10 points)*

_____ **11.** Under which heading would you find out what to do with explosive or combustible products that you own?

  A Preparing to Evacuate
  B Outside Your Home
  C Inside Your Home
  D After the Fire Passes

Following Technical Directions *(20 points; 10 points each)*

12. On a separate sheet of paper, describe the proper way to dress to protect yourself in case you may be exposed to fire.

13. On a seperate sheet of paper, describe what you should do with water hoses, pumps, and containers before evacuating your home.

Identifying the Logic of Functional Documents *(20 points; 10 points each)*

14. Under the header "Preparing to Evacuate," what two logical sequences are used to explain what you should do? Write your answer on a separate sheet of paper.

15. Under "If You Stay in Your Home When a Fire Approaches," what logical sequence is used? Write your answer on a separate sheet of paper.

Collection 11 Summative Test **275**

End-of-Year Test

Reading and Literary Analysis

DIRECTIONS Read the passage below, and answer the following questions.

SAMPLE

For years, scientists have been trying to learn why dinosaurs vanished from the earth some 65 million years ago. Two of the best-known theories for their extinction are the asteroid theory and the volcano theory. The asteroid theory suggests that a gigantic asteroid or comet hit the earth. The explosion from the impact was similar to that of a nuclear bomb and caused immediate *catastrophic* damage. Dust and debris from the impact clogged the skies and blocked out the sun, killing plants, a main source of food for the dinosaurs. The volcano theory suggests that massive volcanic explosions occurred all over the earth. These eruptions may have created the same deadly conditions described in the asteroid theory.

A The word *catastrophic* means —
  A gigantic
  B insignificant
  C disastrous
  D historic

B Which would be the *best* source for finding research information about dinosaur extinction?
  F Science journals
  G News magazines
  H Daily newspapers
  J Dinosaur movies

End-of-Year Test

Reading and Literary Analysis (continued)

DIRECTIONS Read the selection below, and answer the following questions.

from The Tragedy of Julius Caesar

William Shakespeare

Characters
Flavius   a tribune (official appointed to administer the law)
Marullus   a tribune
Carpenter
Cobbler   (a shoemaker)

ACT 1, Scene 1 *A street in Rome.*
Enter FLAVIUS, MARULLUS, *and certain* COMMONERS *over the stage.*

Flavius.
Hence! Home, you idle creatures, get you home!
Is this a holiday? What, know you not,
Being mechanical,° you ought not walk
Upon a laboring day without the sign
5 Of your profession?° Speak, what trade art thou?

Carpenter. Why, sir, a carpenter.

Marullus.
Where is thy leather apron and thy rule?
What dost thou with thy best apparel on?
You, sir, what trade are you?

10 **Cobbler.** Truly, sir, in respect of a fine workman,° I am but, as you would say, a cobbler.°

Marullus.
But what trade art thou? Answer me directly.

Cobbler. A trade, sir, that, I hope, I may use with a safe conscience, which is indeed, sir, a mender of bad soles.

---

3. **mechanical:** working class.
5. **sign of your profession:** your work clothes and tools.
10. **in respect of a fine workman:** in comparison with a skilled laborer;
11. **cobbler:** In Shakespeare's day the word meant both "shoemaker" and "bungler."

Flavius.
15 What trade, thou knave? Thou naughty° knave, what trade?

Cobbler. Nay, I beseech you, sir, be not out with me: yet, if you be out, sir, I can mend you.

Marullus.
What mean'st thou by that? Mend me, thou saucy fellow?

Cobbler. Why, sir, cobble you.

Flavius.
20 Thou art a cobbler, art thou?

Cobbler. Truly, sir, all that I live by is with the awl:° I meddle with no tradesman's matters, nor women's matters; but withal,° I am indeed, sir, a surgeon to old shoes: when they are in great danger, I recover them. As proper men as ever trod upon neat's leather° have gone upon
25 my handiwork.

Flavius.
But wherefore art not in thy shop today?
Why dost thou lead these men about the streets?

Cobbler. Truly, sir, to wear out their shoes, to get myself into more work. But indeed, sir, we make holiday to see Caesar and to rejoice in
30 his triumph.

Marullus.
Wherefore rejoice? What conquest brings he home?
What tributaries° follow him to Rome,
To grace in captive bonds his chariot wheels?
You blocks, you stones, you worse than senseless things!
35 O you hard hearts, you cruel men of Rome,
Knew you not Pompey?° Many a time and oft

---

15. **naughty:** worthless.
21. **awl:** sharp, pointed tool for making holes in wood or leather.
22. **withal:** nevertheless.
24. **neat's leather:** leather from cattle.
32. **tributaries:** captives (captive enemies who have to pay tribute, or tax, to Rome).
36. **Pompey:** Roman politician and general who was defeated by Caesar in 48 B.C. and later murdered.

Have you climbed up to walls and battlements,
To tow'rs and windows, yea, to chimney tops,
Your infants in your arms, and there have sat
40 The livelong day, with patient expectation,
To see great Pompey pass the streets of Rome.
And when you saw his chariot but appear,
Have you not made an universal shout,
That Tiber trembled underneath her banks
45 To hear the replication° of your sounds
Made in her concave shores?°
And do you now put on your best attire?
And do you now cull out a holiday?
And do you now strew flowers in his way
50 That comes in triumph over Pompey's blood?
Be gone!
Run to your houses, fall upon your knees
Pray to the gods to intermit° the plague
That needs must light on this ingratitude.

Flavius.
55 Go, go, good countrymen, and, for this fault,
Assemble all the poor men of your sort;
Draw them to Tiber banks and weep your tears
Into the channel, till the lowest stream
Do kiss the most exalted shores of all.

[*Exeunt all the* COMMONERS.]

---

45. **replication:** echo; copy.
46. **concave shores:** carved-out banks of the river.
53. **intermit:** hold back.

60 See, whe'r their basest mettle° be not moved;
    They vanish tongue-tied in their guiltiness.
    Go you down that way towards the Capitol;
    This way will I. Disrobe the images,°
    If you do find them decked with ceremonies.

Marullus.
65 May we do so?
    You know it is the feast of Lupercal.°

Flavius.
    It is no matter; let no images
    Be hung with Caesar's trophies. I'll about
    And drive away the vulgar° from the streets;
70 So do you too, where you perceive them thick.
    These growing feathers plucked from Caesar's wing
    Will make him fly an ordinary pitch,°
    Who else would soar above the view of men
    And keep us all in servile fearfulness.

[*Exeunt.*]

---

60. **basest mettle:** basic substance; their "stuff."
63. **images:** statues.
66. **Lupercal:** old Roman fertility festival celebrated on February 15.
69. **vulgar:** common people.
72. **an ordinary pitch:** at an ordinary height.

End-of-Year Test continued

READING AND LITERARY ANALYSIS

1 A conversation between characters onstage, such as the one in lines 1–30, is called —

A a monologue
B a soliloquy
C an aside
D dialogue

2 Although the play is a tragedy, the cobbler's witty word play is an element of —

F monologue
G comedy
H soliloquy
J history

3 The cobbler's conversation reveals that he is —

A confident of his abilities
B easily cowed by authorities
C embarrassed by his profession
D a follower, not a leader

4 An appropriate set design for this scene would *most* likely include a —

F large arena
G furnished room
H speaker's platform
J row of shops

5 The scornful treatment by Flavius and Marullus succeeds in —

A making the commoners angry
B winning the commoners to their cause
C driving the commoners from the street
D persuading the commoners to cheer Pompey

6 This scene foreshadows Caesar's murder by —

F showing how the commoners change allegiances
G employing puns and other witty dialogue
H establishing that powerful men dislike Caesar
J describing the commoners' love of Pompey

7 The metaphor at the end of the scene comparing Caesar to a bird shows how —

A the commoners love Caesar
B Caesar moves gracefully
C Caesar acts like a coward
D Caesar has grown too powerful

8 Shakespeare's purpose in writing this opening scene was *most likely* to —

F introduce the main characters
G describe the setting
H outline the relationship between the common people, the soldiers, and Caesar
J present the conflicts between Caesar and Brutus

End-of-Year Test

Reading and Literary Analysis (continued)

DIRECTIONS Read the selection below, and answer the following questions.

A Dog's Tale
by Mark Twain

My father was a St. Bernard, my mother was a collie.... This is what my mother told me, I do not know these nice distinctions myself. To me they are only fine large words meaning nothing.

My mother had a fondness for such; she liked to say them, and see other dogs look surprised and envious, as wondering how she got so much education. But, indeed, it was not real education; it was only show: she got the words by listening in the dining-room and drawing-room when there was company, and by going with the children to Sunday-school and listening there; and whenever she heard a large word she said it over to herself many times, and so was able to keep it until there was a *dogmatic* gathering in the neighborhood, then she would get it off, and surprise and distress them all, from pocket-pup to mastiff, which rewarded her for all her trouble.

If there was a stranger he was nearly sure to be suspicious, and when he got his breath again he would ask her what it meant. And she always told him. He was never expecting this but thought he would catch her; so when she told him, he was the one that looked ashamed, whereas he had thought it was going to be she. The others were always waiting for this, and glad of it and proud of her, for they knew what was going to happen, because they had had experience.

When she told the meaning of a big word they were all so taken up with admiration that it never occurred to any dog to doubt if it was the right one; and that was natural, because, for one thing, she answered up so promptly that it seemed like a dictionary speaking, and for another thing, where could they find out whether it was right or not? for she was the only cultivated dog there was.

By and by, when I was older, she brought home the word Unintellectual, one time, and worked it pretty hard all the week at different gatherings, making much unhappiness and despondency; and it was at this time that I noticed that during that week she was asked for the meaning at eight different assemblages, and flashed out a fresh definition every time, which showed me that she had more presence of mind than culture, though I said nothing, of course.

She had one word which she always kept on hand, and ready, like a life-preserver, a kind of emergency word to strap on when she was likely to get washed overboard in a sudden way—that was the word Synonymous. When she happened to *fetch* out a long word which had had its day weeks before and its prepared meanings gone to her dump-pile, if there was a stranger there of course it knocked him groggy for a couple of minutes, then he would come to, and by that time she would be away down wind on another tack, and not expecting anything; so when he'd hail and ask her to cash in, I (the only dog on the inside of her game) could see her canvas flicker a moment—but only just a moment—then it would belly out taut and full, and she would say, as calm as a summer's day, "It's synonymous with supererogation," or some godless long reptile of a word like that, and go placidly about and skim away on the next tack, perfectly comfortable, you know, and leave that stranger looking profane and embarrassed, and the initiated slatting the floor with their tails in unison and their faces transfigured with a holy joy.

End-of-Year Test continued

READING AND LITERARY ANALYSIS

9 Using a dog as narrator gives the passage a tone of —

- A objectivity
- B formality
- C bitterness
- D humor

10 What literary device is used in the sentence "She had one word which she always kept on hand, and ready, like a life-preserver"?

- F simile
- G metaphor
- H hyperbole
- J onomatopoeia

11 "A Dog's Tale" uses the topic of animal communication in order to —

- A show how dogs really communicate
- B explain how animals learn from humans
- C demonstrate that dogs are smarter than most people
- D poke fun at human behavior

12 Read this sentence from the selection.

> "Whenever she heard a large word she said it over to herself many times, and so was able to keep it until there was a dogmatic gathering in the neighborhood."

In this sentence the word *dogmatic* is used as —

- F an insightful simile
- G a descriptive metaphor
- H an illuminating allusion
- J a humorous play on words

13 In the last paragraph the narrator says his mother would "fetch out a long word." The connotations of the word *fetch* remind the reader that the narrator's mother —

- A is well educated
- B is a dog
- C knows lots of big words
- D likes to show off

The following question is not about the selection. Read and answer the question.

14 In Greek mythology the god Pan, who has the legs, horns, and ears of a goat but the face of a man, inspires great fear in humans. The English word that is derived from the name Pan is —

- F pang
- G panic
- H panel
- J pancake

GO ON

284 Holt Assessment: Literature, Reading, and Vocabulary

Reading and Literary Analysis (continued)

DIRECTIONS Read the passage below, and answer the following questions.

Animal Communication

Animal communication is a relatively new field of scientific study. Scientists, from bioacousticians to zoologists, are now studying how and why animals communicate with one another.

Animals communicate mainly to identify themselves, to give their location, and to influence the behavior of another animal or a person. Though most animal communication is between members of the same species, inter-species communication does occur.

Most of us think of *sounds* when we think of animal communication, but animals communicate in many other ways. In fact, animals use five types of signals or displays: (1) sound or vibrations; (2) visual clues; (3) chemicals; (4) touch; and (5) electricity.

Sound or Vibration Communication

Many animals use sound to communicate. Sound can spread rapidly, and other animals can readily tell from which direction it comes. The most common sounds used by animals are vocalizations, such as the singing of birds, the barking of dogs, and the squeaking of dolphins. However, there are some animal vocalizations that humans can't hear.

Bioacoustics researcher Katy Payne discovered that elephants communicate by "infrasound," sound so low in pitch that humans can't hear it. Extremely low sounds travel long distances much better than high sounds do. Consequently, elephants can communicate over distances of up to two miles.

When Dr. Phillip Lobel of the Marine Biology Lab rigged up some underwater microphones to study the effects of pollution, he was astonished to discover that fish actually talk, or vocalize.

Some animals also use nonvocal sounds. For example, beavers slap their tails on the surface of the water to warn of danger, and gorillas beat their chests to send messages to other gorillas.

Visual Communication

Animals also use "badges," such as a patch of bright color or a set of horns, for visual communication. These badges send messages such as the species, the age, or the gender of the sender. Some species use other visual

GO ON

End-of-Year Test 285

signs to send messages. To mark their territory, rabbits build special dung heaps, and bears leave scars on tree trunks. Honeybees communicate with each other by using movements that resemble dances.

Chemical Communication

Many mammals, fish, and insects use pheromones, a type of chemical, to communicate. For example, ants secrete pheromones to warn their colony of danger. Some pheromones warn animals to stay away, and then may even injure other animals. Other pheromones are intended to attract animals. Some moths use them to attract a mate.

Touching Communication

Some species use touching patterns to communicate. Birds and monkeys often engage in mutual grooming to communicate acceptance. Wolves, dogs, and other canines have mock fights to establish pecking order.

Electric Communication

This type of communication includes various uses of electrical impulses. The electric eel can emit a strong enough electrical impulse to stun prey. Other types of fish use relatively weak electrical discharges to gather information. Some fish use electrical discharges to deter predators.

Researchers have a long way to go before they fully understand how animals communicate, but one thing seems clear: Animal communication is more complex than scientists originally thought.

READING AND LITERARY ANALYSIS

15 The story "A Dog's Tale" uses the topic of animal communication in a humorous way, but this article —

A presents factual information on the topic
B contrasts dogs with other animals
C is amused at the way animals communicate
D focuses on animals' communication by sound

16 Which type of communication listed in this article did the narrator's mother use in "A Dog's Tale"?

F Visual
G Sound
H Electric
J Chemical

17 Which question would be relevant for research based on this article?

A How do elephants care for their young while traveling?
B What chemicals do spiders use to paralyze their prey?
C Are birds' colors portrayed realistically in field guides?
D When did researchers first learn about elephant communication?

18 The word in this article that comes from the Greek words meaning "life" and "hearing" is —

F infrasound
G bioacoustics
H zoologists
J vocalizations

End-of-Year Test

Reading and Literary Analysis (continued)

DIRECTIONS Read the Web site below, and answer the following questions.

Put All the Pieces Together

With *The Puzzler*™

Play Games and Have Fun While Increasing Your Vocabulary and Word Skills!

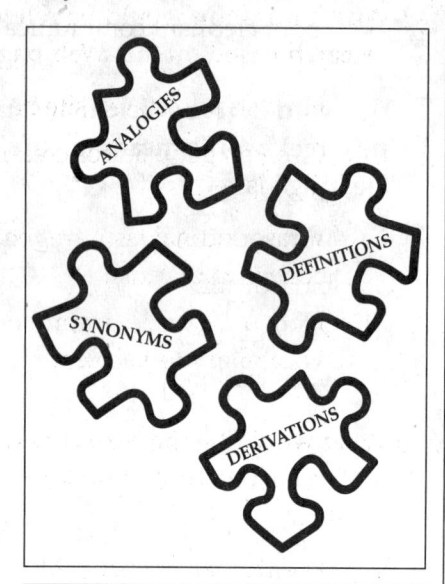

ANALOGIES
DEFINITIONS
SYNONYMS
DERIVATIONS

Twice a week you will receive a new puzzle that will challenge your thinking while increasing your word knowledge. Whether you are preparing for any of the national tests required of college applicants or are seeking to refresh your skills, our *Puzzler* puzzles will develop your abilities and improve your test scores.

Here's a sample of some of our helpful *Puzzlers*:

- Definitely Definitions
- Snappy Synonyms
- Word Play
- At the Root of the Matter
- Don't Ignore the Idioms
- Crossing the Curriculum
- Of Mythic Proportions

REGISTER NOW!

Set up your personal *Puzzler* registration. — There is no charge. Read our Privacy policy. Visit with the faculty who create the word games found at *The Puzzler*. (All our puzzles are created by teachers and wordsmiths!)

Try Out Today's Puzzle
A Plethora of Produce
Finding literary devices among the lettuce and the lentils!

Check out these links to our sponsors and look at all the additional great learning products they offer . . .

- *Scholar Dollars! — Let us help you pay for college*
- *Start the Presses! — Publishing software*
- *Look It Up! — America's No. 1 online encyclopedia*

GO ON

Holt Assessment: Literature, Reading, and Vocabulary

End-of-Year Test *continued*

READING AND LITERARY ANALYSIS

19 What is the first step to take before using *The Puzzler* Web site?

- A Get permission from a teacher.
- B Register for the Web site.
- C Pay a fee to use the Web site.
- D Take a vocabulary test.

20 The company that produces *The Puzzler* defends its claim to quality by —

- F stating that its puzzles are created by teachers
- G inviting readers to visit its sponsors
- H listing a sample of its puzzles' titles
- J criticizing competing Web sites

21 Alliteration is used in this Web page to —

- A make the meaning clear
- B highlight important ideas
- C catch the reader's attention
- D organize information

22 One could imagine the narrator's mother in "A Dog's Tale" consulting this Web site because it —

- F uses different puzzles
- G raises test scores
- H is free
- J increases vocabulary

23 Which question would be relevant for research based on this Web page?

- A How should a Web site be designed?
- B Can you get paid for creating puzzles?
- C What national tests are required of college applicants?
- D Do word puzzles improve vocabulary test scores?

24 What would be the correct way to list this Web page in a bibliography?

- F "The Puzzler." Wordskill Associates. 8 Aug. 2000. 24 Sept. 2003 <http://www.wordskillassoc.com/puzzler/homepage.html>.
- G Wordskill Associates, "The Puzzler," Internet Web page, August 8, 2000.
- H Wordskill Assoc. http://www.wordskillassoc.com/puzzler/homepage.html "The Puzzler." 8 Aug. 2000. 24 September 2003
- J Associates, Wordskill, *The Puzzler*, August 8, 2000.

Reading and Literary Analysis (continued)

DIRECTIONS Read the selection below, and answer the following questions.

Using the Office Phone System

Placing Calls

Internal calls: Lift the handset, and dial the desired four-digit extension number.

Local calls: Lift the handset, and dial "9" plus the outside number.

Long distance: Lift the handset, and dial "9" plus "1" plus the area code plus the number.

Answering Calls

Lift the handset or press the "Speaker" key, and you will be automatically connected to the caller. To answer Line 2, press the button next to the flashing arrow (if you already have a call on Line 1, be sure to put that caller on hold first by pressing the "Hold" key).

Transferring Calls

To activate: With a call in progress, press "Transfer" from the menu display, dial the desired extension number, and press "Connect."

To cancel: If you wish to get the caller back without completing the transfer, press "Good-bye" and the flashing line key.

Three-Way Conference Calls

1. With a call in progress, press "Conf."

2. Dial the next party (internal or external), and wait for an answer.

3. Announce the conference, and press "Connect" from your menu display to connect all parties.

READING AND LITERARY ANALYSIS

25 How are the directions organized under the subheading "Placing Calls"?

A   In chronological order
B   Step by step
C   By the type of call
D   By cost of the call

26 Boldface headings are used in the directions *mostly* to —

F   highlight instructions for different phone functions
G   create visual interest for the reader
H   make the straightforward text interesting
J   show the order in which steps should be completed

27 Under the heading "Three-Way Conference Calls," how do the directions help readers perform the steps in the proper order?

A   The steps are listed in alphabetical order.
B   The steps are listed from easiest to hardest.
C   The steps are listed in numerical order.
D   The steps are listed in order of importance.

28 These instructions would *most* appropriately be listed in a bibliography for a report on —

F   workplace policies
G   use of office equipment
H   communicating with your managers
J   getting a job

29 If you receive a call on Line 2 while you're talking with someone on Line 1, what should you do before pressing the button next to the "flashing" arrow?

A   Press "Transfer" from the menu display.
B   Press the "Speaker" key.
C   Press "Good-bye."
D   Put the Line 1 caller on hold.

30 When transferring a call, what button should you press after dialing the desired extension?

F   Connect
G   Transfer
H   Conf.
J   The flashing Line key

GO ON

End-of-Year Test

End-of-Year Test

Vocabulary

DIRECTIONS Choose the word or words that mean the same, or about the same, as the underlined word. Then, mark the space for the answer you have chosen.

SAMPLE A

Consoling is another word for —

- A applying
- B promising
- C amusing
- D comforting

31 Something that is garbled is —

- A peaked
- B confused
- C supported
- D balanced

32 Someone who is inquisitive is —

- F guilty
- G humble
- H curious
- J quiet

33 Something that is imperial is —

- A generous
- B foreign
- C constant
- D majestic

34 Something that is innocuous is —

- F harmless
- G favorable
- H important
- J quaint

35 Someone who is induced to do something is —

- A required
- B employed
- C persuaded
- D discouraged

36 Jeopardy means about the same thing as —

- F pleasure
- G danger
- H survival
- J anger

GO ON

End-of-Year Test | *continued*

VOCABULARY

37 Something that is <u>squandered</u> is —
- A wasted
- B chosen
- C increased
- D discussed

38 A <u>cataclysm</u> is a —
- F mistake
- G loss
- H threat
- J disaster

39 Something done <u>valiantly</u> is done —
- A easily
- B haltingly
- C bravely
- D narrowly

40 Someone who is <u>aghast</u> is —
- F delighted
- G horrified
- H calmed
- J unified

ENTRY-LEVEL TEST
Answer Sheet

Reading and Literary Analysis

Sample
- A Ⓐ Ⓑ Ⓒ Ⓓ
- B Ⓕ Ⓖ Ⓗ Ⓙ

1. Ⓐ Ⓑ Ⓒ Ⓓ
2. Ⓕ Ⓖ Ⓗ Ⓙ
3. Ⓐ Ⓑ Ⓒ Ⓓ
4. Ⓕ Ⓖ Ⓗ Ⓙ
5. Ⓐ Ⓑ Ⓒ Ⓓ
6. Ⓕ Ⓖ Ⓗ Ⓙ
7. Ⓐ Ⓑ Ⓒ Ⓓ
8. Ⓕ Ⓖ Ⓗ Ⓙ
9. Ⓐ Ⓑ Ⓒ Ⓓ
10. Ⓕ Ⓖ Ⓗ Ⓙ
11. Ⓐ Ⓑ Ⓒ Ⓓ
12. Ⓕ Ⓖ Ⓗ Ⓙ
13. Ⓐ Ⓑ Ⓒ Ⓓ
14. Ⓕ Ⓖ Ⓗ Ⓙ
15. Ⓐ Ⓑ Ⓒ Ⓓ
16. Ⓕ Ⓖ Ⓗ Ⓙ
17. Ⓐ Ⓑ Ⓒ Ⓓ
18. Ⓕ Ⓖ Ⓗ Ⓙ
19. Ⓐ Ⓑ Ⓒ Ⓓ
20. Ⓕ Ⓖ Ⓗ Ⓙ
21. Ⓐ Ⓑ Ⓒ Ⓓ
22. Ⓕ Ⓖ Ⓗ Ⓙ
23. Ⓐ Ⓑ Ⓒ Ⓓ
24. Ⓕ Ⓖ Ⓗ Ⓙ
25. Ⓐ Ⓑ Ⓒ Ⓓ
26. Ⓕ Ⓖ Ⓗ Ⓙ
27. Ⓐ Ⓑ Ⓒ Ⓓ
28. Ⓕ Ⓖ Ⓗ Ⓙ
29. Ⓐ Ⓑ Ⓒ Ⓓ
30. Ⓕ Ⓖ Ⓗ Ⓙ

Vocabulary

Sample A
Ⓐ Ⓑ Ⓒ Ⓓ

31. Ⓐ Ⓑ Ⓒ Ⓓ
32. Ⓕ Ⓖ Ⓗ Ⓙ
33. Ⓐ Ⓑ Ⓒ Ⓓ
34. Ⓕ Ⓖ Ⓗ Ⓙ
35. Ⓐ Ⓑ Ⓒ Ⓓ
36. Ⓕ Ⓖ Ⓗ Ⓙ

Sample B
Ⓐ Ⓑ Ⓒ Ⓓ

37. Ⓐ Ⓑ Ⓒ Ⓓ
38. Ⓕ Ⓖ Ⓗ Ⓙ
39. Ⓐ Ⓑ Ⓒ Ⓓ
40. Ⓕ Ⓖ Ⓗ Ⓙ

END-OF-YEAR TEST

Answer Sheet

Reading and Literary Analysis

Sample
- A (A) (B) (C) (D)
- B (F) (G) (H) (J)

1. (A) (B) (C) (D)
2. (F) (G) (H) (J)
3. (A) (B) (C) (D)
4. (F) (G) (H) (J)
5. (A) (B) (C) (D)
6. (F) (G) (H) (J)
7. (A) (B) (C) (D)
8. (F) (G) (H) (J)
9. (A) (B) (C) (D)
10. (F) (G) (H) (J)
11. (A) (B) (C) (D)
12. (F) (G) (H) (J)
13. (A) (B) (C) (D)
14. (F) (G) (H) (J)
15. (A) (B) (C) (D)
16. (F) (G) (H) (J)
17. (A) (B) (C) (D)
18. (F) (G) (H) (J)
19. (A) (B) (C) (D)
20. (F) (G) (H) (J)
21. (A) (B) (C) (D)
22. (F) (G) (H) (J)
23. (A) (B) (C) (D)
24. (F) (G) (H) (J)
25. (A) (B) (C) (D)
26. (F) (G) (H) (J)
27. (A) (B) (C) (D)
28. (F) (G) (H) (J)
29. (A) (B) (C) (D)
30. (F) (G) (H) (J)

Vocabulary

Sample A
(A) (B) (C) (D)

31. (A) (B) (C) (D)
32. (F) (G) (H) (J)
33. (A) (B) (C) (D)
34. (F) (G) (H) (J)
35. (A) (B) (C) (D)
36. (F) (G) (H) (J)
37. (A) (B) (C) (D)
38. (F) (G) (H) (J)
39. (A) (B) (C) (D)
40. (F) (G) (H) (J)

Answer Sheets

ANSWER SHEETS

Answer Key

Answer Key

Entry-Level Test, page 1
Reading and Literary Analysis
Sample A B
Sample B H

1. A	16. G
2. G	17. D
3. C	18. F
4. G	19. B
5. D	20. J
6. H	21. D
7. A	22. G
8. J	23. C
9. A	24. G
10. H	25. D
11. C	26. H
12. J	27. D
13. B	28. H
14. F	29. B
15. C	30. F

Vocabulary
Sample A C

31. A	36. F
32. H	Sample B B
33. D	37. A
34. G	38. J
35. C	39. C
	40. G

Collection 1

Collection 1 Diagnostic Test
Literature, Informational Text, Vocabulary, page 13

1. B	6. G
2. H	7. A
3. D	8. H
4. J	9. C
5. B	10. J

Contents of the Dead Man's Pocket
by Jack Finney
Selection Test, page 15

Comprehension

1. A	6. H
2. F	7. C
3. B	8. J
4. H	9. D
5. D	10. F

Literary Focus

11. B	13. D
12. F	14. G

Vocabulary Development

15. c	18. a
16. b	19. d
17. e	

Constructed Response

20. Students' responses will vary. A sample response follows:

   Two examples of flash-forward in the story are when Tom looks down to the street below and imagines himself falling and dying and when he imagines what it would be like to wait on the ledge until his wife comes home. In both cases the fear aroused by these glimpses of the future prompts Tom to be more proactive. In both cases, readers' suspense is increased because the flash-forwards make it seem likely that Tom is going to die.

Holt Assessment: Literature, Reading, and Vocabulary

Answer Key

Double Daddy
by Penny Parker

Diary of a Mad Blender
by Sue Shellenbarger

The Child's View of Working Parents
by Cora Daniels

Selection Test, page 18

Comprehension

1. B
2. H
3. D
4. J
5. A

Vocabulary Development

6. autonomy
7. poignant
8. phenomenon
9. integrate
10. colleague

The Leap
by Louise Erdrich

Selection Test, page 20

Comprehension

1. B
2. H
3. A
4. J
5. C
6. H
7. A
8. G
9. D
10. F

Literary Focus

11. C
12. H
13. D
14. G

Vocabulary Development

15. D
16. F
17. B
18. G
19. D

Constructed Response

20. Students' responses will vary. A sample response follows:

    The premature birth and death of the narrator's sister is something that happened before the narrator was born. The author places the event at the end of the long flashback that narrates the experiences of the Flying Avalons and the disaster that ended their career. The preceding event is the disaster, which the mother survives with burns; the subsequent event is the mother's meeting and relationship with the narrator's father. Because the mother was in a hospital after she lost the baby, she met the narrator's father; thus, it's possible that the narrator owes her life to the death of her older sister.

The Pedestrian
by Ray Bradbury

Selection Test, page 24

Comprehension

1. B
2. H
3. A
4. G
5. C
6. J
7. D
8. H
9. B
10. J

Literary Focus

11. A
12. H
13. C
14. F

Vocabulary Development

15. intermittent
16. manifest
17. ebbing
18. regressive
19. antiseptic

Answer Key

Constructed Response

20. Students' responses will vary. A sample response follows:

   The meaning I get from "The Pedestrian" is that it's dangerous to be a free-thinking individual in a technological society. Bradbury's picture of 2053 society is conveyed largely through setting. The congestion of the streets in the daytime is contrasted with their emptiness at night, the eerie silence of residential streets, and the ghostly gray flickering light from innumerable television sets in innumerable blank houses.

   Mead's freedom of thought, meanwhile, is also reflected largely through setting. He walks on the street instead of remaining hidden in his house. He breathes fresh air instead of air-conditioned air. He views the landscape firsthand instead of on an electronic screen. His desire to be in a setting of his own free choice—a setting that gives him personal joy—is something the mechanized guardians of his society find dangerous. So they whisk him away from that setting and place him in the officially approved but certainly destructive setting of the Psychiatric Center for Research on Regressive Tendencies.

Collection 1 Summative Test,
page 27

Vocabulary Skills

1. B
2. F
3. D
4. H
5. B

Comprehension

6. H
7. C
8. J
9. A
10. F

Reading Skills and Strategies: Constructed Response

Making Predictions

11. Students' responses may vary. A sample response follows:

   The father protects his sons; the sons may return the favor. As the father is getting older, perhaps the sons will save his life in turn by rushing him to a hospital if he falls ill.

Analyzing Cause and Effect

12. Students' responses may vary. A sample response follows:

   They are silent because they are overwhelmed and stunned by what they see and by the memory of what they have just experienced. This inference is based on the fact that the storm was a shock that almost caused the boys to panic. In fact, they were silent previously when they huddled around the wagon in fear. The sight of the ice on the roads, the broken windshields, and the memory of the storm must have affected them deeply.

Determining an Author's Purpose

13. Students' responses may vary. A sample response follows:

   The writer wants the reader to know that a father's love for his children is strong, regardless of whether he is rich or poor.

Literary Focus: Constructed Response

14. Students' responses may vary. A sample response follows:

   One of the father's traits that dominates the entire plot is his devotion to his family. If this trait were not so extreme—if it were only moderate—he would not pull the wagon to the garbage dump every Saturday, and thus the story would not even get started. This trait is shown not only in these physical actions but also in the encouraging things he says to his sons when they are hiding from the hailstorm.

Answer Key

He also brings all four sons with him every week even though the trip would surely be easier without them. Combined with this devotion is his trait of relative indifference to his own injuries. His nonchalance is shown in the way he smiles after examining the welts on his back. Both of the father's traits are also reflected in the tone the narrator uses to describe him—a tone of awe directed at a hero. For example, more than once the narrator describes his father as expanding in size: a projection of the huge size the father attains in the sons' minds. If not for the two combined traits, he would not have exposed himself to the full force of the hail as he did, and, thus, the ending of the story would have been completely different. The entire story is told in a flashback as one of his sons remembers the incident.

Collection 2

Collection 2 Diagnostic Test
Literature, Informational Text, Vocabulary, *page 32*

1. B
2. J
3. A
4. F
5. C
6. F
7. C
8. F
9. C
10. G

Everyday Use
by Alice Walker
Selection Test, *page 34*

Comprehension

1. C
2. G
3. A
4. J
5. B
6. G
7. C
8. F
9. B
10. F

Literary Focus

11. A
12. H
13. D
14. F

Vocabulary Development

15. doctrines
16. furtive
17. rifling
18. oppress
19. cowering

Constructed Response

20. Students' responses will vary. A sample response follows:

The passage shows us that the mother knows the difference between who she is and who she would like to be. She knows that she is a good farmer and that she is physically strong and competent. On another level, she would also like to be the kind of person her daughter Dee wishes she were—poised, conventionally attractive, and quick of tongue. However, the mother seems to know that her own inner qualities are admirable. Just the fact that she can analyze her own dream so well implies that she is aware of her own intelligence. But she understands that she is the product of a simpler, more traditional way of life in which appearances aren't that highly valued.

Interview with Alice Walker
by Roland L. Freeman

Interview with Nikki Giovanni
by Roland L. Freeman

"Thinkin' on Marryin'"
by Patricia Cooper and Norma Bradley Allen

A Baby's Quilt to Sew Up the Generations
by Felicia R. Lee
Selection Test, *page 37*

Comprehension

1. A
2. H
3. A
4. F
5. B
6. H
7. D
8. G
9. A
10. F

301

Answer Key

Two Kinds
by Amy Tan
Selection Test, *page 39*

Comprehension
1. A
2. G
3. D
4. H
5. A
6. H
7. C
8. G
9. C
10. J

Literary Focus
11. D
12. F
13. C
14. F

Vocabulary Development
15. e
16. c
17. d
18. b
19. a

Constructed Response

20. Students' responses will vary. A sample response follows:

   At first, Jing-mei tries to please her mother. The girl believes that if she is perfect she'll be loved and admired. Later, however, she rebels, refusing to practice the piano and saying hurtful things to her mother. This conflict is most openly expressed when Jing-mei, in a fit of anger, makes a vindictive remark about her mother's two dead daughters. The mother is shocked into silence. The conflict simmers as Jing-mei feels she is unable to discuss it with her mother. Years later, however, her mother offers her the piano as a gift. This gesture helps resolve the conflict. Although Jing-mei does not accept the piano at first, she develops warmer feelings toward her mother. After her mother's death, she begins to play the piano again.

By Any Other Name
by Santha Rama Rau
Selection Test, *page 42*

Comprehension
1. D
2. J
3. B
4. G
5. C
6. F
7. D
8. J
9. A
10. J

Literary Focus
11. A
12. G
13. C
14. H

Vocabulary Development
15. e
16. c
17. d
18. a
19. b

Constructed Response

20. Students' responses will vary. A sample response follows:

   The scene in which the teacher changes Santha's and Premila's names to Cynthia and Pamela is one of the key interactions between British and Indian cultures in the story. As a representative of the ruling power, the teacher goes beyond the usual bounds of classroom authority and attempts to change her students' names, feeling she is doing the girls a favor. The girls, on the other hand, feel that their identities have been taken away, replaced by new ones they cannot relate to. Santha calmly accepts this process even though she feels detached from it. This reaction fits in with Santha's behavior throughout much of the story: She is relatively passive, obeying directives from her sister as well as her teacher. Ultimately Santha and Premila get their own names back through an act of rebellion in which Premila is active and Santha is again a passive, though observant and insightful, follower.

Answer Key

Collection 2 Summative Test,
page 45

Vocabulary Skills

1. C
2. F
3. A
4. H
5. D

Comprehension

6. J
7. D
8. J
9. B
10. G

Reading Skills and Strategies: Constructed Response

Making Inferences About Motivation

11. Students' responses will vary. A sample response follows:

    Alice laughs loudly in order both to impress Marc's ex-wife and show that she and Marc are having a good time. Perhaps she is also trying to convince herself. Because of this emphasis on appearance, I infer that she is not as sure about her feelings toward Marc as it first seemed. Marc watches his posture also to impress his ex-wife. His desire to impress makes his character seem more insecure than we might have believed.

Making Inferences About Character

12. Students' responses will vary. A sample response follows:

    I infer that Alice is questioning her decision to marry Marc. She thinks that his first wife saw a negative side to him that she does not yet see. The text supports this suspicion by showing that Alice now views Marc's first wife as somehow "superior."

Comparing and Contrasting

13. Students' responses will vary. A sample response follows:

    We see Alice as anxious, insecure, and unsure of her feelings, whereas Marc's ex-wife is relaxed and unconcerned with the opinions of others. Throughout the story, Alice grows increasingly curious, then becomes jealous of the other woman. She thinks that the other woman's self-possessed attitude is evidence of her superiority as well as indicative of Marc's inferiority. In addition, both women have blue eyes, but Alice wears a hat, and the ex-wife does not.

Literary Focus: Constructed Response

14. Students' responses will vary. A sample response follows:

    Basic situation: A French husband and wife are entering a seaside restaurant and must choose which table to sit at.
    Event: Husband refuses table with a sea view and insists on table in crowded inner area.
    Event: Wife asks husband for reason for his table choice.
    Event: Husband reveals that his first wife is sitting at one of the tables outside.
    Event: Throughout dinner, husband and wife discuss husband's first marriage and first wife. Husband gives "incompatibility" as reason for divorce.
    Climax: New wife looks at her husband in a new way—furtively, dubiously.
    Resolution: As the couple leaves, the new wife wonders jealously about the first wife; there are intimations of trouble in the second marriage.

Collection 3

Collection 3 Diagnostic Test

Literature, Informational Text, Vocabulary, *page 51*

1. B
2. H
3. A
4. J
5. D
6. H
7. A
8. G
9. C
10. G

Answer Key   303

Answer Key

By the Waters of Babylon
by Stephen Vincent Benét
Selection Test, page 53

Comprehension

1. C
2. F
3. D
4. G
5. B
6. H
7. A
8. F
9. D
10. H

Literary Focus

11. D
12. G
13. A
14. F

Constructed Response

15. Students' responses will vary. A sample response follows:

   Benét decided to use a first-person narrator to limit what readers experience. This point of view helps maintain the story's suspense. Because readers see all events through John's eyes, this limitation makes readers as naive and frightened as John is by the startling revelations about the Place of the Gods. Further, the first-person point of view gives the story an immediacy and freshness that underscores the tension. John is the ideal narrator for this story because he is inexperienced and innocent but intelligent. These qualities add to his credibility and sharpen the story's startling ending, as readers realize that the civilized world has been destroyed by a war or a catastrophe.

The Storyteller
by Saki
Selection Test, page 56

Comprehension

1. B
2. F
3. C
4. H
5. D
6. J
7. A
8. F
9. D
10. H

Literary Focus

11. A
12. G
13. C
14. F

Vocabulary Development

15. c
16. d
17. b
18. e
19. a

Constructed Response

20. Students' responses will vary. A sample response follows:

   The omniscient point of view allows readers to see the interior life of more than one character. Readers learn that the aunt is a moralistic and unimaginative woman. The bachelor, in contrast, is not restricted to the sentimental, moral pieties of his day. As a result, he delights in telling the children a "horribly good" story in which goodness does not triumph. The children are stereotypical: bored and annoying when not amused but alert and well-behaved when entertained.

   By using an omniscient narrator rather than restricting the point of view to the first person or the third person limited, readers get the full effect of Saki's humor and satire, which provides the emotional energy not only to drive the plot forward but also to give it meaning. Readers see the aunt squirm at the bachelor's "immoral" tale, and the children delight in it. Readers also see the bachelor's smug pleasure at upstaging the aunt.

The Cold Equations
by Tom Godwin
Selection Test, page 59

Comprehension

1. A
2. H
3. C
4. G
5. B
6. F
7. D
8. J
9. A
10. H

Answer Key

Literary Focus
11. B 13. C
12. H 14. F

Vocabulary Development
15. increments
16. recoiled
17. paramount
18. annihilate
19. irrevocable

Constructed Response
20. Students' responses will vary. A sample response follows:

If Marilyn had been the narrator, the story would have had an emotional tone rather than a calm one. The third-person-limited point of view allows readers to feel compassion for Barton as well as for Marilyn. He has no choice but to jettison her. Otherwise he and the settlers will die along with her. If readers were to see events from the first-person point of view, through Marilyn's eyes, they would likely be more sympathetic toward her and less sympathetic toward Barton.

Taste—The Final Frontier
by Esther Addley
Selection Test, page 62

Comprehension
1. B 4. J
2. G 5. C
3. D

Vocabulary Development
6. palatable
7. mutiny
8. judicious
9. rancid
10. habitat

Typhoid Fever
from Angela's Ashes
by Frank McCourt
Selection Test, page 64

Comprehension
1. C 6. H
2. G 7. B
3. A 8. J
4. G 9. B
5. D 10. G

Literary Focus
11. C 13. A
12. H 14. F

Vocabulary Development
15. induced
16. potent
17. torrent
18. clamoring
19. induced

Constructed Response
20. Students' responses will vary. A sample response follows:

"The Highwayman" is similar to the story of Patricia and Frankie in several ways. First, both the memoir and the poem describe the tragic death of a young woman. In "Typhoid Fever," Patricia dies from diphtheria and an African disease. Her death is tragic not only because she is so young but also because today we can usually prevent or treat these diseases. In "The Highwayman," Bess also dies tragically, sacrificing herself to save her lover. Second, "The Highwayman" is romantic, as is McCourt's story of the budding affection between Patricia and Frankie. Bess and the highwayman love each other; Patricia and Frankie feel affection as well as kinship in their shared isolation and illness.

Answer Key

An Ancient Enemy Gets Tougher
by Karen Watson
Selection Test, *page 67*
Comprehension

1. A
2. G
3. C
4. J
5. B
6. F
7. C
8. J
9. A
10. F

Collection 3 Summative Test,
page 69
Vocabulary Skills

1. D
2. F
3. A
4. G
5. A

Comprehension

6. J
7. B
8. F
9. C
10. F

Reading Skills and Strategies
Drawing Conclusions

11. C
12. G

Literary Focus: Constructed Response

13. D
14. F
15. Students' responses will vary. A sample response follows:

   If William Clark had narrated the tale, the story would be very different. Sacajawea uses simple, straightforward language. Most likely Clark would have written in the more ornate language typical of his culture and time. Sacajawea interprets events from a Native American perspective. She knows the importance of bravery to her culture and thinks it crazy that Americans do not want the Indian nations to war. She knows how gifts are valued and understands why the Brule would see a small gift as an insult. Clark does not know these things. Most likely he would explain these things from his perspective. He would explain why the "Great White Father" ordered the nations to stop fighting. He would explain the reason for not trading arms with the Indians and for giving them only small gifts. Sacajawea's narrative helps us see things from the Native American perspective. Clark's would help us see things from the white American perspective.

Collection 4

Collection 4 Diagnostic Test
Literature, Informational Text, Vocabulary, *page 74*

1. C
2. J
3. D
4. H
5. A
6. G
7. A
8. F
9. B
10. H

Catch the Moon
by Judith Ortiz Cofer
Selection Test, *page 76*
Comprehension

1. B
2. G
3. C
4. H
5. A
6. G
7. B
8. J
9. C
10. H

Literary Focus

11. C
12. F
13. A
14. J

Vocabulary Development

15. relics
16. sarcastic
17. ebony
18. vintage
19. dismantled

Answer Key

Constructed Response

20. Students' responses will vary. A sample response follows:

If Judith Ortiz Cofer had written this story as a poem, it would have had the same characters, setting, topic, and theme. Transformed into a narrative poem, the work of literature would still describe Luis's maturation as he comes to accept his mother's death and deals with the grief it has caused him. If the story had been a poem, however, it may have been shorter and more allusive. Readers would have to read between the lines to infer the theme. As a poem the work's rhythm would probably be more regular.

The Bass, the River, and Sheila Mant
by W. D. Wetherell
Selection Test, page 79

Comprehension

1. C
2. J
3. A
4. H
5. D
6. J
7. A
8. H
9. B
10. F

Literary Focus

11. A
12. F
13. B
14. J

Vocabulary Development

15. c
16. d
17. b
18. e
19. a

Constructed Response

20. Students' responses will vary. A sample response follows:

The bass might represent missed opportunities—the result of the choices we make. The narrator can't decide between the huge fish and Sheila. He decides to let the fish go and stay with Sheila. When she deserts him soon after they arrive at the concert, he realizes that he has made the wrong choice. The "one that got away" becomes a symbol, not just of all the opportunities that he has missed and can never have again but also of his true heart's desire and the pull he must follow his whole life.

And of Clay Are We Created
by Isabel Allende
Ill-Equipped Rescuers Dig Out Volcano Victims
Bradley Graham
Selection Test, page 82

Comprehension

1. D
2. F
3. A
4. H
5. C
6. G
7. D
8. F
9. B
10. J

Literary Focus

11. D
12. F
13. B
14. J

Vocabulary Development

15. magnitude
16. tenacity
17. pandemonium
18. ingenuity
19. commiserate

Constructed Response

20. Students' responses will vary. A sample response follows:

Both accounts describe the same tragedy, but Allende's version is fiction while the newspaper account is fact. Allende's account has a clear plot: a beginning, a middle, and an end. Her account also has a theme, or insight into life. The newspaper account, in contrast, presents the facts in order of importance, from most important to least important. The article has a main idea but no theme. The main idea concerns the scope of the tragedy, not an insight into life.

Answer Key

The Man in the Water
by Roger Rosenblatt

The Parable of the Good Samaritan
King James Bible

A State Championship Versus Runner's Conscience
by John Christian Hoyle

Selection Test, *page 86*

Comprehension

1. C
2. G
3. B
4. H
5. A
6. F
7. D
8. J
9. B
10. G

Literary Focus

11. A
12. G
13. D
14. F

Vocabulary Development

Students' responses will vary. A sample response follows:

15. swinging; waving wildly
16. modest; frugal
17. continuing; constant
18. set against
19. flexible; tolerant; changeable

Constructed Response

20. Students' responses will vary. A sample response follows:

    All three selections were written to make a point. In "The Man in the Water," Rosenblatt does not state the point outright until the end. Instead, he lays a foundation for his message by providing many details that enable readers to infer his point. This approach creates a more subtle style in which a powerful statement has a good chance of acceptance by readers. Parables, in contrast, are written to teach a lesson.

    Here the lesson is directly stated in the last sentence: "Which now of these three, thinkest thou, was neighbor unto him that fell among thieves?" The personal essay directly states the main idea, as does the parable. Readers can find it in the conclusion: "Basking in personal glory on the altar of ego, I figure, is never worth it."

If Decency Doesn't, Law Should Make Us Samaritans
by Gloria Allred and Lisa Bloom

Good Samaritans U.S.A. Are Afraid to Act
by Ann Sjoerdsma

Selection Test, *page 89*

Comprehension

1. D
2. G
3. C
4. F
5. A

Vocabulary Development

6. c
7. d
8. a
9. e
10. b

Collection 4 Summative Test, *page 91*

Vocabulary Skills

1. B
2. J
3. A
4. F
5. C

Comprehension

6. G
7. A
8. F
9. B
10. J

Answer Key

Reading Skills and Strategies: Constructed Response

Determining an Author's Purpose

1. Students' responses will vary. A sample response follows:

   R. A. Sasaki's purpose in this passage from *Another Writer's Beginnings* is to explain why she decided to become a writer. She is not trying to persuade anyone else to become a writer, nor is she merely telling a story about her childhood. The events that led her to become a writer are important, as are the events that lead anyone into a career. She wants readers to consider how seemingly small events and turns of fate can influence the course of an entire life.

Making Inferences About Character

12. Students' responses will vary. A sample response follows:

    Goal—Wanting to become a Mouseketeer. **Motivation**—Desire to be popular. **Outcome**—Abandons the plan.

    Goal—Showing her mother the school picture. **Motivation**—Wants to be reassured that she is pretty. **Outcome**—Realizes that she is not pretty after all.

    Goal—Deciding to become a writer. **Motivation**—Recognition that she cannot rely on beauty. **Outcome**—Becomes a writer.

Summarizing the Main Idea

13. Students' responses will vary. A sample response follows:

    R. A. Sasaki conveys the main idea that she decided to become a writer when she realized that she could not rely on her appearance to carry her through life. Details include her mother's "devastating" response to the author's unattractive fifth-grade school picture. The mother's inability to find one nice thing to say confirms what the author had long suspected: that she was not attractive. This conclusion clearly shows the main idea: "So for the first time I considered the possibility that I might not make it as a Mouseketeer after all. Looks would never be my meal ticket. I would have to develop other talents."

Literary Focus: Constructed Response

14. Students' responses will vary. A sample response follows:

    Form: As a novel—novel. **As an essay**—essay.

    Length: As a novel—long. **As an essay**—short.

    Content: As a novel—fictionalized. **As an essay**—all true.

    Purpose: As a novel—to entertain. **As an essay**—to explain.

    Statement about life: As a novel—theme. **As an essay**—main idea.

Collection 5

Collection 5 Diagnostic Test

Literature, Informational Text, Vocabulary, *page 95*

1. C
2. J
3. A
4. G
5. C
6. G
7. D
8. F
9. B
10. H

Lamb to the Slaughter
Roald Dahl
Selection Test, *page 97*

Comprehension

1. C
2. G
3. D
4. F
5. B
6. F
7. C
8. J
9. B
10. F

Literary Focus

11. A
12. J
13. A
14. F

Answer Key 309

Answer Key

Vocabulary
15. d
16. a
17. b
18. c
19. e

Constructed Response

20. Students' responses will vary. A sample response follows:

   Dramatic irony occurs when the reader knows more about a situation than the character does. This story contains many examples of dramatic irony. For instance, we know that Mary is going shopping to provide herself with an alibi. Situational irony occurs when the reader's expectations are reversed. One example is that at the beginning of the story we see a content housewife who loves her husband; the fact that she murders him comes as a surprise.

R.M.S. Titanic
Hanson W. Baldwin

A Fireman's Story
Harry Senior

From a Lifeboat
Mrs. D. H. Bishop

Selection Test, *page 100*

Comprehension
1. C
2. G
3. C
4. G
5. C
6. F
7. B
8. F
9. B
10. H

Literary Focus
11. A
12. F
13. A
14. H

Vocabulary Development
15. e
16. b
17. c
18. d
19. a

Constructed Response

20. Students' responses will vary. A sample response follows:

   The situational irony in the essay comes from the fact that the tragic events he describes—the sinking of the *Titanic*—were exactly the opposite of what was supposed to happen. The dramatic irony comes from the fact that the passengers we are reading about do not know, as the readers do, what is about to happen to them. Two examples of dramatic irony are: first, when the radio operator tells the *Californian* to "shut up"; second, when a lifeboat lowers less than half full. Examples of situational irony include the men exercising in the gym and the clerks trying to save the mail.

from Into Thin Air
Jon Krakauer

Selection Test, *page 103*

Comprehension
1. C
2. H
3. D
4. F
5. D

Literary Focus
6. J
7. A
8. G
9. C

Vocabulary Development
10. d
11. b
12. e
13. a
14. c

Constructed Response

15. Students' responses will vary. A sample response follows:

   It is ironic that Krakauer was lucky enough to find someone to lower his oxygen intake, but, as it turns out, the oxygen level was increased. Consequently his feelings of vitality and strength indicate his imminent danger of running out of oxygen too soon. Another example of situational irony and contradiction is that if Harris had

Answer Key

not said the oxygen bottles were empty at the Hillary Step, more lives might have been saved because the expedition team leader Rob Hall would have been able to plan a careful descent.

Explorers Say There's Still Lots to Look For
Helen O'Neill
Selection Test, page 106

Comprehension

1. C
2. F
3. B
4. J
5. B

Vocabulary Development

6. b
7. d
8. a
9. c
10. e

Notes from a Bottle
James Stevenson
Selection Test, page 108

Comprehension

1. C
2. G
3. A
4. J
5. B
6. H
7. C
8. J
9. B
10. F

Literary Focus

11. A
12. J
13. A
14. F

Vocabulary Development

15. c
16. e
17. b
18. d
19. a

Constructed Response

20. Students' responses will vary. A sample response follows:

　　An instance of ambiguity and subtlety in the story is that even though the city is clearly flooding, everybody is enjoying themselves. Throwing records through the air and engaging in other wild acts make the situation seem comic, not serious. But by the time the people are on the roof, the mood seems rather sad and a little scary. It is ambiguous because at first it seems the story is written to make the reader laugh, then it somehow doesn't. Because readers don't really know what is going on at first, they are inclined to accept the party atmosphere at face value. The diary format is instrumental in creating a distance between the reader and the action. Because of the fragmentary nature of the information given, readers don't know quite what to think, and the ambiguity is increased. Readers must simply accept the information as presented and react to the story's shifting emotional ground.

Collection 5 Summative Test,
page 111

Vocabulary Skills

1. A
2. G
3. B
4. J
5. C

Comprehension

6. G
7. C
8. J
9. A
10. G

Reading Skills and Strategies: Constructed Response

Making Inferences

11. Students' responses will vary. A sample response follows:

　　I think this story uses situational irony—the kind where you think one thing is true, but then the opposite turns out to be true. My conclusion is supported by the surprise at the end, when it turns out the dry skull went through the same thing that the hunter did. It is not dramatic irony because that's when the reader knows something the characters don't know; that doesn't happen here.

Answer Key　　　　　　　　　　　　　　　　311

Answer Key

Understanding Text Structures

12. H. Students' responses will vary. A sample response follows:

   When the dead hunter says, "Talking brought me here," he repeats exactly what the dry skull said to him when he found it—a situation that suggests that the point of this story is that the hunter never should have told the king in the first place; he should have kept his mouth shut. So the moral is that you shouldn't take a risk by telling people things you do not understand and getting in over your head.

Understanding Cause and Effect

13. Students' responses will vary. A sample response follows:

   The action the hunter takes, which is the cause, is to tell the king he found a talking skull. The effect is to put the hunter in the same position as the talking skull. This connection is made clear at the end when the hunter winds up telling the skull exactly what the skull had told him: "Talking brought me here!"

Making Predictions

14. H. Students' responses will vary. A sample response follows:

   The way the story is written seems to suggest its pattern has repeated itself in the past and will continue to repeat itself, so I predict that another hunter will come along and find the new talking skull.

Literary Focus: Constructed Response

15. Students' responses will vary. A sample response follows:

   b. The hunter tells the king about the skull.
   c. The king asks if anyone knows of such a thing.
   d. The king sends the hunter with guards to prove his story.
   e. The skull doesn't speak, and the guards kill the man.
   f. A hunter goes into the forest.

Collection 6

Collection 6 Diagnostic Test

Literature, Informational Text, Vocabulary, *page 115*

1. B	6. J
2. F	7. C
3. D	8. G
4. G	9. B
5. A	10. H

Through the Tunnel
by Doris Lessing

Selection Test, *page 117*

Comprehension

1. D	6. J
2. H	7. D
3. B	8. G
4. G	9. C
5. A	10. H

Literary Focus

11. B	13. A
12. H	14. J

Vocabulary Development

15. d	18. a
16. b	19. c
17. e	

Constructed Response

20. Students' responses will vary. A sample response follows:

   Jerry accomplishes a difficult feat by swimming through the tunnel, and he emerges as a stronger person both physically and emotionally. At the beginning of the story, the rocks at the wild bay "lay like discolored monsters under the surface." In front of the local boys, Jerry is described as experiencing "hot shame, feeling the pleading grin on his face like a scar that he could never remove. . . ." He has not yet earned his place among the boys.

Answer Key

When he swims through the tunnel, the rocks are no longer monsters. Instead, "Sunlight was falling through it, showing the clean, dark rock of the tunnel. . . ." Through the exercise of will, self-control, strength, and intelligence, Jerry has earned his rite of passage. In the light of his accomplishment, he sees the rocks as they really are—not as monsters that intimidated him as a young boy. Compared to the silly, exaggerated way Jerry acted before he could make it through the tunnel, he feels self-assured at the end of the story. In his newly found maturity, he does not even feel the need to boast of his accomplishment to his mother. Instead, he tells her only that he's learned to hold his breath underwater.

Coming of Age, Latino Style: Special Rite Ushers Girls into Adulthood
by Cindy Rodriguez

Vision Quest
from Encyclopaedia Britannica

Crossing a Threshold to Adulthood
by Jessica Barnes

Selection Test, *page 120*

Comprehension

1. B
2. F
3. D
4. H
5. A

Vocabulary Development

6. inevitable
7. formidable
8. vigil
9. indigenous
10. solitary

The Masque of the Red Death
by Edgar Allan Poe

The Black Death
from When Plague Strikes
by James Cross Giblin

Selection Test, *page 122*

Comprehension

1. B
2. J
3. C
4. F
5. A
6. J
7. C
8. H
9. A
10. H

Literary Focus

11. D
12. F
13. C
14. J

Vocabulary Development

15. C
16. G
17. D
18. F
19. B

Constructed Response

20. Students' responses will vary. A sample response follows:

   One term used for bubonic plague was *Black Death*. In Edgar Allan Poe's story, a plague is considered the Red Death. In history the Black Death was carried by an invisible bacteria that caused humans to become suddenly very ill and die horribly. In the story, the strangely masked and costumed creature at the party vanishes and leaves only its costume and mask behind. The uninvited guest, who is actually the Red Death, is invisible. It is this invisible force that affects all the party guests and kills them, one by one. "The Black Death" points out three ways in which people in Florence reacted to the plague, according to the *Decameron* by Giovanni Boccaccio. Some people in Florence "adopted an attitude of 'play today for we die tomorrow.'" This was Prince Prospero's approach to the appearance of the plague in his realm.

Answer Key

Unfortunately, all his power and cleverness could not control the power of the disease that would lead to his death.

Stopping by Woods on a Snowy Evening
by Robert Frost

After Apple-Picking
by Robert Frost

Selection Test, *page 126*

Comprehension

1. A
2. H
3. C
4. J
5. D
6. G
7. A
8. J
9. A
10. H

Literary Focus

11. C
12. J
13. D
14. F

Constructed Response

15. Students' responses will vary. A sample response follows:

"Stopping by Woods on a Snowy Evening" begins with the delight the speaker feels at seeing the snowy woods. The speaker considers that the owner of the woods is probably at home in his village house while the speaker and his horse enjoy some time in the snowy countryside. About the owner the speaker says, "He will not see me stopping here / To watch his woods fill up with snow." By the end of the poem, though, the speaker thinks about his entire life, not just this day's journey. He says, "But I have promises to keep," which refers to promises for his whole life, not just this day. Then the speaker repeats the line "And miles to go before I sleep" to emphasize his life journey in addition to the day's journey through the snow. Thus, the speaker arrives at a wisdom that looks beyond immediate concerns.

Collection 6 Summative Test,
page 129

Vocabulary Skills

1. C
2. G
3. A
4. H
5. B

Comprehension

6. G
7. D
8. H
9. B
10. F

Reading Skills and Strategies: Constructed Response

Understanding Symbols

11. Students' responses will vary. A sample response follows:

a. Symbol—glass; **Functions**—"implies sight," "suggests depth," "mirrors and makes real," "is sought and is seen," "reflects."
Symbol—shoe; **Functions**—"implies miles," "suggests length," "measures," "makes solid," "wears," "is worn."

b. Like the fairy tale the poem is teaching about love and how to attain it.

c. The poet has taken the fairy tale's emblematic shoe and split it in two. The famous glass slipper becomes two symbols, each based on one of its functions.

The poet links the shoe to the prince. A shoe is utilitarian and practical; it "wears and is worn." The prince wants someone who can fulfill practical functions, and he is equally willing to perform practical functions in a relationship. He seeks someone who wants to make this exchange.

To the speaker, the Cinderella figure, the poet assigns the function of glass. Here the poet inserts a twist. She makes the glass a mirror—a looking glass. The primary function of a looking glass is to show the "gazer" himself or herself. Thus, the poet shows that Cinderella knows that the prince seeks more than a practical relation-

Answer Key

ship, a functional marriage of convenience—he seeks the knowledge of his true self.

The sisters relate to the prince on his level: the shoe's practical reality. Only Cinderella knows that the essential relationship exists elsewhere—in his own *images* of love and their relationship. It is this knowledge that enables her to mirror his own self to him and thus win, if not love, at least marriage.

12. Students' responses will vary. A sample response follows:

    The sisters symbolize the ego—one's idea of self. The ego may be seen as either positive or negative. The poet presents the sisters negatively. They represent that aspect of the personality that seeks its own fulfillment rather than the fulfillment of another.

    They are women whose idea of love is not selflessness. Because their ideals do not match the ideals of their lovers, the women try to change their lovers' ideals, not themselves. However, their princes perceive these efforts as an attack, and they dispose of the sisters. Like the sisters the princes only want self-fulfillment and will find it only in a perfect match. Cinderella is that match because she is the mirror image of their own ideal self.

    The wisdom of the sisters or the speaker may be debatable, but one thing is not: Those who are concerned merely with the presentation of self will not find love. The last line leaves the reader wondering how long the prince will be satisfied with a reflection of his own self. Thus, the poet has presented the paradox and problem of love: In love one seeks and finds one's true self; yet true love is selfless.

Literary Focus: Constructed Response

13. Students' responses will vary. A sample response follows:

    Glass is first mentioned in the third line of the poem. There glass is compared to both the sharpness of love and "the point of a knife." Thus, through a simile, love, glass, and the knife are linked. The figurative connection between the three is further complicated in the third stanza, where a metaphor introduces a riddle: "Glass is not glass." A particular kind of glass may be found "in the language of love." By the end of the stanza, the riddle is solved—this special kind of glass is a mirror, a psychological reflection of self.

    The last line of the stanza—"A queen must be made of glass"—introduces a new connection that makes the meaning of the metaphor clear. In love a person must be a mirror who reflects his or her partner's ideal love. Thus, through the figurative meaning of *glass*, in a few lines the poet expresses some of the complexities of human relationships.

Collection 7

Collection 7 Diagnostic Test

Literature, *page 133*

1. C	6. J
2. F	7. A
3. D	8. H
4. H	9. B
5. B	10. G

A Storm in the Mountains
by Aleksandr Solzhenitsyn
Selection Test, *page 135*

Comprehension

1. C	6. H
2. J	7. C
3. B	8. F
4. F	9. B
5. A	10. J

Literary Focus

11. C	13. B
12. J	14. H

Answer Key

Constructed Response

15. Students' responses will vary. A sample response follows:

Both a newspaper article and a prose poem are written in prose in paragraph form. A newspaper article strives to report objective facts by answering the questions *who? what? when? where? why?* and *how?* A prose poem's powerful images are subjective, and its elusive message is open to interpretation. Solzhenitsyn expresses what the storm in the mountains means to him when he states: "Insignificant yet grateful, we became part of this world—a primal world in creation before our eyes." In contrast, a well-written news article states only the facts and does not editorialize or interpret the meaning of an event.

Same Song
by Pat Mora
Selection Test, *page 138*

Comprehension

1. C
2. G
3. D
4. H
5. A
6. G
7. B
8. J
9. C
10. H

Literary Focus

11. B
12. J
13. D
14. H

Constructed Response

15. Students' responses will vary. A sample response follows:

The narrator's daughter performs her beauty rituals at six o'clock in the morning. The son's routine starts at nine o'clock in the evening. The daughter's routine involves curling her hair and applying makeup, while his is about bodybuilding. Both are disappointed when they look in "the mirror, mirror on the wall," perhaps because their appearance is not "fair" enough to live up to the American ideal of beauty.

Eating Together
by Li-Young Lee
Grape Sherbet
by Rita Dove
Selection Test, *page 141*

Comprehension

1. C
2. G
3. A
4. G
5. A
6. G
7. D
8. J
9. A
10. F

Literary Focus

11. D
12. H
13. B
14. G

Constructed Response

15. Students' responses will vary. A sample response follows:

In the past, the speaker thought of Memorial Day as a time of fun when her father cooked out and her family ate together. In fact, visiting a cemetery on Memorial Day seemed to be a kind of joke and an opportunity to play around the tombstones. Now that she is older and her father is dead, she sees Memorial Day as a serious occasion to remember those we loved and their unique contributions.

The Legend
by Garrett Hongo
Selection Test, *page 144*

Comprehension

1. C
2. H
3. D
4. G
5. C
6. F
7. D
8. F
9. B
10. F

Answer Key

Literary Focus
1. B
2. H
13. D
14. G

Constructed Response
15. Students' responses will vary. A sample response follows:

At first the speaker feels indifferent to the death of someone he doesn't know. Then he is ashamed that he feels so distinct from the man and that he favors reason over emotion, just as Descartes did. He recognizes his compassion for the dead man, who he hopes will be comforted by the "weaver girl" who will "take up his cold hands."

Simile
by N. Scott Momaday
Selection Test, *page 147*

Comprehension
1. B
2. J
3. D
4. J

Literary Focus
5. A
6. G
7. D
8. G
9. B

Constructed Response
10. Students' responses will vary. A sample response follows:

The speaker and his companion have had a fight and are now wary of each other. They are alert to danger—the danger of hurt feelings and broken hearts. They are listening to ("ears forward") and watching ("eyes watchful") each other for any word or action that might hurt and cause them to go their separate ways ("in whose limbs there is latent flight").

I Am Offering This Poem
by Jimmy Santiago Baca

since feeling is first
by E. E. Cummings
Selection Test, *page 149*

Comprehension
1. A
2. H
3. D
4. G
5. C
6. G
7. C
8. F
9. B
10. H

Literary Focus
11. C
12. J
13. A
14. G

Constructed Response
15. Students' responses will vary. A sample response follows:

The gift expresses simple true love and generosity. "Keep it like a warm coat," "like a pair of thick socks," "it is a pot full of yellow corn / to warm your belly," and "warm yourself by this fire, / rest by this fire, and make you feel safe" are examples of simile and metaphor that show how love makes you feel warm and cozy, nourished and safe.

Heart! We will forget him!
by Emily Dickinson

Three Japanese Tankas
by Ono Komachi
Selection Test, *page 152*

Comprehension
1. A
2. J
3. B
4. J
5. D
6. H
7. B
8. F
9. C
10. G

Answer Key 317

Answer Key

Literary Focus

11. D
12. J
13. B
14. H

Constructed Response

15. Students' responses will vary. A sample response follows:

   The speaker in the first tanka asks a man if they should pass up the chance to light up each other's life with love. In the second tanka, the speaker has been "drenched / in cold waves" ever since she fell in love. She compares her man's love to a "drifting ship" on which she has placed her heart, meaning that he has moved away from her even though she still loves him. In the third tanka, the speaker compares her loveless life to an empty husk of grain to express her hopelessness and despair.

Shall I Compare Thee to a Summer's Day?
by William Shakespeare
Selection Test, *page 155*

Comprehension

1. C
2. G
3. B
4. J
5. D
6. H
7. D
8. J
9. A
10. H

Literary Focus

11. A
12. F
13. C
14. G

Constructed Response

15. Students' responses will vary. A sample response follows:

   The speaker asserts that through his poem he will make his beloved immortal. Certainly poetry has this power. When we read a poem about a person, that person comes to life—even though he or she may be long dead. In "Shall I Compare Thee to Summer's Day?" it is interesting that the person the speaker wants to immortalize is unnamed. Although he creates a vivid portrait of his beloved, we are never told who this person is. Therefore, the speaker seems to defeat his purpose.

Ode to My Socks
by Pablo Neruda
Selection Test, *page 158*

Comprehension

1. B
2. J
3. C
4. G
5. D
6. F
7. A
8. J
9. B
10. H

Literary Focus

11. B
12. H
13. B
14. J

Constructed Response

15. Students' responses will vary. A sample response follows:

   The speaker uses several metaphors to describe how the socks make his feet feel. He calls them "two fish made / of wool," "two long sharks," "two immense blackbirds," and "two cannons." These are things that move and explode, so to speak. They make his feet feel as though they might burst—into flight, into the air, or into a run. Such a wonderful gift as these socks arouses reverential feelings in the speaker. He uses a simile to describe the worshipful attitude he has toward his socks. He says that he puts them on "Like explorers / in the jungle who hand / over the very rare / green deer / to the spit / and eat it / with remorse."

Answer Key

Sea Fever
by John Masefield
Selection Test, page 161

Comprehension

1. C
2. G
3. C
4. H
5. A
6. G
7. B
8. H
9. B
10. H

Literary Focus

11. B
12. H
13. A
14. F

Constructed Response

15. Students' responses will vary. A sample response follows:

You can hear the rhythm of the sea swells in the alliteration ("windy," "with," and "white"; "spray," "spume," and "sea"), the rhythm, the rhyme ("flying" / "crying"), and the rise and fall of the following lines: "And all I ask is a windy day with the white clouds flying, / And the flung spray and the blown spume, and the sea gulls crying." Similarly, the repetition of "And" simulates the repeating motion of the waves.

Bonny Barbara Allan
by Anonymous
Selection Test, page 164

Comprehension

1. C
2. F
3. C
4. G
5. D
6. G
7. A
8. H
9. D
10. G

Literary Focus

11. D
12. J
13. B
14. H

Constructed Response

15. Students' responses will vary. A sample response follows:

"Bonny Barbara Allan" is a story that is told in song. It has a strong meter (iambic tetrameter, except for the fourth, fifth, sixth, and twelfth stanzas) and a refrain ("Hardhearted Barbara Allan"). It also contains phrases and images common to folk ballads, such as "in the merry month of May" and "A red, red rose grew out of his grave."

The Flying Cat
by Naomi Shihab Nye
Selection Test, page 167

Comprehension

1. B
2. J
3. C
4. F
5. D
6. G
7. A
8. H
9. B
10. G

Literary Focus

11. D
12. G
13. B
14. G

Constructed Response

15. Students' responses will vary. A sample response follows:

The free-verse poem, "The Flying Cat," uses long and short sentences and many run-on lines (for example, "as if / the explosion of cats were another") to imitate the rhythms of everyday speech. For example, Nye asks questions ("Will the baggage compartment be pressurized?" "Will a soldier's footlocker fall on the cat during take-off?") and puts them into the context of telephone conversations ("You ask these questions one by one, in different voices / over the phone").

Answer Key

Ex–Basketball Player
by John Updike

miss rosie
by Lucille Clifton
Selection Test, page 170

Comprehension

1. C
2. J
3. B
4. F
5. D
6. H
7. D
8. H
9. A
10. H

Literary Focus

11. B
12. J
13. D
14. F

Constructed Response

15. Students' responses will vary. A sample response follows:

Although both poems seem like free verse and sound conversational, "Ex–Basketball Player" is written in the tight structure of iambic pentameter. It uses internal rhyme ("Their rubber elbows hanging loose and low. / One's nostrils are two S's, and his eyes / An E and O. . . .") and alliteration ("trolley tracks."). Both poems use figurative language (personification of gas pumps in "Ex–Basketball Player"; simile in "Miss Rosie": "when I watch you / wrapped up like garbage"). "Miss Rosie" also uses idiom: "i stand up," meaning "I support" or "I stand up for you."

Remember
by Joy Harjo
Selection Test, page 173

Comprehension

1. D
2. F
3. C
4. H
5. A
6. G
7. A
8. J
9. C
10. J

Literary Focus

11. A
12. F
13. B
14. H

Constructed Response

15. Students' responses will vary. A sample response follows:

The repetition of the refrain "Remember" creates a coaxing rhythm that conveys a tone of reverence for oneself, all living things, the earth, and the universe. "Remember the sky," "Remember the moon," "Remember the sun's birth," "Remember your birth," and "Remember sundown" are examples of the refrain pointing out natural phenomena that the "you" of the poem is to heed and be one with.

We Real Cool
by Gwendolyn Brooks
Selection Test, page 176

Comprehension

1. B
2. G
3. D
4. H
5. C

Literary Focus

6. H
7. D
8. F
9. C

Constructed Response

10. Students' responses will vary. A sample response follows:

"We Real Cool" is free verse that imitates the beat of the street through internal rhyme and alliteration, which set the rhythm as well as the tone of the poem. Examples of internal rhyme and alliteration are "Thin gin," "Lurk late," "Strike straight," "Sing sin," and "Jazz June." Brooks introduces an ironic twist to the tone in the final rhyme: "We / Jazz June. We / Die soon." This twist, which is closely tied to the sound effects, tells readers that Brooks means the opposite of what

Answer Key

she is saying. She actually wants the pool players, who think they are cool, to abandon the self-destructive path they have chosen and not die soon.

Jazz Fantasia
by Carl Sandburg
Selection Test, page 178

Comprehension

1. C
2. J
3. D
4. H
5. B

Literary Focus

6. J
7. A
8. G
9. B

Constructed Response

10. Students' responses will vary. A sample response follows:

   The playful tone of "Jazz Fantasia" is conveyed through onomatopoeia. Examples of onomatopoeia in the poem include "ooze," "husha- / husha-hush," "bang-bang," and "hoo-hoo-hoo-oo." The playful tone mirrors Sandburg's meaning: Jazz engages the full range of human emotion.

Collection 7 Summative Test,
page 180

Comprehension

1. B
2. H
3. B
4. G
5. C

Reading Skills and Strategies: Constructed Response

Using Prior Knowledge

6. Students' responses will vary. A sample response follows:

   The word *star* indicates hope and dreams of aspiration, as in "Hitch your wagon to a star." The phrase "guiding star" implies an object that gives life meaning and lights one's way, much the way a mother should in the life of her child.

Paraphrasing

7. Students' responses will vary. A sample response follows:

   Child, your untroubled innocence makes me want to give you the world; you deserve all of its beauty, and fascination. I want to fill your life with only wonderful and positive things, not the sort of dark depression that I experience.

Literary Focus

8. G
9. A
10. H
11. B

12. Students' responses will vary. A sample response follows:

   "Little stalk without wrinkle": innocent child untouched by life's complications

   "this dark Ceiling without a star": the dark, troubled world of depression, in which there is no light to help you find your way out

Collection 8
Collection 8 Diagnostic Test
Literature, Informational Text, Vocabulary, page 184

1. C
2. J
3. B
4. F
5. D
6. H
7. A
8. G
9. B
10. H

Geraldo No Last Name
by Sandra Cisneros
Selection Test, page 186

Comprehension

1. B
2. H
3. A
4. J
5. A
6. F
7. A
8. G
9. D
10. H

Answer Key

Literary Focus
11. D
12. F
13. C
14. G

Constructed Response
15. Students' responses will vary. A sample response follows:

   Marin feels frustrated and helpless about Geraldo's death. She didn't know him well, but, as a human being, he deserved to live and to be helped after the accident. In the story, Marin states that Geraldo might have been saved if a surgeon had been at the hospital. Although she could do nothing to help Geraldo medically, she remained in the hospital, waiting for hours and feeling helpless. Marin hardly knew Geraldo, but his sudden and tragic death shocked her greatly.

Night Calls
by Lisa Fugard

Waiting for *E. gularis*
by Linda Pastan
Selection Test, *page 189*

Comprehension
1. A
2. J
3. C
4. J
5. B
6. G
7. B
8. G
9. B
10. F

Literary Focus
11. C
12. F
13. C
14. H

Vocabulary Development
15. patina
16. avid
17. abutting
18. opulent
19. indigenous

Constructed Response
20. Students' response will vary. A sample response follows:

   Lisa Fugard creates a mysterious mood through the use of poetic language that includes many figures of speech. During the flashback at the beginning of the story, she says her father's hands "seemed to hang off the ends of his arms like two chunks of meat." We learn that the father is emotionally lifeless because he is trapped in the grief brought on by the death of his wife years earlier in a car accident. The narrator uses other figures of speech to create more mystery surrounding her father. For example, "I saw that my father's eyes had gone dull like a dead animal's" and "I'd seen him crisscrossing the veld, like a rabid dog." At the end of the story, the father and daughter work through their grief over the mother's death. The author extends the mood of mystery and poetry by using another figure of speech about the father's hands. This time, instead of being lifeless, the father's hands "fluttered like giant, tawny moths in the moonlight."

Call of the Wild—Save Us!
by Norman Myers
Selection Test, *page 193*

Comprehension
1. B
2. F
3. C
4. H
5. D

Vocabulary Development
6. d
7. a
8. e
9. b
10. c

Answer Key

A Very Old Man with Enormous Wings
by Gabriel García Márquez

Sonnet for Heaven Below
by Jack Agüeros

Selection Test, *page 195*

Comprehension

1. D
2. G
3. A
4. G
5. B
6. J
7. A
8. G
9. C
10. H

Literary Focus

11. C
12. J
13. C
14. G

Vocabulary Development

15. B
16. H
17. D
18. F
19. D

Constructed Response

20. Students' response will vary. A sample response follows:

 The people of Macondo need to understand who and what the angel is and what his purpose among them is. Because he doesn't speak the language of the people, he can't talk to them about himself; they are left to create stories about him. When the spider woman arrives and tells her story, the people lose interest in the angel. They hear her story, understand it, are intrigued by it, and believe it.

Collection 8 Summative Test,
page 199

Vocabulary Skills

1. D
2. F
3. D
4. G
5. C

Comprehension

6. G
7. A
8. H
9. C
10. G

Reading Skills and Strategies: Constructed Response

Evaluating Style

11. Students' responses will vary. A sample response follows:

 Colette's writing style in "The Bracelet" is thought provoking. The story begins with incomplete sentences, indicated by ellipses, in which Mrs. Augelier recalls gifts from previous anniversaries. She takes her time describing the act of putting on the bracelet, an anniversary gift from her husband. Colette writes complex sentences in which semicolons and dashes extend thoughts and connect fragments of thoughts related to Mrs. Augelier's initial response to the gift. Colette uses sophisticated expressions, such as "the pretty bijou of a connoisseur," to refer to a collector's jewel. Detailed descriptions and multisyllabic, sophisticated terms provoke the reader to think about the importance of the bracelet as well as the greater meaning it may have in Mrs. Augelier's life.

Evaluating Figurative Language

12. Students' responses will vary. A sample response follows:

 When Mrs. Augelier puts the diamond bracelet on her hand for the first time, Colette describes the effect of the jewels as "tiny rainbows, blazing with color" that "danced on the white tablecloth." Then, Colette mentions a natural bracelet of wrinkles that Mrs. Augelier discovers on her wrist, describing them as "three finely engraved creases encircling her wrist above the glittering snake." The idea that a diamond bracelet looks like a snake provokes the reader to consider that the gift may not evoke such wonderful thoughts and feelings in Mrs. Augelier. Possibly, the

Answer Key

beauty of the bracelet is like her lost youth—a frightening thought for Mrs. Augelier. These figures of speech enhance the thought-provoking style of the entire story.

Literary Focus: Constructed Response

13. Students' responses will vary. A sample response follows:

    Tone: analytical, serious

    Left circle—*Words and phrases for tone from the story*—"counted and recounted," "she believed herself guilty of not loving him enough," "repeated intently," "the dissimulation of a lunatic"

    Mood: depressed

    Right circle—*Words and phrases for mood from the story*—"she believed herself guilty of not loving him enough," "she was already tired of her new bracelet," "I don't know what's wrong with me," "Being fifty is a bore," "genius who creates . . . the marvels of childhood, who gradually weakens, then dies mysteriously within us, did not even stir"

    Middle section—*Some tone and mood words and phrases from the story:* "convalescent whose appetite the fresh air has yet to restore"; "Madame Augelier fell back, bruised, into the present, into reality"; "Resigned, Madame Augelier thus came to know how old she really was"

Collection 9

Collection 9 Diagnostic Test

Literature, Informational Text, Vocabulary, *page 204*

1. B
2. F
3. D
4. G
5. A
6. J
7. B
8. H
9. C
10. F

Where Have You Gone, Charming Billy?
by Tim O'Brien

The Friendship Only Lasted a Few Seconds
by Lily Lee Adams

Selection Test, *page 206*

Comprehension

1. C
2. F
3. A
4. J
5. B
6. G
7. A
8. H
9. A
10. H

Literary Focus

11. B
12. H
13. C
14. H

Vocabulary Development

15. skirted
16. inertia
17. stealth
18. agile
19. diffuse

Constructed Response

20. Students' responses will vary. A sample response follows:

    U.S. soldiers in Vietnam had to deal with a land and a people they were utterly unfamiliar with in terms of climate, culture, geography, and language. Because of this, the soldiers were at a disadvantage. Because the fighting in Vietnam was guerilla style, a familiarity with the land was central to survival. In addition, the morale of the U.S. soldiers was low: Many did not believe in the war and knew of the strong antiwar sentiment at home.

Answer Key

The War Escalates
from The American Nation
by Paul Boyer

Dear Folks
by Kenneth W. Bagby

from Declaration of Independence from the War in Vietnam
by Martin Luther King, Jr.

Selection Test, *page 210*

Comprehension
1. C
2. J
3. B
4. F
5. B

Vocabulary Development
6. J
7. B
8. G
9. C
10. J

The Sword in the Stone
from Le Morte d'Arthur
by Sir Thomas Malory
retold by Keith Baines

"The Magic Happened"
by John Steinbeck

Selection Test, *page 212*

Comprehension
1. B
2. H
3. D
4. G
5. A
6. G
7. A
8. G
9. D
10. H

Literary Focus
11. A
12. F
13. D
14. J

Vocabulary Development
15. e
16. c
17. a
18. b
19. d

Constructed Response

20. Students' responses will vary. A sample response follows:

Arthur is a true hero of his time because he lives by the qualities of honor, loyalty, and generosity. Arthur displays honor when he keeps all his promises to Sir Kay, despite Sir Kay's deceit. Arthur shows his loyalty when he tells Sir Ector that he will always consider him a father, even though his own father, as it turns out, was King Uther. Arthur shows generosity when, at his coronation, he forgives the knights and nobles who did not originally support him.

The Tale of Sir Launcelot du Lake
from Le Morte d'Arthur
by Sir Thomas Malory
retold by Keith Baines

The Romance: Where Good Always Triumphs
by David Adams Leeming

Selection Test, *page 215*

Comprehension
1. B
2. F
3. D
4. H
5. B
6. G
7. D
8. H
9. B
10. F

Literary Focus
11. D
12. J
13. C
14. J

Vocabulary Development
15. fidelity
16. champion
17. diverted
18. wrath
19. oblige

Answer Key

Constructed Response

20. Students' responses will vary. A sample response follows:

    Sir Launcelot's behavior is based on bravery, honor, loyalty, and generosity. These are the traits of a romantic hero and form the basis of the chivalric code. Sir Launcelot is loyal to Queen Gwynevere, and honors his oath to her by resisting the four queens who imprison him. He generously helps Sir Belleus after a fight over mistaken identity. He also honors his promise to the daughter of King Bagdemagus by bravely fighting the knights of the Round Table. Sir Launcelot magnanimously offers his service to the daughter of King Bagdemagus even though he has fulfilled his oath.

Theseus
retold by Edith Hamilton

"All We Need Is That Piece of String"
by Bill Moyers with Joseph Campbell

Selection Test, *page 219*

Comprehension

1. B
2. G
3. C
4. F
5. D
6. F
7. B
8. F
9. A
10. H

Literary Focus

11. D
12. F
13. D
14. H

Constructed Response

15. Students' responses will vary. A sample response follows:

    Theseus is a daring young man who is more interested in finding and meeting challenges than in enjoying the results of victory. He prefers to take the most dangerous route to Athens, and during his travels he succeeds in slaying the dangerous bandits. Although Theseus is made heir to his father's kingdom, he prefers to take on a challenge that all Athenians dread: confronting the Minotaur. After Theseus, with the help of Ariadne, defeats the Minotaur, he travels back to Greece. But somehow he does not raise the signal to his father, King Aegeus, prompting the king's suicide. As the new monarch of Athens, Theseus asks only to be commander in chief, a position that will bring him greater challenges in the future. True to his character, Theseus wants a government that represents all Athenians.

Sigurd, the Dragon Slayer
retold by Olivia E. Coolidge

Selection Test, *page 222*

Comprehension

1. C
2. J
3. C
4. F
5. A
6. F
7. A
8. J
9. C
10. F

Literary Focus

11. B
12. H
13. D
14. G

Constructed Response

15. Students' responses will vary. A sample response follows:

    One of the themes of "Sigurd, the Dragon Slayer" is that without wisdom, even the strongest hero may not survive. That lesson becomes clear when Sigurd slays the dragon. He has no idea that Regin is about to slay him until, by accident, he tastes the roasted dragon heart. The heart now injects dragon wisdom into Sigurd, and he uses that knowledge to destroy greedy Regin. This lesson implies that Vikings treasured wisdom as much as they respected great strength. Without wisdom,

Answer Key

Norse people would not have survived. They believed that the heroes of their mythology protected the world from destruction with their wisdom.

Collection 9 Summative Test, page 225

Vocabulary Skills

1. B
2. F
3. D
4. H
5. B

Comprehension

6. H
7. B
8. J
9. A
10. H

Reading Skills and Strategies: Constructed Response

Analyzing Heroes and History

11. Students' responses will vary. A sample response follows:

    A hero is someone who is courageous and trustworthy. Tomotada must be thought of as courageous, because he is a samurai. He has proved himself a good soldier and scholar, and he is trusted by the Lord of Noto, who sends him on the quest. But Tomotada does not act heroically when he breaks his word and selfishly gives up his quest to live with Green Willow in the mountains. Tomotada, therefore, cannot be considered a true and complete Japanese samurai hero.

Analyzing the Relationship of History and Its Tales and Myths

12. Students' responses will vary. A sample response follows:

    An important aspect of Japanese society I learned from reading "Green Willow" is the sense of courtesy and modesty practiced by people from all walks of life. The old couple address Tomotada as "Honored Sir" and describe their house as a "hovel" and their daughter as a "poor, ignorant girl." Tomotada does not agree with the old man, claiming that he is "lucky indeed to be served by so lovely a maiden" and then reciting a poem to Green Willow. Much later, when Green Willow becomes ill, she addresses Tomotado not by his name but as "my dear husband" or "my lord," which are terms of respect.

Literary Focus: Constructed Response

13. Students' responses will vary. Sample responses follows:

    A The young girl represents the beauty and delicacy of nature, because she is really a willow tree. When someone cuts down "her" tree, she dies.

    B Tomotada thinks he has found perfect happiness that will last for many years, but his young wife dies suddenly.

    C The young girl is so beautiful that Tomotada feels lucky to have her. Then he finds out that she is not really human, making her just an ideal of what he thought a woman should be.

    D The young girl represents the ideal of love at first sight. Tomotada is immediately enchanted by the girl, and she returns his admiration. Although they hardly know each other when they get married, their union is filled with great joy.

14. Students' responses will vary. A sample response follows:

    Row 1—quest; Tomotada sets out on a special quest to the Lord of Kyoto. Because of a storm, he takes refuge in the old couple's home and ultimately abandons his quest.

    Row 2—magical elements; the old couple and the young girl are not actually human but willow trees in the form of humans.

Answer Key

Collection 10

Collection 10 Diagnostic Test
Literature, Informational Text, Vocabulary, *page 231*

1. C
2. H
3. B
4. J
5. C
6. G
7. D
8. F
9. A
10. H

The Brute: A Joke in One Act
by Anton Chekhov
Selection Test, *page 233*

Comprehension

1. B
2. H
3. B
4. H
5. B
6. H
7. A
8. F
9. B
10. H

Literary Focus

11. D
12. F
13. B
14. H

Vocabulary Development

15. C
16. F
17. D
18. G
19. C

Constructed Response

20. Students' responses will vary. A sample response follows:

   Like all comedies, farces are usually about a relationship between people. Like other characters in farces, Smirnov exaggerates his responses and emotions in his relationship with Mrs. Popov. He refuses to leave when he learns that Mrs. Popov cannot pay him for a few days. He states that women show no logic and then exaggerates by saying, "I'd rather sit on a barrel of dynamite" than deal with a woman. Later, in conversation, he again exaggerates his emotional response to Mrs. Popov's refusal to pay him by demanding a duel with her. When she accepts (to his utter surprise), he falls madly in love with her—another of the many exaggerated emotional responses that add up to a totally farcical love story.

The Tragedy of Julius Caesar, Act I
by William Shakespeare
Selection Test, *page 237*

Comprehension

1. D
2. G
3. C
4. G
5. C
6. G
7. D
8. J
9. A
10. G

Literary Focus

11. C
12. G
13. C
14. J

Constructed Response

15. Students' responses will vary. A sample response follows:

   Cassius sees the storm as a call to end Caesar's tyranny. It is the gods' harsh commentary on Caesar's growing ambition and a warning that a horrible disaster will descend if Caesar isn't stopped. Casca questions, "Who ever knew the heavens menace so?" Cassius responds, "Those that have known the earth so full of faults." The faults may be interpreted as the overly ambitious career of Caesar. In a monologue spoken to Casca about the storm being a message from angered gods (lines 77–78), Cassius talks about a man like Caesar as "prodigious grown / And fearful, as these strange eruptions are." Cicero, on the other hand, believes people interpret strange events in whatever manner they choose. Yet, he, too, refrains from venturing into the political storm that is about to erupt. Perhaps, were he to believe in omens, he might foretell his own death.

Answer Key

The Tragedy of Julius Caesar, Act II
by William Shakespeare
Selection Test, *page 240*

Comprehension
1. A
2. H
3. D
4. J
5. C
6. J
7. A
8. H
9. C
10. G

Literary Focus
11. B
12. G
13. D
14. G

Constructed Response
15. Students' responses will vary. A sample response follows:

   Brutus is physically unwell and unable to sleep at the beginning of the act, due to his inner turmoil over whether or not to kill Caesar. He is caught in a waking nightmare. In the same way, the heavens are in turmoil as the conspirators make plans to upset civil order. When Brutus leaves his home, having decided to take part in the assassination of Caesar, thunder sounds outside. Also, while Caesar discusses whether or not to appear at the Senate that day, thunder and lightning strike outside of his house, reminding the characters and the audience that Rome, as well as Brutus himself that day, are unwell. The insurrection will culminate with Caesar's murder followed by civil unrest.

The Tragedy of Julius Caesar, Act III
by William Shakespeare
Selection Test, *page 243*

Comprehension
1. B
2. J
3. D
4. H
5. B
6. J
7. B
8. J
9. A
10. F

Literary Focus
11. B
12. F
13. B
14. H

Constructed Response
15. Students' responses will vary. A sample response follows:

   Antony repeats the phrase "he is an honorable man" until it appears ridiculous in contrast with the nobility of the slain Caesar. Antony teases the crowd with Caesar's will, appealing to their curiosity and self-interest. Antony breaks down emotionally before the crowd, showing himself to be loyal and loving; while Brutus, who has coolly delivered his speech, seems selfish, unfeeling, and calculating. Antony holds up Caesar's torn cloak as a way of showing how excessively violent the murder was; Antony also treats the cloak as if it were Caesar himself. While telling touching tales of Caesar, Antony keeps bringing up the will until the crowd insists he read it. The will reveals Caesar's legacy to every citizen, which incites the crowd and makes them exact revenge on the conspirators.

Answer Key

The Tragedy of Julius Caesar, Act IV
by William Shakespeare
Selection Test, *page 246*

Comprehension

1. B
2. H
3. A
4. F
5. D
6. H
7. C
8. G
9. D
10. J

Literary Focus

11. B
12. F
13. D
14. G

Constructed Response

15. Students' responses will vary. A sample response follows:

   The ghost's appearance could represent the vengeance that Antony has sworn he will get for Caesar. It could also be understood as Brutus's troubled conscience rather than as a literal ghost. The ghost scene serves to demonstrate, as the storm in the first act does, the displeasure of the gods with the conspirators' actions.

The Tragedy of Julius Caesar, Act V
by William Shakespeare

The Fear and the Flames
by Jimmy Breslin
Selection Test, *page 249*

Comprehension

1. A
2. J
3. A
4. H
5. B
6. F
7. C
8. H
9. A
10. G

Literary Focus

11. D
12. J
13. C
14. G

Constructed Response

15. Students' responses will vary. A sample response follows:

   There are many contradictions stated by characters in this play much like the experiences of people in real life. Anthony calls Brutus the noblest Roman although he had taunted him earlier for leading them to war. Brutus takes his own life even though he had said earlier that he disapproved of his father-in-law's suicide. Octavius speaks of the "glories" of the day although what we have just seen is a great deal of violence and death. The image of eagles and vultures in Cassius's omens is a contradiction reflected in the roles of Antony and Octavius: both men are eagles (victors), but they achieve victory only through the deaths of Cassius and Brutus; thus, the eagles become vultures.

Julius Caesar in an Absorbing Production
by John Mason Brown
Selection Test, *page 252*

Comprehension

1. D
2. G
3. C
4. J
5. B

Vocabulary Development

6. J
7. A
8. G
9. B
10. F

Collection 10 Summative Test,
page 254

Vocabulary Skills

1. D
2. G
3. A
4. G
5. B

330

Holt Assessment: Literature, Reading, and Vocabulary

Answer Key

Comprehension

6. J
7. B
8. H
9. D
10. G

Reading Skills and Strategies: Constructed Response

Paraphrasing

11. Students' responses will vary. A sample response follows:

    What beast made you suggest this plan to me? When you dared to go through with the plan, you were a real man. And if you take action, you will be twice the man. Before, you didn't know when or where you might kill the king, but you were still willing to find a time and place. Now, by chance, you have an opportunity to kill him, and because you actually have to act, you have lost your courage. I have raised children, and I know how wonderful it is to nurse a baby. If I had promised to kill my own baby, just as you promised to kill King Duncan, I would have torn it from me and smashed its head open—even while it smiled at me.

Literary Focus: Constructed Response

12. Students' responses will vary. A sample response follows:

    The dialogue shows that Lady Macbeth dominates Macbeth. In the beginning of the conversation, Macbeth is about to say that he is concerned that the plan will not succeed. Lady Macbeth interrupts him in midsentence and tells him that if he remains courageous, they will not fail. She thus shames Macbeth into agreeing to the plan she then describes. However, Macbeth still hesitates. Afraid of getting caught, he asks Lady Macbeth whether she really thinks the murder will be pinned on the guards. Lady Macbeth gives him the answer he needs, assuring him that no one will "dare" think otherwise. Macbeth gives in to his wife's plan and, in the end of the excerpt, seems eager to carry it out.

13. Students' responses will vary. A sample response follows:

    B—Lady Macbeth's determination to see that Macbeth keeps their bloody bargain is fierce, especially as expressed in her image of dashing out the brains of her own child.

    D—Lady Macbeth's implacable ambition to see Macbeth king and herself queen drives her to urge—even insist—that Macbeth murder King Duncan.

14. Students' responses will vary. A sample response follows:

    Both men allow others to persuade them to commit certain acts (Brutus by Cassius; Macbeth by Lady Macbeth). Brutus wants to kill Caesar out of fear that Caesar will become a dictator and that all Romans will lose their freedom. Brutus believes that his act of murder will be honorable. Macbeth, however, wants power only for himself and his family. Brutus meets with tragedy because of his inability to clearly recognize the baser motives of others. Macbeth, on the other hand, meets his tragic end because he doesn't have the strength to resist his own baser motives and the single-minded ambition of his wife.

Collection 11

Collection 11 Diagnostic Test

Informational Text, *page 259*

1. C
2. G
3. A
4. H
5. D
6. F
7. B
8. J
9. C
10. G

Evaluating the Logic of Functional Documents

Selection Test, *page 261*

Comprehension

1. D
2. H
3. A
4. H
5. B

Answer Key

Reading Informational Text

6. G
7. C
8. J
9. D
10. G

Following Technical Directions
Selection Test, page 263

Comprehension

1. D
2. G
3. A
4. H
5. A

Reading Informational Text

6. G
7. A

Analyzing Functional Workplace Documents
Selection Test, page 265

Comprehension

1. C
2. G
3. D
4. F
5. B

Reading Informational Text

6. G
7. A
8. H
9. C
10. F

Citing Internet Sources
Selection Test, page 267

Comprehension

1. B
2. H
3. D
4. H
5. B

Reading Informational Text

6. J
7. C
8. J
9. C
10. J

Reading Consumer Documents
Selection Test, page 269

Comprehension

1. C
2. J
3. B
4. H
5. B

Reading Informational Text

6. H
7. B
8. H
9. A
10. G

Collection 11 Summative Test,
page 271

Vocabulary Skills

1. B
2. F
3. C
4. G
5. D

Comprehension

6. J
7. B
8. J
9. C
10. J

Reading Functional Documents

Understanding the Format of Functional Documents

11. C

Following Technical Directions

12. Students' responses may vary somewhat. A sample response follows:
    1. Wear long pants and long-sleeve shirts or jackets made of wool or cotton.
    2. Wear gloves and carry a damp cloth.
    3. Do not wear clothes made of synthetic fibers.

13. Students' responses may vary somewhat. A sample response follows:
    1. Attach garden hoses to spigots and place them so they can reach any area of your house.
    2. Fill trash cans and buckets with water and put them where firefighters can find them.

Answer Key

3. Set up any workable pumps to provide water from swimming pools or other water reservoirs, and mark their location.
4. Fill sinks, bathtubs, and buckets with water.

Identifying the Logic of Functional Documents
14. step-by-step; point-by-point
15. point-by-point

End-of-Year Test, *page 276*
Reading and Literary Analysis
Sample A C
Sample B F

1. D
2. G
3. A
4. J
5. C
6. H
7. D
8. H
9. D
10. F
11. D
12. J
13. B
14. G
15. A

16. G
17. D
18. G
19. B
20. F
21. C
22. J
23. D
24. F
25. C
26. F
27. C
28. G
29. D
30. F

Vocabulary
Sample A D
31. B
32. H
33. D
34. F
35. C

36. G
37. A
38. J
39. C
40. G

Skills Profile

Skills Profile

Student's Name _____ Grade _____

Teacher's Name _____ Date _____

For each skill, write the date the observation is made and any comments that explain the student's development toward skills mastery.

▶ SKILL	▶ NOT OBSERVED	▶ EMERGING	▶ PROFICIENT
▶ **Literature**			
Analyze the characteristics of different forms of dramatic literature such as comedy, tragedy, drama, and dramatic monologue.			
Compare and contrast similar themes across genres.			
Analyze influences on characters (such as internal and external conflicts and motivation) and the way those influences affect the plot.			
Determine characters' traits from what the characters say about themselves.			
Compare and contrast works that express a universal theme, and provide evidence to support that theme.			
Analyze the development of time and sequence, including the use of foreshadowing and flashback.			
Analyze various literary devices, including figurative language, imagery, allegory, and symbolism.			
Identify ambiguities, contradictions, and ironies in the text.			
Analyze the way voice, tone, persona, and choice of narrator affect characterization and plot.			

SKILL	NOT OBSERVED	EMERGING	PROFICIENT
Analyze the function of dialogue, scene design, soliloquies, asides, and character foils in dramatic literature.			
Evaluate the aesthetic qualities of style, including the effect of diction, figurative language, tone, and mood.			
Analyze the way a work of literature relates to the themes and issues of its historical period. (Historical approach)			

▶ Informational Text

SKILL	NOT OBSERVED	EMERGING	PROFICIENT
Analyze the way authors use the structure and format of workplace documents to achieve their purposes.			
Prepare a bibliography of reference materials using a variety of consumer, workplace, and public documents.			
Generate relevant research questions after reading about an issue.			
Synthesize the content from several sources or works by a single author on a single issue.			
Analyze and elaborate on ideas presented in primary and secondary sources.			
Follow technical directions to use technology.			
Evaluate the logic of functional documents.			
Evaluate the credibility of an author's argument by examining generalizations, the scope of the evidence, and the intentions of the author.			

▶ Vocabulary

SKILL	NOT OBSERVED	EMERGING	PROFICIENT
Identify the literal and figurative meanings of words, and understand word derivations.			

Skills Profile

NAME _____ CLASS _____

SKILL	NOT OBSERVED	EMERGING	PROFICIENT
Distinguish between the denotative and connotative meanings of words.			
Use knowledge of Greek, Roman, and Norse mythology to understand the origin and meaning of new words.			